INSTANT REPLAY

365 Days of North Carolina Sports Trivia

INSTANT REPLAY

365 Days of North Carolina Sports Trivia

Jimmy Tomlin

BANDIT BOOKS

Winston-Salem, North Carolina

Copyright © 2011 by Jimmy Tomlin
All rights reserved
Printed in the United States of America

Cover photos: clockwise, from top left—Kay Yow, courtesy of N.C. State Athletics; Carolina Hurricanes win the Stanley Cup, courtesy of Carolina Hurricanes/Gregg Forwerck; Tim Biakabutuka of the Carolina Panthers, courtesy of High Point Enterprise/David Holston; Michael Jordan, courtesy of the Hugh Morton Collection, North Carolina Collection, University of North Carolina Library at UNC-Chapel Hill

Library of Congress Control Number 2011908769
ISBN 978-1-878177-21-6 (print edition)
      978-1-878177-22-3 (ebook edition)

Bandit Books, Inc.
P.O. Box 11721
Winston-Salem, NC 27116-1721
(336) 785-7417

Distributed by John F. Blair, Publisher
(800) 222-9796
www.blairpub.com

Cover Design by Angela Harwood

*In memory
of my good friend Tom Berry,
who encouraged and supported this book,
and who probably knew more sports trivia
off the top of his head
than I've included in this whole book*

CONTENTS

Introduction	i
Acknowledgments	iii
January	1
February	25
March	49
April	75
May	105
June	127
July	151
August	171
September	191
October	215
November	239
December	263

Team buttons and a program cover from the
Jan. 1, 1942 Rose Bowl, held in Durham

Program courtesy of Duke University Athletics; team buttons courtesy of Lew Powell Memorabilia Collection, North Carolina Collection, Wilson Library, UNC-Chapel Hill

Introduction

OK, so I lied.

Right there on the cover of the book, where everyone can see it, the title says, *Instant Replay: 365 Days of North Carolina Sports Trivia*. Do you realize what a bold, ambitious claim that is, thinking there might be an entertaining nugget of North Carolina sports history for every single day of the year? Did you really think this book could possibly deliver 365 days' worth of North Carolina sports trivia?

Well, it doesn't. It delivers *366* days' worth.

Yep, North Carolina's sports heritage is so rich that I couldn't stop at 365 days, so I included Leap Day—which, as you'll discover, provides one of the most intriguing items in the whole book, and one of my favorites. You see, on Feb. 29, 1964, two boys' high-school basketball teams in North Carolina played a game that lasted an astonishing *13 overtimes*, a national record which, nearly 50 years later, still hasn't been—and may never be—broken.

Why write a book of North Carolina sports trivia? The short answer is that I love North Carolina, I love sports and I love trivia, so it's a topic that's right up my alley. As a professional journalist, though, I also recognize the impact of a compelling story, and believe me, the world of North Carolina sports—the athletes, the coaches, the events and even the fans—has more compelling stories than Richard Petty has racin' trophies. And that's saying something.

Speaking of Petty and compelling stories, you won't believe who filed a formal protest that negated what would've been The King's first professional win as a racecar driver. You'll also get a kick out of what Petty's earnings were when he finally did get that monkey off his back and win a race. And speaking of monkeys—how's that for a segue?—don't miss the story of the monkey co-driver (yes, a *monkey*!) who found himself in Victory Lane one day at the Hickory Motor Speedway. His driver booted him off the team two weeks later, though, when he snapped under the pressure—the monkey, that is, not the driver—but hey, that's just racin'.

Of course, as much as we love our basketball and racing, North Carolina's sports history has so much more to offer than just rebounds and restrictor plates: Ferocious football. Golf greats. Boffo baseball. Terrific tennis. Softball studs. Super swimmers. Remarkable runners. Heavenly hurdlers. Amazing angling. Sizzling soccer. Stunning skaters. Even a big-time bobsledder.

I've tried to incorporate as many sports as possible, and at every level. At the professional level, for example, you'll find quite a few of Michael Jordan's feats—he had a pretty decent career, you know—but you'll also discover some of the astonishing exploits of the state's high-school athletes, from the baseball player who hit five home runs in a single game to the softball pitcher who pitched a perfect doubleheader—back-to-back perfect games on the same day! Fans of college a single game to the softball pitcher who pitched a perfect double-header—back-to-back perfect games on the same day! Fans of college athletics will find plenty of stories at that level, too, and not just at the so-called "Big Four" schools of Duke, North Carolina, N.C. State and Wake Forest, but also at smaller schools such as Guilford College, Belmont Abbey, Barton and St. Andrews Presbyterian.

You'll find funny stories, such as the tale of the beauty queen who survived a beanball unleashed by a mayor throwing out the first pitch at a minor-league baseball game; whimsical stories, such as the NFL quarterback whose Hollywood aspirations landed him on an episode of "Gilligan's Island"; and sad stories, such as a professional football player who went to prison for having his pregnant girlfriend killed, and two pro football players who were killed by their wives.

As I said, I've tried to include a little bit of everything.

Having said that, however, let me also say this: *Instant Replay* is not an encyclopedia, nor was it ever meant to be. Even though I'm exhausted—writing a thoroughly researched book of more than 1,100 trivia items will do that to a man—this book is not exhaustive. I'm certain readers will think of athletes I omitted, fantastic finishes I somehow left out, championship teams I failed to praise. I offer no apologies because, as I said, this is not an encyclopedia—there's simply no way I could've included *every* athlete, *every* team, *every* game, *every* Olympian, *every* state and national record. And the fact that I couldn't include everything speaks volumes about our state's rich athletic heritage.

So it's my hope that you won't fret over what you *don't* find on these pages, but that you'll thoroughly enjoy what you *do* find. After all, as the title says, it's a full 365 days of North Carolina sports trivia.

Wink, wink.

– Jimmy Tomlin

Acknowledgments

At the risk of leaving someone out, which I'm afraid I most certainly will do, I must say a few thank-yous to the folks who helped make this book possible: To Becky, Ashley and Caroline, the loves of my life, for all the times they had to endure me sitting at the computer; to Mom, one enthusiastic cheerleader; to Sandy Berry, for support, encouragement and, of course, all those media guides; to all who assisted with research, especially my faithful friends Mary Best and Diane Silcox-Jarrett; to Brett and Linda Piper, for photography assistance; to co-workers Dwight Davis and Vince Wheeler, for support and story tips; to all of the media relations professionals who assisted with my research and helped provide photos; to my publisher, Barry McGee of Bandit Books, for taking a chance on me and for answering countless questions; to Angela Harwood for a terrific cover design; and to anyone else who assisted in any way, please know that your help was anything but trivial.

Bones McKinney, Wake Forest University basketball coach from 1958-1965
Courtesy of Wake Forest Media Relations

JANUARY

January 1

1919

Horace Albert "Bones" McKinney, the future colorful basketball coach of the Wake Forest Demon Deacons, is born in Lowlands, North Carolina. As a college basketball player, McKinney will have the rare distinction of playing for both North Carolina State (two years), and then—after his playing career is interrupted by World War II—the University of North Carolina (one year). That UNC team, the 1946 squad, will go to the Final Four. McKinney will coach Wake Forest from 1958 to 1965, leading the Demon Deacons to their only Final Four appearance in 1962. He will later coach the Carolina Cougars of the American Basketball Association (ABA). McKinney will die in 1997, at the age of 78.

January 1 continued

1942

Less than a month after the Japanese bombed Pearl Harbor, Duke University hosts the Rose Bowl—the only time in nearly 100 games that the granddaddy of all college football games has been played away from Pasadena, California—out of fears that a game played on the West Coast might be vulnerable to another attack by Japanese warplanes. The game caps off a hectic two weeks during which Duke officials prepared to host a game that had looked as if it wouldn't be played at all.

The second-ranked Blue Devils, with their 9-0 record, had longed to redeem themselves for their heartbreaking, last-minute 7-3 loss to Southern California in the 1939 Rose Bowl; this time, their opponents would be the 7-2 Oregon State Beavers, ranked 12th nationally, and Duke couldn't wait for the gridiron showdown. Anticipation turned to disappointment, however, on December 13, when U.S. military leaders called for the game to be cancelled in the interest of national defense. Only a day later, Duke coach Wallace Wade invited Rose Bowl officials to play the game in Durham, and they eagerly accepted the invitation, as did Oregon State.

Chief among the hurried preparations for the game was bumping up the Duke stadium's seating capacity from 35,000 to 56,000 by bringing in borrowed bleachers from its three in-state rivals: the University of North Carolina, North Carolina State and Wake Forest. Makeshift press-room facilities were also installed to accommodate the approximately 200 sportswriters who would cover the game. Meanwhile, the grass on the field was replanted, and the Carolina Inn in Chapel Hill agreed to

An aerial photo of the 1942 Rose Bowl in Durham
Courtesy of Duke University Athletics

host the visiting Beavers. Duke printed up more than 50,000 tickets and sold them all—at $4.40 apiece—in a span of about forty-eight hours.

In light of everything that went into preparing for the game to be played in Durham on such short notice, the game itself almost seems anticlimactic. Duke plays an uncharacteristically sloppy game, committing seven turnovers—four interceptions and three fumbles. Still, the Blue Devils trail only 20-14 going into the fourth quarter. On three occasions they drive deep into Oregon State territory, but come away empty each time. Duke manages a safety late in the game, but it's not enough, and Oregon State gets a 20-16 upset.

1946

Wake Forest takes on South Carolina in the inaugural Gator Bowl in Jacksonville, Florida, coming away with a 26-14 win.

January 2

1939

Duke's highly touted football team comes within 41 seconds of a perfect, unscored-upon season, before allowing Southern California a 19-yard touchdown pass in the final minute of the Rose Bowl. The Blue Devils lose the heartbreaker 7-3, in the process frittering away their perfect season.

January 3

1991

High Point native Luke Appling, who played his entire career for the Chicago White Sox, was a two-time American League batting champion and was elected to the Baseball Hall of Fame, dies at the age of 83.

2004

Carolina Panthers kicker John Kasay becomes only the fifth player in NFL history to kick five field goals in a playoff game, performing the feat in Carolina's 29-10 win over the Dallas Cowboys in the NFC Wild Card game.

2007

The Charlotte Sting, one of the WNBA's eight original franchises in 1997, folds, citing low attendance and loss of revenue. Players will be sent to the league's remaining teams via a dispersal draft.

January 3 continued

2011

Speedskater Heather Richardson, born and raised in High Point, wins the 500 meters and 1,000 meters at the 2011 U.S. Speedskating Championships in Kearns, Utah, setting a U.S. record in the 500 meters with a time of 37.58 seconds. Richardson competed in the 2010 Winter Olympics and hopes to compete in the 2014 Olympics as well.

January 4

1935

Future two-time world heavyweight boxing champion Floyd Patterson is born in Cleveland County.

1986

The University of North Carolina at Wilmington's men's basketball team earns a dubious distinction when Navy's David Robinson blocks 14 of the Seahawks' shots in a single game, at the time an NCAA record.

1986

The University of North Carolina men's basketball team wins its final game in Carmichael Auditorium—beating N.C. State, 90-79—before moving to the newly completed Dean E. Smith Student Activities Center. Following the game, colorful Wolfpack coach Jim Valvano grabs the game ball and shoots a layup, jokingly explaining later that he wanted to make the final basket in Carmichael Auditorium.

2001

Former North Carolinian Michael Jordan, now playing for the Washington Wizards, becomes only the fourth player in NBA history to score 30,000 career points.

Did You Know?

Harlem Globetrotters legend—and Wilmington native—Meadowlark Lemon, known as "The Clown Prince of Basketball," is an ordained minister. He was ordained in 1986 and received his doctorate of divinity from Vision International University in 1998. He also hosts a Christian-based talk show, "The Meadowlark Lemon Show," through the Trinity Broadcasting Network.

January 5

1988
Basketball legend Pete Maravich, who played for Raleigh's Broughton High School before having outstanding college and NBA careers, dies of a heart attack at the age of 40 while playing in a pickup game in Pasadena, California. Following his death, the basketball arena at Louisiana State University where he played his college ball will be named the Pete Maravich Assembly Center.

2000
Durham native Morgan Wootten, the legendary basketball coach at DeMatha Catholic High School in Hyattsville, Maryland, enters his sixth decade of coaching, having directed teams in the 1950s, 1960s, 1970s, 1980s, 1990s and now the 2000s. By the time he retires in 2002, he will be the winningest head coach in the history of basketball at any level.

January 6

1940
Duke University dedicates its new $400,000 basketball arena, Duke Indoor Stadium, and the Blue Devils celebrate the occasion with a 36-27 win over Princeton. In 1972, the name of the arena will be changed to Cameron Indoor Stadium—for longtime basketball coach Eddie Cameron—which eventually will lead to Duke's rowdy fans being nicknamed "Cameron Crazies."

1959
Lawrence "Cotton" Clayton of Kittrell Zeb Vance grabs 46 rebounds against Knightdale, a state high-school record.

1965
Following a loss at Wake Forest, the fourth consecutive loss of the season, the North Carolina basketball team returns to Chapel Hill late at night to find a burning effigy of fourth-year head coach Dean Smith hanging from a tree outside Woollen Gymnasium on campus. A group of students, clearly displeased with the Tar Heels' mediocre 6-6 record, angrily chants, "We want Smith! We want Smith!" The young coach tells players to keep their seats while he addresses the surly crowd alone, but star center Billy Cunningham can't contain his anger, jumps off the bus, runs to the effigy and tears it down. Players will later point to the incident as a turning point in the season that pulls the team together. Meanwhile, Smith will survive the season and go on to become the most

January 6 continued

revered figure in Tar Heel basketball history, to the point that UNC's new basketball arena that opens in 1986 will be named for him.

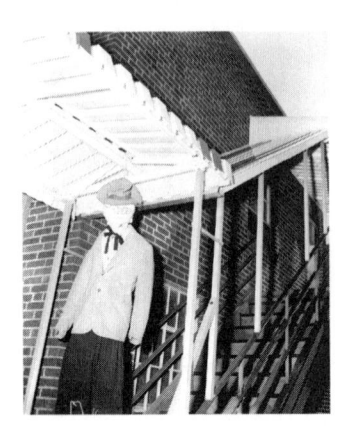

Although the burning dummy representing Dean Smith has become the state's best-known case of fans hanging a coach in effigy and calling for his dismissal, it was not the first time such an incident occurred in North Carolina. In the winter quarter of 1957 at Appalachian State Teachers College, now Appalachian State University, in Boone, an effigy of basketball coach Francis Hoover (above) was found hanging outside one of the gymnasiums on campus. Hoover, who had graduated from the college in 1939 and was in his 11th season as basketball head coach, eventually would be inducted into the Appalachian Athletic Hall of Fame in 1977, but at least in 1957, he apparently was not a popular figure on campus. While information from ASU's Historical Photographs Collection states that "circumstances surrounding the creation and hanging of the effigy are unknown," it could've had something to do with the Mountaineers' dismal 4-20 record that season.

(Photo courtesy of Prichett Collection, University Archives and Records, Appalachian State University, Boone, NC)

1973

A poll by the Golf Writers Association of America names Ben Hogan, Bobby Jones, Walter Hagen, Jack Nicklaus and former Wake Forest University star Arnold Palmer the five greatest golfers of all time.

1999

In a battle of Charlotte rivals, Olympic High School's George Leach blocks 19 shots against Myers Park, a state high-school record.

January 7

1978
The North Carolina Tar Heels set an NCAA record for field goal percentage in a half, making 16 of 17 shots—a sizzling 94.1 percent—in the second half of a game against Virginia.

1992
Michelle Richardson of Columbia High School snares 36 rebounds against Cape Hatteras, a state high-school record for girls' basketball.

1994
After six overtimes—a state record for girls' high-school basketball—Freedom High School of Morganton finally defeats Hickory, 66-64.

January 8

1955
Public television channel UNC-TV makes its broadcasting debut in North Carolina. Though the station will come to be known for its educational programming, UNC-TV airs a sporting event, the North Carolina vs. Wake Forest men's basketball game, as one of its first programs. The Tar Heels, playing at home in a sold-out Woollen Gym, get the win, 95-78.

1991
Williamston native Gaylord Perry, one of the most successful pitchers in major-league history, is elected to the National Baseball Hall of Fame. Perry ended his lengthy career in 1983 with more than 300 wins and more than 3,500 strikeouts, and he was the first pitcher to win the Cy Young Award in both the American League and National League.

Did You Know?
You can take the star athlete out of North Carolina, but you can't take North Carolina out of the star athlete. Even as he was leading the Chicago Bulls to six NBA championships, former University of North Carolina star Michael Jordan wore a pair of Tar Heel shorts beneath his Bulls shorts for good luck.

January 9

1965

Tyrone "Muggsy" Bogues, who will star for Wake Forest University and later the Charlotte Hornets, is born in Baltimore, Maryland. At only 5-feet-3-inches, he will be the shortest player in NBA history.

Muggsy Bogues
Courtesy of Wake Forest Media Relations

1968

Former University of North Carolina basketball star Larry Brown, now playing for the ABA's Denver Rockets, scores 17 points and wins the MVP Award in the inaugural ABA All-Star Game.

January 10

1980

Former North Carolina State football coach Bo Rein dies when the small, private plane he's in crashes into the Atlantic Ocean. The 34-year-old Rein had coached at State from 1976 to 1979, compiling a 27-18-1 record and leading the Wolfpack to two bowl-game victories. After the 1979 season, he was hired away by Louisiana State University to take over as that school's head coach, but he would die in the plane crash before ever coaching a game there. NCSU will honor Rein's memory by presenting the annual Bo Rein Award to an unsung Wolfpack football player who makes vital contributions to the team.

8   ≡   Instant Replay

1982
Kinston native Dwight Clark, who played football at Garinger High School in Charlotte and is now a Pro Bowl receiver for the San Francisco 49ers, stuns the Dallas Cowboys with his leaping fingertip catch of a Joe Montana pass in the back of the end zone with less than a minute left in the NFC Championship Game, tying the score at 27; the extra point gives the 49ers the dramatic win, sending the team to Super Bowl XVI. "The Catch," as Clark's amazing reception will come to be known in NFL lore, will also make the cover of *Sports Illustrated.*

2003
The NBA announces that Charlotte, former home of the New Orleans Hornets franchise, has been awarded NBA and WNBA expansion franchises. Those teams become the NBA's Charlotte Bobcats and the WNBA's Charlotte Sting, which eventually will fold.

January 11

2000
Former Duke University basketball star Grant Hill, now with the Detroit Pistons, is named one of the final three selections for the 2000 USA Basketball Men's Senior National Team, which will participate in the 2000 Olympic Games in Sydney, Australia. Previously named to the team were former Wake Forest star Tim Duncan, now of the San Antonio Spurs, and former N.C. State star Tom Gugliotta, now of the Phoenix Suns.

2005
Bessemer City sharpshooter Ty Carter gets hot from behind the 3-point line, knocking down a state high-school record 14 treys.

Did You Know?
From 1999 to 2002, Roanoke High School's Deborah Cherry recorded 885 steals during her high-school career, tops in the nation at the time.

January 12

1960
Future NBA Hall of Famer Jacques Dominique Wilkins is born in Paris, France. His family will move to Washington, North Carolina,

January 12 continued

where he will lead Washington High School to consecutive state championships in 1978 and 1979.

2000
Charlotte Hornets star Bobby Phills, only 30 years old, dies in an automobile accident in Charlotte. The Hornets' game that evening against the Chicago Bulls is postponed and rescheduled.

January 13

1981
Mocksville native Joe Gibbs is named head coach of the Washington Redskins. Gibbs will lead the Redskins to three Super Bowl titles—in the 1982, 1987 and 1991 seasons—earning himself induction into the Pro Football Hall of Fame.

1999
Michael Jordan announces his retirement—for the second time—from the NBA. As with his first retirement, though, he is not done playing.

2001
The Atlanta Hawks retire Dominique Wilkins' No. 21 jersey, making him only the third Hawk to be so honored.

January 14

1973
North Carolina State introduces the country to a new tradition—a nationally televised college basketball game on the Sunday afternoon of the Super Bowl (in this case, Super Bowl VII)—with a thrilling 87-85 win over the Maryland Terrapins. More than twenty-five million fans watch the game on a syndicated network as the Wolfpack's superb sophomore, David Thompson, racks up 37 points, including a put-back shot at the buzzer to win the game.

1984
The "Cameron Crazies," Duke University's rowdy basketball fans who have gained a national reputation for their antics, making Duke's Cameron Indoor Stadium one of the toughest venues in the country for opponents, take things too far this time. When the Maryland Terrapins

come to Durham, the students predictably target the Terps' Herman Veal, a standout who had been accused of sexually assaulting a Maryland coed the previous week. When Veal is introduced before the game, the crowd showers him with panties and condoms, as well as vulgar taunts. One sign reads, "Hey, Herman...did you send her flowers?" but most other signs are far uglier. Such abuse of opponents was nothing new for the Crazies, particularly when it came to opposing players' brushes with the law. When North Carolina State's Tommy Burleson confessed to breaking into three pinball machines, the Duke pep band serenaded him with a rendition of "Pinball Wizard." And when State's Lorenzo Charles was charged with robbing a pizza delivery boy, the fans bombarded him with empty pizza boxes.

But the Veal incident disturbs university officials, because it re-enforces the reputation Duke's student section is developing for crude behavior. Three days after the Maryland game, university president Terry Sanford will send Duke students a letter encouraging them to restrain from such tasteless behavior. Titled "An Avuncular Letter" and signed "Uncle Terry," the letter suggests students have crossed the "recognizable line between enthusiasm and cheapness." Sanford encourages students to be clever but not crude—that they be "G-rated for television"—because, as he writes, "Resorting to the use of obscenities in cheers and chants at ball games indicates a lack of vocabulary, a lack of cleverness, a lack of ideas, a lack of class, and a lack of respect for other people. We are, I am sorry to report, gaining an unequaled reputation as a student body that doesn't have a touch of class."

Sanford's letter apparently strikes a chord with students. One week after greeting Veal with a barrage of panties and condoms, the Duke fans greet their arch rival, the North Carolina Tar Heels, with...halos? Yep, the Blue Devils' faithful look like angels in their makeshift halos, fashioned from coat hangers and aluminum foil. Moreover, they hold up signs dripping with mock hospitality, such as "Welcome, Honored

The Cameron Crazies
Courtesy of Duke University Athletics

January ≡ 11

January 14 continued

Guests" and "A Hearty Welcome to Coach Dean Smith and the North Carolina Tar Heels." And when they disagree with a referee's call, instead of using vulgarities, the crowd chants, "We beg to differ! We beg to differ!"

1987

Hertford native Jim "Catfish" Hunter, one of the most celebrated pitchers in major-league history, is elected to the National Baseball Hall of Fame.

A Catfish Hunter button
Courtesy of the Lew Powell Memorabilia Collection, North Carolina Collection, Wilson Library, UNC-Chapel Hill

2008

Lewisville native and former Wake Forest University star Chris Paul, now playing for the New Orleans Hornets, collects 33 points, 10 rebounds, 11 assists and seven steals, narrowly missing a rare quadruple-double, in the Hornets' 104-97 win over the Dallas Mavericks.

January 15

1996

Kay Yow, N.C. State's venerable women's basketball coach, notches her historic 500th win, a 68-63 victory over West Virginia State University.

1997

Former Tar Heel basketball star Sam Perkins, now with the NBA's Seattle Supersonics, ties an NBA single-game record by shooting 8-for-8 from behind the 3-point line in Seattle's 122-78 win over Toronto.

2000
Morgan Wootten, longtime coach of the famed DeMatha Catholic High School boys' basketball team—and a Durham native—records his 1,200th win, becoming the first basketball coach at any level (high school, college or pro) to reach that milestone.

January 16

1988
CBS fires Jimmy "The Greek" Snyder, an oddsmaker and personality on "The NFL Today" for a dozen years—and a resident of Durham—for racially offensive comments he made to a television reporter. Commenting on the superiority of black athletes in America, Snyder said, "During the slave period, the slave owner would breed his big black with his big woman so that he could have a big black kid—that's where it all started." The public furor over his comments so stresses Snyder that he complains of chest pains and spends a few days in a Durham hospital.

1991
The first basketball meeting of the season between rivals North Carolina and North Carolina State, scheduled to be played in Chapel Hill, is postponed when war breaks out in the Persian Gulf. School officials make the difficult decision so close to game time that the two teams are already on the court warming up. To make up the game, the teams will play a rare back-to-back doubleheader—February 6 in Raleigh and February 7 in Chapel Hill. In each game, the home team gets the win.

2006
Two dozen students from rivals Duke and North Carolina set a world record for the longest continuous basketball game ever played—57 hours, 17 minutes and 41 seconds—with Duke getting the win, 3,688-3,444. The real winner, though, is a charity called the BounceBack Kids, which receives more than $60,000 from the fundraising game.

Did You Know?
Before the Wolfpack became North Carolina State's official nickname for athletic teams, they were referred to by such nicknames as the Aggies, the Techs, the Farmers and the Red Terrors. Local newspapers first began referring to some of the athletic teams as the Wolfpack as early as 1921, but the transition from the Red Terrors wasn't complete until the mid-1940s.

January 17

1948
Only hours before a men's basketball game between North Carolina State and Duke, the Raleigh city building inspector condemns Thompson Gymnasium on the NCSU campus. For the Wolfpack's final game in Thompson, against High Point College, the doors are locked and the game's only spectators are college officials and a few reporters. From then until the new Reynolds Coliseum opens in 1949, Raleigh's Memorial Auditorium will serve as State's home court.

1979
North Carolina defensive specialist Dudley Bradley makes arguably the most memorable steal in the state's rich college basketball history. With the N.C. State Wolfpack clinging to a one-point lead, Bradley swipes the ball from Wolfpack guard Clyde "The Glide" Austin at midcourt, then dribbles downcourt for the go-ahead dunk with only seven seconds remaining. State misses a shot at the buzzer, giving the Tar Heels the heart-stopping win.

1988
In Cleveland sports lore, it will come to be known simply as "The Fumble." Cleveland Browns running back Earnest Byner, who played college football at East Carolina University, commits the most famous fumble in Browns history, losing the ball at the Denver Broncos' 3-yard-line in the closing minutes of the AFC Championship Game. The Browns, trailing 38-31, appear headed for a game-tying touchdown when Byner is stripped of the ball and Denver recovers. The Broncos will give up an intentional safety and hold on for a 38-33 win.

January 18

1986
The No. 1-ranked North Carolina Tar Heels christen their cavernous new basketball arena, the Dean E. Smith Student Activities Center, with a thrilling 95-92 win over arch rival Duke. UNC forward Warren Martin scores the Heels' first basket in the new arena.

2004
The Carolina Panthers win their first NFC Championship, beating the Philadelphia Eagles 14-3 in Philadelphia to advance to the Super Bowl. Carolina's Ricky Manning Jr. ties an NFL Championship game record with three interceptions.

2011
The North Carolina Tar Heels extend the NCAA's longest home winning streak against one team to 55 in a row with their 75-65 win over Clemson at the Smith Center. Amazingly, the Tigers have never won a men's basketball game in Chapel Hill, a streak that goes all the way back to 1926.

January 19

2000
Former Tar Heel basketball star Michael Jordan, who led the Chicago Bulls to six NBA championships, returns to the NBA as part owner and president of basketball operations for the Washington Wizards.

January 20

1964
Wake Forest basketball coach Horace "Bones" McKinney, a restless, excitable coach known for his sideline histrionics, introduces a new strategy for keeping himself under control during games—an automotive seat belt. "If I'm going to stay in this business, I'm going to have to do

Bones McKinney with his seat belt
Courtesy of Forsyth County Public Library Photograph Collection

January 20 continued

something about the tension," he explains. So for Wake Forest's home game against Maryland, McKinney straps himself to the bench with a red seat belt—to match the bright red socks he wears for good luck—to keep himself from doing anything that might earn him a technical foul. For most of the game the seat belt does its job, but with nine minutes to go in the game and the Demon Deacons falling apart, an official's call that McKinney disagrees with sends him over the edge. Off comes the seat belt and up pops the incredulous coach for the rest of the game. Wake winds up losing, 91-82.

1966

Catawba College guard Dwight Durante, a 5-foot-8 scoring machine, lights up Western Carolina for 58 points, leading the Indians to an 89-81 win over the Catamounts. Durante's big night is a single-game scoring record for college games played in North Carolina (though Winston-Salem State's Cleo Hill once scored 63 points in a game on the road). About seven weeks earlier, Durante had scored 39 against Western Carolina, but the Catamounts had won the game in a blowout, 105-81. After that game, with tears in his eyes, Durante had vowed to coach Sam Moir, "Coach, we'll never lose to them again," and they never would during Durante's stellar career, which will include being named a first-team NAIA All-American. After graduation, Durante will be drafted by the New York Knicks in the sixth round of the 1969 draft, but fearing he might not be given a fair shake because of his height, he signs instead with the Harlem Globetrotters.

2003

More than 16,000 fans—a state record for high-school basketball—flood the Greensboro Coliseum for the North Carolina Scholastic Classic, a five-game event featuring some of the nation's top high-school teams. The main attraction? Future NBA superstar LeBron James, whose St. Vincent-St. Mary High School squad rolls over Winston-Salem's R.J. Reynolds, 85-56. King James lives up to the hype with his 32 points, 10 rebounds and two assists.

2009

Barack Obama is inaugurated as president of the United States, and standing with him is his "body man"—or personal assistant—Reggie Love, a former Duke University football and basketball player.

2011

Charlotte native Davis Love III, who played golf collegiately at the University of North Carolina, is named captain of the U.S. Ryder Cup team for 2012, fulfilling a dream he'd had for years.

January 21

1992
Former N.C. State football star Bill Cowher becomes the 15th head coach in Pittsburgh Steelers history, succeeding Chuck Noll. He will coach the team for 15 seasons and lead the Steelers to the Super Bowl XL championship.

January 22

1933
Lennie Rosenbluth, who will lead the University of North Carolina basketball team to the 1957 NCAA championship—and be named that year's Collegiate Player of the Year over Wilt Chamberlain of Kansas—is born in New York City. He will set numerous scoring records at UNC, and will be inducted into the Helms College Basketball Hall of Fame.

Lennie Rosenbluth
Courtesy of UNC Athletic Communications

1972
The Indoor Stadium at Duke University, home of the Blue Devils basketball team, is officially renamed Cameron Indoor Stadium. The name change honors former Duke basketball coach Eddie Cameron (1929-1942), who drew up the original plans for the stadium, which

January 22 continued

opened in 1940. The unranked Blue Devils commemorate the event with a 76-74 upset of third-ranked North Carolina.

2010

Professional golfer Jim Thorpe, a Roxboro native, is sentenced to a year in prison for failure to pay more than $2 million in income taxes. Thorpe, who won three PGA tournaments during his career, pleaded guilty in September to two counts of failing to pay income taxes. Following his prison term, he will return to the Champions Tour.

January 23

1971

The Greensboro Coliseum plays host to the 1971 ABA All-Star Game. The East team bests the West, 126-122, before a crowd of more than 14,000, but the West's Mel Daniels of the Indiana Pacers earns MVP honors with his 29 points. The winning East team features Carolina Cougars star Joe Caldwell (21 points) and former North Carolina Tar Heel star Charlie Scott (7 points).

1995

New expansion team the Carolina Panthers hire Pittsburgh Steelers defensive coordinator Dom Capers as the team's first head coach.

January 24

1920

North Carolina and Duke—at the time still known as Trinity College—meet on the basketball court for the first time in what will become one of the nation's most heated rivalries. Playing in the small Angier B. Duke Gymnasium on the Trinity campus, the visiting Tar Heels pull off a surprising 36-25 win over the previously 6-0 Trinity squad.

1990

Clarence (Big House) Gaines, in his 44th year as head basketball coach at Winston-Salem State University, joins former Kentucky coaching legend Adolph Rupp as the only coaches to reach the 800-win milestone. Gaines accomplishes the feat when his Rams defeat Livingstone College, 79-70.

2009

North Carolina State women's basketball coach Kay Yow, one of the most respected figures in all of college basketball, dies of breast cancer at the age of 66. Yow, a Gibsonville native, became N.C. State's first full-time women's basketball coach in 1975 and won 680 games against only 325 losses; her overall collegiate coaching record, which included four seasons at Elon College, was 737-344. Yow never won a national championship, but she led the Wolfpack to 20 NCAA tournaments, including a trip to the Final Four in 1998. She also coached the U.S. women's team to a gold medal in the 1988 Olympics in Seoul, Korea, and in 2002 she was inducted into the Naismith Memorial Basketball Hall of Fame, only the fifth female coach to be so honored. In February 2007, the basketball court at State's Reynolds Coliseum was renamed Kay Yow Court in her honor. During a memorable funeral service on January 30, mourners will watch a video of Yow that she recorded before her death.

Kay Yow
Courtesy of N.C. State Athletics

Did You Know?

The top three career assist leaders in NCAA history all played their college basketball in North Carolina—and at schools within a 30-mile radius. They are Bobby Hurley, Duke University, with 1,076 assists; Chris Corchiani, N.C. State, 1,038 assists; and Ed Cota, the University of North Carolina, 1,030 assists.

January 25

1994
Pat Crawford, the last surviving member of the famed St. Louis Cardinals "Gashouse Gang," dies at age 91 in Morehead City. Crawford, whose early professional career included stints with the Kinston Highwaymen and the Charlotte Hornets—and who earned a degree from Davidson College—was the leading pinch hitter for the Cardinals, who won the 1934 World Series.

1996
Former Duke basketball star Grant Hill, now with the Detroit Pistons, leads all vote-getters in NBA All-Star balloting for the second straight year. Hill edges former Tar Heel Michael Jordan as the top vote-getter, 1,358,004 to 1,341,422.

January 26

1977
Future Tar Heel basketball star Vince Carter, who will go on to stardom in the NBA—including winning the league's Rookie of the Year honor in 1999—is born in Daytona Beach, Florida.

1995
Grant Hill becomes the first NBA rookie ever to lead all players in All-Star voting, getting votes on 1,289,585 ballots.

> **Did You Know?**
> Olympic gold-medalist skier Picabo Street, who had an unusual habit of naming her skis, dubbed one pair her "Earnies," in honor of Kannapolis-born NASCAR star Dale Earnhardt.

January 27

1911
The North Carolina Tar Heels beat Virginia Christian, 42-21, in UNC's first varsity basketball game. About 200 curious spectators show

up for the game on the UNC campus. That inaugural team, coached by track and field coach Nat Cartmell, will go on to finish the season 7-4.

The 1910-11 UNC basketball team
Courtesy of UNC Athletic Communications

1945

Stanly County native Nancy Isenhour, a 19-year-old student at High Point College, is featured in a *Collier's Weekly* magazine article recognizing her as the nation's first female to play on a men's college basketball team. Men's head coach Virgil Yow, faced with a manpower shortage caused by World War II, recruited the petite Isenhour—a gritty player with a consistent shot, who also happened to be the school's May Queen—to play for his Panthers. The article, titled "Panther Girl," alludes to Isenhour's unique, endearing method of checking into a game—she gives the player she's replacing a light kiss on the

Nancy Isenhour
Courtesy of High Point University

January ≡ 21

January 27 continued

cheek—and then goes on to describe her impact. High Point's opponents "gaped, stumbled and fumbled for the next five minutes" after Isenhour entered the game. "This was one problem no one had ever prepared them for," the story reads. Yow laments that while his players have embraced the idea of having a woman on the team—and have gone out of their way to help her improve her overall game—they don't do a good enough job of setting screens for her, so she can take advantage of her shooting ability. According to Yow, his 1942 team, which won the Southeastern championship and went to the national tournament in Kansas City, would've flourished even more with Isenhour on the floor. "If Nancy had been on the team I took to the Kansas City tournament in 1942," he says, "she'd have been one of the leading scorers in the country."

1976

Legendary former N.C. State basketball star David Thompson, now with the Denver Nuggets, wins the MVP Award of the final ABA All-Star Game, leading Denver to a 144-138 win over a team of all-stars. At halftime, he competes in the inaugural slam-dunk contest, but loses in the finals to Julius Erving.

January 28

1974

Swimmers warming up for a swim meet at N.C. State between the Wolfpack and South Carolina get quite a shock—literally—when electric timers in the pool malfunction, shocking the swimmers and causing them to scream and jump out of the pool.

1979

NBC, making its first visit to Duke's rowdy Cameron Indoor Stadium for a national telecast, the Blue Devils vs. Marquette, insists the game be broadcast on a time delay, so network officials can censor any crowd actions they deem too outrageous.

January 29

1983

Michael Jordan scores 39 points—his career high at the University of North Carolina—in leading the Tar Heels to a 72-65 win over Georgia Tech.

2011
The fastest shot in National Hockey League history is recorded during the All-Star Game's skills competition in Raleigh, when Zdeno Chara of the Boston Bruins blasts a 105.9-mph slap shot.

January 30

1972
Fisherman James Hussey lands a world-record bluefish—weighing in at 31 pounds, 12 ounces—at Hatteras Inlet. Nearly 40 years later, Hussey's catch will still be the world record.

1999
Former Tar Heel football star Lawrence Taylor, one of the best defensive players in NFL history, is elected to the Pro Football Hall of Fame in his first year of eligibility. Some voters feel that Taylor's history of drug abuse should have prevented him from going into the Hall of Fame, but his on-the-field excellence got him elected.

Lawrence Taylor in action
Courtesy of UNC Athletic Communications

2007
Former major-leaguer Max Lanier, a native of Denton, dies at age 91 in Dunellon, Florida. A two-time All-Star for the St. Louis Cardinals, Lanier led the National League with a stellar 1.90 earned run average in 1943.

January 31

1970

Basketball showman "Pistol Pete" Maravich, who starred at Raleigh's Broughton High School in the mid-1960s and now plays for Louisiana State, surpasses the great Oscar Robertson as the all-time NCAA Division I scoring leader. Maravich makes a 15-foot jumper in LSU's 109-86 win over Mississippi to break Robertson's career total of 2,973 points. Playing without the benefit of the 3-point shot, which has not yet been introduced in college basketball, he will finish his legendary career with 3,667 points, still tops in NCAA Division I history.

1993

An immensely popular and entertaining McDonald's commercial featuring Michael Jordan and Larry Bird playing a game of H-O-R-S-E makes its debut during the Super Bowl.

2005

Jordan Snipes of Guilford College rebounds a missed free throw with 0.6 of a second left and quickly heaves a length-of-the-court prayer that swishes, giving the Quakers a stunning 91-89 overtime victory over Randolph-Macon. The improbable shot caps an amazing night for Snipes, who finishes with a career-best 34 points, including making 6-of-7 from the 3-point line. That night on ESPN's "SportsCenter," the shot will air as five of the show's top ten plays of the night. "I just took the ball and threw it," Snipes says. "I didn't know what else to do."

FEBRUARY

February 1

1977

With no shot clock to force the action, Durham's Hillside High School defeats Roxboro Person 2-0 in boys' basketball, achieving the lowest combined point total in North Carolina high-school history. Hillside scores a basket a few seconds after the opening tipoff to account for the game's only points. Person then holds the ball for one shot—a strategy the underdog Rockets would employ in all four quarters of the game—but they never make a basket. "Hillside came out in a zone and I was trying to force them out of it, but they wouldn't come," explains Person Coach Reid Davis, "so we just tried to play for one shot." Person manages a flurry of three shots in the final 38 seconds of the game, but cannot connect, giving Hillside's Hornets the win. Nationwide, only three high-school boys' basketball games have produced fewer points, all of which ended 1-0.

February 1 continued

2004

After posting a dismal 1-15 record only two seasons earlier, the Carolina Panthers play the New England Patriots for the NFL's most coveted prize—a Super Bowl trophy—in Super Bowl XXXVIII. The Panthers, who defeated the Dallas Cowboys, the St. Louis Rams and the Philadelphia Eagles to get to the big game, fall 32-29 to the Patriots in what *Sports Illustrated* writer Peter King will call "the greatest Super Bowl of all time." After Carolina ties the game at 29 with 1:08 remaining in regulation, the game appears headed for overtime—the first in Super Bowl history—but New England moves quickly down the field, and Adam Vinatieri kicks a 41-yard field goal with only four seconds left to give the Patriots the win. As a consolation, the Panthers chalk up one impressive statistic: Quarterback Jake Delhomme's 85-yard touchdown pass to Muhsin Muhammad goes down as the longest offensive play from scrimmage in Super Bowl history.

Thomasville native Brad Hoover
Courtesy of High Point Enterprise/*David Holston*

February 2

1929

New Duke University basketball coach Eddie Cameron's first squad knocks off North Carolina, 36-20. Duke had lost 16 straight to UNC, a losing streak that went back to 1921, when Duke was still known as Trinity College.

1993

Former North Carolinian Dominique Wilkins, who grew up in Beaufort County, scores 34 points against Seattle to become the Atlanta

Hawks' all-time leading scorer—passing Hall of Famer Bob Pettit—with 20,885 points.

2000
In Fayetteville, Pine Forest High School's Padra Strong plays the role of defensive enforcer, blocking 19 shots—a state record for girls' high-school basketball—against cross-town rival Douglas Byrd.

February 3

1949
Lexington pro Dugan Aycock plays a unique cross-country round of golf, teeing off from downtown Lexington and heading toward the ninth hole of Hinkle Golf Course in Thomasville, about eight miles away. After teeing off one block from the city square, Aycock follows a course of mostly fields and farmland, requiring about five and a half hours to reach his destination. Aycock had come up with the idea as a novel fundraiser for the March of Dimes and its campaign to help develop a polio vaccine; people were invited to donate $1 and enter a guess as to how many strokes Aycock would require. Guesses range from as low as 61 strokes to as high as 2,166, but five guessers—three men and two women—get it exactly right, guessing 114 strokes. Aycock's prediction, which he had placed in a sealed envelope before he started, was 113 strokes.

1986
Never short on heart, 5-foot-7-inch point guard Anthony "Spud" Webb—who rose to national acclaim playing for the N.C. State

Spud Webb
Courtesy of N.C. State Athletics

February 3 continued

Wolfpack—shocks the NBA world by winning the league's annual slam dunk contest over defending champion—and another former North Carolinian—Dominique Wilkins, who played his high-school ball at Washington High School in Beaufort County. Showing off his 42-inch vertical leap, Webb dazzles spectators and the judges with such eye-popping dunks as an off-the-backboard one-handed jam, a 360-degree helicopter one-handed jam, and a 180-degree reverse double-pump slam. The win over the 6-foot-8 Wilkins makes Webb the shortest man ever to win the competition.

1994

Duke and North Carolina, who have played so many monumental men's basketball games, square off for the first time when the teams are ranked #1 and #2, respectively, in the national polls. Playing at home, the Tar Heels win this one, 89-78.

February 4

1959

Lawrence Julius Taylor is born in Williamsburg, Virginia. After an All-American career as a linebacker at the University of North Carolina, Taylor—or "L.T."—will join the New York Giants and become one of the greatest defensive players in NFL history, earning himself a spot in the Pro Football Hall of Fame.

1961

Basketball stars Art Heyman of Duke (ranked No. 4 in the nation) and Larry Brown of North Carolina (ranked No. 5) ignite one of the most famous brawls in NCAA basketball history during the two teams' heated game at Duke's Indoor Stadium. After Heyman makes two free throws to give Duke an 80-75 lead with 15 seconds left, Brown takes the inbounds pass and heads for the basket, where Heyman grabs him hard by the shoulders as he tries to shoot. Brown responds angrily, throwing first the ball at Heyman, then a punch. When Heyman retaliates with a swing of his own, Carolina reserve Donnie Walsh sprints from the bench and cold-cocks Heyman from behind, knocking him to the floor. More UNC players jump on him, and while no Blue Devils come to Heyman's defense, incensed fans charge onto the floor and join the melee. It takes Durham police more than 10 minutes to restore order. Officials eject Heyman for fighting—but, surprisingly, not Brown, who makes his two free throws. Duke makes a free throw in the final seconds and wins the game 81-77. Heyman, Brown and Walsh will be suspended for the remainder of the Atlantic Coast Conference regular season.

February 5

1987
Pete Maravich, aka "Pistol Pete," is inducted into the Naismith Memorial Basketball Hall of Fame. Maravich, the all-time leading NCAA Division I scorer, and later an accomplished guard in the NBA, starred at Raleigh's Broughton High School when his dad, Press Maravich, coached at N.C. State University.

2006
Pittsburgh Steelers head coach Bill Cowher, a former defensive star at North Carolina State University, leads the Steelers to a 21-10 win over the Seattle Seahawks in Super Bowl XL. After one more season with Pittsburgh, Cowher will step down—after 15 seasons as the Steelers' head coach—finishing with a record of 161-99-1. Also in the Super Bowl, Steelers running back Willie Parker, a Clinton native who played his college ball at the University of North Carolina, breaks loose for a 75-yard touchdown in the third quarter to give Pittsburgh a 14-3 lead. Parker's TD is the longest run from scrimmage in Super Bowl history.

Bill Cowher
Courtesy of N.C. State Athletics

February 6

1906
In what is believed to be the state's first intercollegiate basketball game, played at Guilford College, Guilford defeats Wake Forest, 26-19.

February 6 continued

1927
Forrest Harrill "Smoky" Burgess, who will set a major-league record for career pinch hits, is born in Caroleen. In his 18-year baseball career, Burgess will get 145 pinch hits, which will be the major-league record from 1967 until 1979.

1988
Michael Jordan avenges his 1985 loss to fellow North Carolinian Dominique Wilkins in the NBA Slam Dunk Contest, defeating him in the final round of one of the most high-flying, entertaining dunking competitions of all time. The win marks Jordan's second consecutive dunking title.

2009
In one of the most stunning collapses in NCAA history, the Campbell University men's basketball team blows a late 18-point lead and loses to Belmont University, 87-84. With only 3:22 to play, Campbell had led 75-57.

Did You Know?
Former Davidson College guard Stephen Curry set an NCAA record for three-pointers in a season, making 162 during the 2007-08 season. The following season, he averaged 28.6 points per game to lead all Division I scorers, en route to being named a first-team All-American.

February 7

1970
Louisiana State's Pistol Pete Maravich, the former Raleigh high-school hoops star, lights up Alabama for a record 69 points—the most ever scored against a Division I team—but Alabama still gets the win, 106-104.

1987
Michael Jordan claims the first of his two NBA Slam Dunk Contest titles, defeating Jerome Kersey in the finals during All-Star Weekend in Seattle. The highlight comes when Jordan takes off from the free throw line and soars for a mesmerizing dunk.

Michael Jordan
Courtesy of the Hugh Morton Collection, North Carolina Collection, University of North Carolina Library at Chapel Hill

1988
Chicago Bulls star—and former Tar Heel—Michael Jordan wins the MVP Award in the NBA All-Star Game, pouring in 40 points to lead the East to a 138-133 victory.

1994
Explaining that he's pursuing his late father's dream for him to play major-league baseball, Michael Jordan signs a minor-league contract with the Chicago White Sox. The dream will not pan out, however, and Jordan eventually will return to the NBA.

2011
Wake Forest University baseball coach Tom Walter donates a kidney to one of his players, freshman Kevin Jordan, after Jordan was diagnosed with a rare kidney disorder. "I'm definitely going to play hard for Coach," Jordan tells reporters at Emory University Hospital in Atlanta following the procedure. "I can't say no to him. I've got his body part in me."

Did You Know?
Shea Ralph of Fayetteville's Terry Sanford High School was named the 1996 *USA Today* National High School Player of the Year, and in 2000—playing for the University of Connecticut—was named *Sports Illustrated for Women*'s Player of the Year.

February 8

1911
A&M College—later to be known as North Carolina State University—plays its first official basketball game, losing at Wake Forest, 33-6.

1970
Alonzo Harding Mourning Jr. is born in Chesapeake, Virginia. After a stellar college career at Georgetown University, Mourning will be drafted in 1992 by the NBA's Charlotte Hornets and, in his rookie season, lead the team to the playoffs.

1998
Michael Jordan becomes the oldest player to win the MVP Award in the NBA All-Star Game, earning the award only nine days shy of his thirty-fifth birthday. He finishes the game with 23 points, six rebounds and eight assists.

February 9

1956
Phil Jackson Ford Jr. is born in Rocky Mount. Ford will become one of the North Carolina Tar Heels' most beloved basketball stars, piloting the team's famed Four Corners offense of the mid to late 1970s and becoming the school's all-time scoring leader (a crown he will yield to Tyler Hansbrough in 2008).

Phil Ford
Courtesy of UNC Athletic Communications

1985
After eliminating the likes of Julius Erving and Larry Nance, two North Carolinians, Michael Jordan and Dominique Wilkins, face each other in the finals of the 1985 NBA Slam Dunk Contest. Wilkins gets the better of Jordan—scoring two perfect 50s in the final round—to claim the title.

1991
Sugar Ray Leonard, Wilmington's flashy boxing champion, announces his retirement right after absorbing a horrific beating at the hands of World Boxing Council (WBC) junior middleweight title-holder Terry Norris at Madison Square Garden. The 34-year-old Leonard gets knocked to the canvas twice—suffering cut lips and an eye swollen shut—en route to a 12-round decision that's not even close. His professional career ends with a 36-2-1 record.

1991
During the NBA's All-Star Weekend at the Charlotte Coliseum, Craig Hodges of the Chicago Bulls drills 19 consecutive shots to win the annual three-point shootout, obliterating Larry Bird's previous record of 11 straight shots in 1986. Also, Dee Brown uses his "Peek-A-Boo" dunk—with his forearm covering his eyes—to win the Slam Dunk Contest.

1997
Michael Jordan scores 14 points, grabs 11 rebounds and dishes out 11 assists to become the first player ever to record a triple-double in the NBA All-Star Game.

2000
The Charlotte Hornets retire Bobby Phills' No. 13 jersey during a halftime ceremony at the Charlotte Coliseum, making his the first jersey the franchise has ever retired. Phills had died in a car crash in Charlotte about a month earlier.

2011
Michelle Williams of Northwest Guilford High School drains eleven 3-pointers in a game against Parkland, tying a state record for girls' high-school basketball.

February 10

1962

Former University of North Carolina track star Jim Beatty, competing at a track and field meet in Los Angeles, becomes the first man to break the four-minute mile barrier on an indoor track, finishing in 3:58.9. The second-place runner finishes more than 8 seconds—at least 50 yards—behind him. Beatty, a former Charlottean, will finish the year with seven new U.S. distance running records and one world record, earning him the 1962 James E. Sullivan Award as the nation's top amateur athlete. That same year, he'll also become the first person chosen as Athlete of the Year by "ABC's Wide World of Sports," and he'll eventually be inducted into the USA Track & Field Hall of Fame.

Jim Beatty
Courtesy of UNC Athletic Communications

1990

Dominique Wilkins, who grew up in Washington, North Carolina, wins his second NBA Slam Dunk Contest, defeating former University of North Carolina star Kenny Smith in the finals. Meanwhile, in the 3-Point Shootout, former Tar Heel Michael Jordan posts a 5-point round, the lowest score in the history of the competition.

2010

The University of North Carolina retires Tyler Hansbrough's No. 50 basketball jersey. Hansbrough was the 2007-08 National Player of the Year his junior year, and as a senior he led the Tar Heels to the 2009 NCAA championship. He is only the eighth player in Tar Heel history to have his jersey retired.

February 11

1996
Michael Jordan scores 20 points in only 22 minutes of playing time to earn the MVP Award of the NBA All-Star Game. Jordan's East squad defeats the West, 129-118.

February 12

2000
Former high-flying Tar Heel Vince Carter etches his name on the NBA Slam Dunk Contest trophy, beating Steve Francis and even his own cousin—Tracy McGrady, a graduate of Durham's Mount Zion Christian Academy—in the finals. Carter registers three perfect 50 scores along the way.

2010
Supermodel Brooklyn Decker, who lived in Charlotte and was discovered as a teenager at a Charlotte shopping mall, graces the cover of the annual *Sports Illustrated* swimsuit issue. Decker, known as a diehard Tar Heel fan, first appeared in the famous swimsuit edition in 2006, but this marks her first time making the cover.

February 13

1947
Michael William Krzyzewski is born in Chicago, Illinois. Krzyzewski will become one of the winningest college basketball coaches of all time, leading the Duke Blue Devils to four NCAA championships.

2006
Greensboro native Joey Cheek, a former inline speed skater, wins the gold medal in the men's 500-meter speed-skating competition at the Winter Olympics in Turin, Italy. He'll also win the silver medal in the 1,000-meter event and will be voted by his Olympic teammates to carry the U.S. flag into the closing ceremonies. Cheek makes more headlines by donating his U.S. Olympic Committee bonus money—$25,000 for the gold medal, $15,000 for the silver—to an international humanitarian organization called Right To Play.

February 14

1988

NASCAR legend Richard Petty, a native of Randleman, amazingly escapes serious injury in a spectacular crash on the 106th lap of the Daytona 500. After being bumped from behind by Phil Barkdoll, Petty's car goes airborne and rolls over about eight times before settling in the middle of the track and being struck by Brett Bodine's car. Despite the frightening crash, Petty walks away unscathed.

February 15

1978

Leon Spinks, who took up boxing as a Marine at Camp Lejeune, wins the heavyweight boxing title by defeating reigning champ Muhammad Ali in a 15-round decision in Las Vegas. The win is widely considered to be one of the biggest upsets in boxing history. By winning the heavyweight title in only his eighth professional fight, Spinks becomes the fastest ever to win the title.

1981

Richard Petty wins his record seventh Daytona 500. No other driver has more than four wins at the storied racetrack.

Richard Petty
Courtesy of High Point Enterprise/*Sonny Hedgecock*

1998
After two decades of trying, Kannapolis native Dale Earnhardt finally gets that elusive win at the Daytona 500, beating Bobby Labonte to the checkered flag. Following his win, in an unusual show of respect, crew members of the other NASCAR drivers line pit road to shake Earnhardt's hand as he heads toward Victory Lane.

2004
Dale Earnhardt Jr. of Kannapolis wins the Daytona 500, six years to the day after his legendary father and namesake won the race.

February 16

2000
East Bladen and East Columbus high schools score a total of nine points—the lowest combined scoring output in the history of North Carolina high-school girls' basketball—with East Bladen getting the win, 5-4.

2001
Former UNC basketball star Larry Brown, now coaching the NBA's Philadelphia 76ers, joins a select group by picking up his 1,000th professional basketball coaching win, as the 76ers beat the Los Angeles Clippers, 108-93. Brown earned 229 of those wins coaching in the ABA, including a stint with the Carolina Cougars.

February 17

1963
Michael Jeffrey Jordan is born in Brooklyn, New York, but the future basketball superstar—whose family will move to Wilmington when he's just a toddler—will come to be known as one of North Carolina's favorite sons, playing basketball at Wilmington's Laney High School and then the University of North Carolina. Jordan will widely be considered the best basketball player ever.

1964
Chicago White Sox shortstop Luke Appling, a native of High Point, is elected to the Baseball Hall of Fame. Among his many achievements, Appling holds the single-season record for highest batting average for shortstops, having hit .388 in 1936.

February 17 continued

1974

Polk County native—and University of North Carolina track star—Tony Waldrop sets a world record for the indoor mile, finishing his race at the San Diego indoor games in 3:55. The run is part of an amazing streak in which he'll run 11 straight mile runs in under four minutes, and his 3:55 remains the NCAA record for the indoor mile. Waldrop will be named the Atlantic Coast Conference Athlete of the Year for 1974, over N.C. State basketball star David Thompson.

Tony Waldrop
Courtesy of UNC Athletic Communications

2001

Charlotte Hornets guard Baron Davis makes the longest shot in NBA history, nailing an 89-footer with 0.7 seconds remaining in the third quarter at Milwaukee.

February 18

1990

Tantalizingly close to his elusive first Daytona 500 win, Kannapolis native Dale Earnhardt has the lead on the final lap when, in the final turn, he runs over a piece of metal and cuts a tire, dropping him back to a heartbreaking fifth-place finish. Derrike Cope, who had been four seconds behind Earnhardt, takes the checkered flag. Earnhardt's disappointed team will take the flat tire and hang it in the Earnhardt garage as a reminder of how close the team had come to winning the famed race.

1999

Carolina Hurricanes player Paul Coffey plays in his 1,300th NHL game, joining fellow Hurricane Ron Francis as the only teammates in league history to reach 1,300 games in the same season. Francis reached the milestone on February 9.

2001

Racing fans experience one of the darkest days in NASCAR history, when 49-year-old Dale Earnhardt dies in a crash at the Daytona 500. The crash occurs as Earnhardt heads into Turn 3 of the final lap and makes contact with Sterling Marlin. As his Number 3 car careens out of control, it is hit again, this time by the car of Ken Schrader, and slams into a retaining wall at an estimated 160 mph. Though Earnhardt is taken to Halifax Medical Center, it is believed he died instantly. NASCAR president Mike Helton will tell the world at a press conference a few hours later, "Undoubtedly, this is one of the toughest announcements I've personally had to make. We've lost Dale Earnhardt."

Dale Earnhardt
Courtesy of High Point Enterprise/*Sonny Hedgecock*

2006

Nate Robinson, standing only 5-feet-9 inches, becomes the second-shortest man to win the NBA Slam Dunk Contest. Ironically, Robinson wows the judges with a perfect 50-point dunk when he leaps *over* the competition's smallest-ever champion—5-foot-7 Spud Webb, the former N.C. State star who won the 1986 dunk contest—and slams it home.

February ≡ 39

February 18 continued

2007

Duke University basketball coach Mike Krzyzewski gets his 700th win—a 71-62 victory over Georgia Tech—making him the second-fastest to reach the 700 milestone (behind Adolph Rupp of Kentucky).

February 19

1968

William English shatters the state's collegiate basketball scoring record—and outscores the opponents' entire team—pouring in 77 points to lead Winston-Salem State to a 146-74 romp over Fayetteville State at Winston-Salem State's Whitaker Gymnasium. English's performance easily surpasses the 68 points scored by his former teammate, Earl "The Pearl" Monroe, against Fayetteville State the previous season. He scores 37 points in the first half despite sitting out the final four minutes, and, with his teammates constantly feeding him the ball, adds 40 more in the second half. He makes 34 of 46 field goals—a sizzling 74 percent—and 9 of 13 free throws. "We didn't have to use any strategy tonight," Winston-Salem State head coach Clarence "Big House" Gaines says after the game. "All they had to do was give it to English, and he made the points." English goes home with a keepsake—the game ball, with "77" written on it to commemorate his record-breaking night.

William English
Courtesy of Winston-Salem State University Athletics

2006

Charlotte resident Jimmie Johnson wins the Daytona 500. However, Johnson fails a post-race inspection, resulting in a four-race suspension of his crew chief, Chad Knaus, and a $200,000 fine. Johnson will go on to win the 2006 NASCAR points championship.

February 20

1943
Scoring phenom Rudolph "Rocky" Roberson of the North Carolina College for Negroes (now North Carolina Central University) in Durham sets a national scoring record with 58 points against Shaw. His performance tops the previous record of 50 points, set in 1938 by Hank Luisetti. Roberson will lead the nation in scoring for three straight years between 1943 and 1945.

1972
Former UNC hoops star Larry Brown, now playing for the ABA's Denver Rockets, sets the ABA record for assists in a game with 23, as Denver beats the Pittsburgh Condors, 146-123.

2000
Newton native Dale Jarrett wins his third Daytona 500, having also won the race in 1993 and 1996.

Dale Jarrett
Courtesy of High Point Enterprise/*Sonny Hedgecock*

2011
Lexington resident Jack Hege, believed to be the only person to have witnessed every single running of the Daytona 500 as a spectator, extends his amazing streak to 53 straight Daytonas. Hege, 84, had pretty much ruled out attending this year's race because he was recovering from a broken left arm, but when a doctor gave him clearance to go, Richard Childress Racing agreed to fly him down to Daytona for the race. Hege's first race at Daytona was actually in 1958, the last race on the beach course, and then the next year he began his incredible streak of Daytona 500s.

February 21

1993

Speaking at a celebration commemorating the tenth anniversary of North Carolina State's magical 1983 NCAA title, former Wolfpack coach Jim Valvano—his body riddled with cancer—tells a packed Reynolds Auditorium, "Don't give up, don't ever give up." Reflecting on that championship team, Valvano says, "The '83 team taught me about dreaming, and that team taught me persistence, the idea of never, *ever* quitting. Don't ever give up! Don't ever stop fighting!"

Did You Know?

Former Duke basketball star J.J. Redick holds the career record for three-pointers, having made 457 from behind the arc between 2003 and 2006. He also set an NCAA mark for free-throw percentage—shooting 91.2 percent—en route to winning numerous National Player of the Year awards during his senior season.

February 22

1934

George "Sparky" Anderson is born in Bridgewater, South Dakota. Though never much of a player, Anderson will find his niche as a manager—including spending the 1968 season as manager of the minor-league Asheville Tourists—and will get elected to the Baseball Hall of Fame for his success as a major-league manager.

1959

In a photo finish, drivers Johnny Beauchamp and Randleman native Lee Petty cross the finish line side by side in the inaugural running of the Daytona 500, now considered the most prestigious race on the NASCAR schedule. Both drivers believe they won the race. "I had him by two feet," Beauchamp says. "I glanced over to Lee Petty's car as I crossed the finish line, and I could see his headlight slightly back of my car. It was so close I didn't know how they would call it, but I thought I won." Petty, on the other hand, states, "I had Beauchamp by a good two feet. In my own mind, I know I won." Beauchamp is initially declared the winner—NASCAR officials positioned at the finish line thought he had won by about twelve inches—but Petty files a formal protest. Three days later, after examining photographs and newsreel footage of the finish, officials will reverse their decision and declare Petty the winner.

Lee Petty
Courtesy of North Carolina State Archives

2008
Robeson County native Kelvin Sampson, the head basketball coach at Indiana University, resigns amid allegations of a number of serious NCAA violations.

February 23

1893
In an effort to promote the school's fledgling football team, UNC students launch a one-page tabloid called *The Tar Heel*. In its early years, the publication—which eventually will become *The Daily Tar Heel*—reports predominantly on school sports events.

1963
Duke All-American basketball star Art Heyman—a.k.a. "King Arthur"—goes out with a bang, scoring a career-high 40 points in his final home game, a 106-93 win over rival North Carolina. He will go on to be named National Player of the Year.

1987
Raleigh native Nate McMillan, who played his college ball at North Carolina State, ties the NBA rookie assist record. The Seattle Supersonics guard records 25 assists in a win over the Los Angeles Clippers.

February 23 continued

1991

North Carolina becomes the first college basketball program to reach the 1,500-win milestone.

2002

Winston-Salem native—and former Duke University football and track star—Randy Jones becomes the first black male to win a Winter Olympics medal for the United States when his four-man bobsled team grabs the silver medal. The medal also ends a 46-year drought during which the United States did not medal in Olympic bobsledding competition. After graduating from Duke, Jones tried out for and made the U.S. bobsled team at the encouragement of his track coach.

February 24

1952

Tommy Burleson, who will help lead the North Carolina State Wolfpack to the 1974 NCAA basketball title, is born in Crossnore.

1979

The University of North Carolina's Rich Yonakor misses a shot so badly at Duke's Cameron Indoor Stadium that it inspires Duke fans to serenade him with a mocking chant: "Airrr ballll!!" Before long, the chant will be heard at basketball arenas throughout the country.

February 25

1947

Raleigh's fire chief forces the N.C. State basketball team to forfeit a game against UNC, because the Wolfpack's Thompson Gymnasium is overcrowded—a fire code violation—and students refuse to leave the building.

1955

Duke and North Carolina square off in their heated rivalry—the best rivalry in all of college basketball—but curiously, neither team is nationally ranked when they play this time, a rarity that has not happened again since. Duke gets the win.

1977
Pete Maravich sets the NBA record for scoring by a guard when he pours in 68 points. The record will be broken in 1990 by another former North Carolinian—Michael Jordan.

1978
North Carolina's All-American point guard Phil Ford scores a career-high 34 points in his final game at Carmichael Auditorium, leading the Tar Heels to an 87-83 win over arch-rival Duke. Ford, a Rocky Mount native, hits 13 of 19 shots and adds five assists.

February 26

1955
Wake Forest senior basketball star Dickie Hemric, a native of Jonesville, passes Furman University's Frank Selvy to become the NCAA's all-time career scoring leader during a game at Clemson. Selvy had 2,538 points, and Hemric will end his career with 2,587. He will remain the career scoring leader until Feb. 6, 1960, when he will be surpassed by Oscar Robertson of Cincinnati.

Dickie Hemric
Courtesy of Wake Forest Media Relations

2002
Former North Carolina State forward Chucky Brown takes the floor for his 12th team—the Sacramento Kings—to set the NBA record for having played with the most teams. The record will eventually be tied by two other players.

February 27

1961

James Ager Worthy is born in Gastonia. He will become an All-American basketball player at Ashbrook High School, lead the North Carolina Tar Heels to an NCAA title in 1982 and be a major part of the Los Angeles Lakers dynasty of the 1980s en route to his induction into the Basketball Hall of Fame.

February 28

1922

In the first college conference basketball tournament ever held, the University of North Carolina defeats Mercer, 40-26, to win the Southern Conference tournament championship. The team is led by future All-American Cartwright Carmichael.

1931

Dean Edwards Smith is born in Emporia, Kansas, the son of a high-school basketball coach. He will go on to become the most famous

Dean Smith
Courtesy of UNC Athletic Communications

and successful basketball coach the University of North Carolina has ever known, winning 879 games and retiring as the winningest coach in NCAA history (though he will later be passed for that honor).

1960

Future NASCAR king Richard Petty, a.k.a. "The Randleman Rocket," gets his first win in a Grand National race—in his 35th career start—winning by six car-lengths on a dirt track in Charlotte. The win earns the 22-year-old a whopping $800. *The Charlotte Observer* will report in a headline, "Dick Petty Wins Fairgrounds Race."

1981

Mr. Wuf and Ms. Wuf, the mascots for the N.C. State Wolfpack, are married in a mock wedding ceremony during halftime of a men's basketball game at Reynolds Coliseum. Wake Forest's mascot, the Demon Deacon, performs the ceremony, and NCSU Chancellor Joab Thomas gives the bride away.

1981

During player introductions at his final game in Cameron Indoor Stadium, Duke basketball star Gene Banks dramatically throws roses to the crowd as a gesture of gratitude. Before the day is over, he'll leave a couple more sweet-smelling memories for the Blue Devil fans—a jump shot from the top of the key as time expires, sending the game into overtime, and a put-back at the end of the overtime period to give Duke a 66-65 win over their arch rivals, the North Carolina Tar Heels. Banks finishes with a game-high 25 points.

2008

The University of North Carolina at Greensboro retires the No. 42 jersey of basketball star Kyle Hines after a stellar four-year career. Though largely unheralded on the national radar, Hines is one of only six NCAA players to record 2,000 points, 1,000 rebounds and 300 blocks in a career. The elite group includes another North Carolina collegian, Tim Duncan of Wake Forest, as well as Alonzo Mourning, David Robinson, Pervis Ellison and Derrick Coleman.

2009

UNC's Tyler Hansbrough sets a new NCAA record for most free throws made in a career, going eight for eight at the line against Georgia Tech and finishing the game with 907 career free throws. The previous record was 905, set by Wake Forest's Dickie Hemric. Hansbrough will go on to finish his career with 968 free throws made.

February 29

1964

How fitting that on Leap Day, when the calendar gives us an extra day, a basketball game would go into extra periods. In one of the strangest basketball games ever—at any level—the Boone Trail Pioneers defeat the Angier Bulldogs, 56-54, in an outlandish *13-overtime* game, the longest sanctioned basketball game in hoops history. Playing for the Harnett County boys' championship, neither of the cross-county rivals substitutes the entire game, meaning all 10 players on the court play 71 minutes (four eight-minute quarters and 13 three-minute overtime periods). Played in Carter Gymnasium on the campus of Campbell College, the Saturday night game runs so long that the referees actually stop the action after seven overtimes to call the N.C. High School Athletic Association and ask for permission to continue the game into the wee hours of Sunday morning. The game is tied at 46 at the end of regulation, and with both teams attempting to hold the ball in overtime, points come very sparingly during the extra periods. Nobody scores in the first, fourth, fifth, sixth, seventh, ninth, 10th, 11th or 12th overtimes. "Once we got to overtime, the team that won the tap pretty much held the ball for the last shot," Angier player Phil Ferrell will tell the *Fayetteville Observer* years later. "The thing I remember most is the feeling that nobody wanted to be the one to make the mistake that cost his team the game." Finally, in the lucky 13th overtime, Boone Trail outscores Angier 4-2 to bring the marathon game to an end. "By the 13th overtime, it reached the point where we didn't think the game was ever going to end," Angier's Ron Ashley will tell the *Fayetteville Observer*. "When it was finally over, there was more a sense of relief than anything else. I think everybody realized they had been part of something special."

Did You Know?

The Dean E. Smith Student Activities Center in Chapel Hill is obviously named for the Tar Heels' former coach, but Smith reportedly resisted efforts to name the building after him. Only when the UNC administration convinced Smith that fundraising efforts for the dome could fail without him did he consent to letting his name go on the building.

MARCH

March 1

1889
The University of North Carolina football team gets its first win—avenging an earlier loss to Wake Forest College—by defeating Wake Forest, 33-0, in a game played at Raleigh Athletic Park.

1978
Gardner-Webb standout John Drew, now of the Atlanta Hawks, sets a dubious NBA record when he commits 14 turnovers in a game against the New Jersey Jets.

1986
The New York Knicks retire Earl "The Pearl" Monroe's No. 15 jersey. Monroe, who played his college ball at Winston-Salem State University, starred on New York's 1973 championship squad.

March 1 continued

2008

Duke men's basketball coach Mike Krzyzewski becomes only the sixth coach in NCAA history to record 800 wins, as the Blue Devils knock off North Carolina State, 87-86.

March 2

1962

On the night when Wilt Chamberlain famously scores 100 points in the Philadelphia Warriors' 169-147 win over the New York Knicks, Philadelphia's second-leading scorer—completely lost in Chamberlain's immense shadow—is Al Attles, the former North Carolina A&T star, who finishes with 17 points.

1974

In another bizarre chapter of the storied Duke-North Carolina rivalry, the Tar Heels overcome an eight-point deficit with only 17 seconds remaining to force the game into overtime, then go on to win in the extra period. Duke, only 10-15 on the season, seems to have the upset over the 20-4 Tar Heels in hand, leading 86-78 with 17 seconds left. But then comes a string of Carmichael Auditorium serendipity: a pair of UNC free throws cuts the lead to six. A quick steal results in a layup, cutting it to four. When Duke fumbles its inbounds pass out of bounds, Carolina takes possession and scores another quick basket, trimming the Duke lead to only two points, with six seconds left. On the ensuing inbounds play, Carolina fouls Duke's Pete Kramer, who misses the front end of a one-and-one free throw opportunity; the Tar Heels rebound and take a timeout with three seconds left. UNC completes the stunning comeback when freshman Walter Davis catches the inbounds pass near midcourt, takes three dribbles and banks in a 30-footer at the buzzer to tie the game at 86. Carolina actually trails again in overtime, 92-89, but scores the game's final seven points for the 96-92 victory, one of the most stunning comebacks in college basketball history.

1991

North Carolina State point guard Chris Corchiani becomes the first player in NCAA history to record his 1,000th assist, reaching the milestone during the Wolfpack's 89-84 loss to Wake Forest.

1997

Dean Smith, head coach of the North Carolina men's basketball team since 1961, coaches his final game in Chapel Hill, a 91-85 victory over arch-rival Duke. No one knows it at the time—not even Smith—but he will announce his retirement before the beginning of the 1997-98 season.

2010
The University of North Carolina basketball program gets its 2,000th win—becoming only the second school to reach that historic milestone (after Kentucky)—with a 69-62 win over Miami in Chapel Hill.

March 3

1984
In what will be his final game at the University of North Carolina's Carmichael Auditorium, Michael Jordan—en route to National Player of the Year honors—scores 25 points to lead the Tar Heels to a 96-83 double-overtime win over Duke. After the season, Jordan will announce that he's skipping his senior season to turn pro.

March 4

1924
The University of North Carolina men's basketball team, nicknamed the White Phantoms, wins the Southern Conference championship. The team's perfect 26-0 record will also earn UNC the Helms Foundation's national championship, the first of UNC's six national titles. The team is led by such stars as Cartwright Carmichael, Jack Cobb and Monk McDonald.

The 1923-24 UNC men's basketball team
Courtesy of UNC Athletic Communications

March 4 continued

1960

Greensboro gets the state's first big-time hockey team when Central Carolina Sports Inc. pays $2,500 for a franchise that will move to Greensboro from Troy, Ohio. The team will be known as the Greensboro Generals. Charlotte will get a franchise later in the same year.

1974

Is streaking a sport? Probably not, but that doesn't deter the country's most popular sports magazine, *Sports Illustrated*, from hailing Western Carolina University as the national streaking champion, "on the basis of 141 streakers—113 men and 28 women."

1984

Durham native Rick Ferrell, a longtime major-league catcher who played college ball at Guilford College, is elected to the National Baseball Hall of Fame. When Ferrell retired from the game in 1947, he had caught more games—1,806—than any other American Leaguer, a record that stood for more than 40 years. He also had a .281 lifetime batting average, and his average topped .300 four times.

1993

Former North Carolina State basketball coach Jim Valvano, in the midst of a yearlong battle against cancer, receives the inaugural Arthur Ashe Courage and Humanitarian Award at the ESPY Awards. During his acceptance speech, he announces the creation of The V Foundation for Cancer Research, an organization dedicated to finding a cure for cancer. The organization's motto will be, "Don't give up ... don't ever give up!"

In his memorably funny, inspirational speech that perfectly captures Valvano's larger-than-life personality, he encourages his audience to do three things every day—laugh, think and be moved to tears. "Think about it: If you laugh, you think and you cry, that's a full day. That's a heck of a day. You do that seven days a week, you're going to have something special."

Valvano concludes by saying, "Cancer can take away all my physical abilities. It cannot touch my mind, it cannot touch my heart, and it cannot touch my soul. And those three things are going to carry on forever."

He will die less than two months later.

2006

Approximately 3.78 million households tune in to ESPN and ESPN2 to watch rivals Duke and North Carolina square off, making it the most-watched college basketball game ever. It's Senior Night at Cameron Indoor Stadium for the No. 1-ranked Blue Devils and their star seniors J.J. Redick and Shelden Williams, but UNC freshman Tyler Hansbrough leads the Tar Heels to an 83-76 upset.

2007
Duke's Gerald Henderson breaks the nose of Tyler Hansbrough when he catches the North Carolina star's face with a hard right elbow in the closing seconds of the Tar Heels' 86-72 win over the Blue Devils. Henderson is ejected from the game and receives a one-game suspension for a "combative foul."

March 5

1922
Famed Wild West sharpshooter Annie Oakley, at age 61, shatters the record for women's trap shooting, breaking 98 out of 100 clay targets thrown at 16 yards during a competition at the Pinehurst Gun Club in Pinehurst. She breaks the first 50 targets before finally missing the 51st, then later misses the 67th, but hits all the rest.

1973
New York Yankee teammates and best friends Fritz Peterson and Mike Kekich stun the baseball world by announcing that they have swapped families—wives, children and even their dogs. The phenomenon of wife-swapping wasn't totally unheard of in the early 1970s, but teammates and team officials were shocked nonetheless. Yankees general manager Lee MacPhail will quip, "We may have to call off Family Day." Peterson, who played minor-league baseball in North Carolina with the Shelby Yankees in 1964 and the Greensboro Yankees in part of 1965, will eventually marry Kekich's wife, and they will have four children together.

2001
UNC-Wilmington misses out on a berth in the NCAA Tournament by losing to George Mason, 35-33, in the finals of the men's Colonial Athletic Association Tournament. The game, in which each team has a scoring drought longer than 7½ minutes, is the second-lowest-scoring game in the NCAA's shot-clock era.

Did You Know?
Talk about grand theft. In 1992, Sureka Hammonds of Parkwood High School in Monroe set a national record with 24 steals in a game against Indian Land, South Carolina.

March 6

2005

A record 22,125 spectators pack the Dean E. Smith Center in Chapel Hill to watch the Tar Heels battle arch-rival Duke. It's the largest crowd ever to see a basketball game on a college campus in North Carolina. Carolina wins, 75-73, thanks to a late put-back hoop and free throw by freshman Marvin Williams.

March 7

1914

Nineteen-year-old George Herman "Babe" Ruth, a rookie pitcher in the Baltimore Orioles organization—and the future major-league home run king—swats his first professional homer during an intrasquad game at the Cape Fear Fairgrounds in Fayetteville, where the team is holding spring training. Playing in his first game, the young left-handed hitter goes 2-for-3, but the home run is what local fans will remember, describing it as the longest home run they've ever seen. Some will claim the

Cape Fear Fairgrounds, where Babe Ruth
hit his first professional home run
Courtesy of VisitFayettevilleNC.com

ball landed in a cornfield beyond the rightfield fence, while others will say it soared over the cornfield and landed in a millpond. As for Ruth's recollection, he will later say of his first home run, "I hit it as I hit all the others—by taking a good gander at the pitch as it came up to the plate, twisting my body into a backswing, and then hitting it as hard as I could swing." Within a few months, Ruth will already be in the majors—breaking in with the Boston Red Sox and playing most of his career with the New York Yankees—where he will hit 714 career homers. Nearly 40 years after Ruth's historic home run in Fayetteville, Maurice Fleishman, who witnessed the homer as an 11-year-old batboy, will lead the campaign to have a state historic marker erected near the spot of the homer.

Courtesy of VisitFayettevilleNC.com

It's also in Fayetteville that Ruth's teammates will give him his famous nickname, "Babe," although there are several explanations as to how it happened. One version claims that Ruth's older teammates teased him because of his relative youth and his cherubic face, and began calling him Babe. Another explanation holds that one day Ruth was tagging along behind team manager and owner Jack Dunn, and the player said, "There goes Dunn's new babe," which led to Ruth's moniker. A variation of that story claims that an assistant manager warned players to stop teasing Ruth so much, because he's "one of Jack Dunn's babes." Regardless of which version is correct, there seems to be no dispute that Ruth's famous nickname was born in Fayetteville.

1982

Dean Smith's North Carolina Tar Heels use their signature "Four Corners" offense to preserve a close—but also boring—47-45 win over Virginia in the championship game of the ACC Tournament. Leading 44-43 with 7:34 remaining, UNC holds the ball for more than seven minutes before taking a shot. The win gives the Heels momentum heading into the NCAA Tournament, which they will win three weeks later, but it makes for dull viewing for the national audience tuned in to watch the battle. As a result, the Atlantic Coast Conference—with the NCAA's blessing—will experiment with a 30-second shot clock and a 3-point shot the next season, and the delay game will never be heard from again.

1996

West Iredell's David Heintz knocks down 23 consecutive free throws in a game against A.L. Brown, a state record for boys' high-school basketball.

March 8

1960

Charles Linwood "Buck" Williams, who will star at the University of Maryland and go on to become the all-time scoring leader for the New Jersey Nets, is born in Rocky Mount.

1968

In one of the more bizarre games in college basketball history—an ACC Tournament semifinal at the old Charlotte Coliseum—North Carolina State holds the ball...and holds it...and holds it...against heavily favored Duke. The tactic works, as State erases Duke's 4-2 halftime lead – *4-2!* – and pulls off a 12-10 upset over the No. 6-ranked Blue Devils. The 22 total points make it the lowest-scoring game in ACC Tournament history. A few bored, disgruntled fans show their displeasure by throwing coins on the court, and at one point the North Carolina radio network takes a commercial break *during the action*—if you can call it that—because there are no timeouts. When the network returns to the air, announcer Bill Currie assures listeners they haven't missed a thing, famously quipping that the game is "about as exciting as artificial insemination." The next day, State will lose in the tourney finals to North Carolina, 87-50.

March 9

1974

University of North Carolina senior distance runner Tony Waldrop extends his jaw-dropping streak of sub-4-minute indoor miles to seven, running a 3:59.5 in the national collegiate championships. The previous record for consecutive sub-4-minute indoor miles was only three.

1974

With an NCAA Tournament bid on the line, North Carolina State—the top-ranked basketball team in the country—beats fifth-ranked Maryland, 103-100, in an overtime thriller widely considered to be one of the greatest games in college basketball history. The game is for the Atlantic Coast Conference Tournament championship, with the winner getting the conference's only bid to the NCAA Tournament—and the loser going home. Maryland jumps out to a 25-12 lead, but the Wolfpack slowly, methodically gets back into the game before finally winning it in overtime. State's 7-foot-4 center Tommy Burleson leads the way with 38 points, and the Wolfpack will carry the momentum all the way to an NCAA championship a couple of weeks later.

March 10

1946
Jim Valvano, the future wisecracking, inspirational coach who will lead the North Carolina State Wolfpack to an unexpected NCAA basketball title in 1983, is born in New York City.

1973
North Carolina State knocks off Maryland, 76-74, in the finals of the ACC Tournament to complete a perfect 27-0 season. The Wolfpack is ineligible to play in the NCAA Tournament because of a recruiting violation.

2010
Disgraced Olympian—and former University of North Carolina basketball star—Marion Jones attempts to make a basketball comeback, joining the WNBA's Tulsa Shock. Now 34 and a mother of three, Jones was stripped of the five medals she won in the 2000 Summer Olympics after admitting she had used performance-enhancing drugs. She received a six-month prison sentence after admitting she had lied to federal prosecutors about her drug use.

March 11

1979
Back-to-back upsets in the second round of the NCAA Tournament's East Regional inspire the moniker "Black Sunday." First, St. John's knocks off No. 2 seed Duke, 80-78; then, Pennsylvania takes out No. 1 seed North Carolina, 72-71.

1979
Future Duke University basketball star Elton Brand, who will earn National Player of the Year honors in 1999, is born in Cortlandt Manor, New York.

Did You Know?

Former Greensboro prep basketball star Danny Manning, who played his college ball at Kansas University from 1985 to 1988, holds the NCAA career record for most games scoring in double figures with 132.

March 12

1944

The South's first integrated college-level basketball game—an unpublicized competition that will come to be referred to decades later as "The Secret Game"—is played in a gymnasium on the campus of the North Carolina College for Negroes (now North Carolina Central University) in Durham. The all-black Eagles of the North Carolina College for Negroes defeat a strong, all-white intramural team from the Duke Medical School, 88-44. The medical school players, several of whom played college basketball before enrolling in med school, prove to be no match for the Eagles' high-octane, fast-break brand of basketball. John McLendon, the Eagles' coach, had arranged for the game to be played in secret on a Sunday morning—when most people would be in church—on the North Carolina College for Negroes' campus. A referee and game clock would be employed to make the game legitimate. At the end of regulation, the two squads integrate even more, with players switching teams for a second game, this one shirts vs. skins. Neither the *Durham Morning Herald* nor the *Durham Sun* will learn of the clandestine game. *The Carolina Times*, Durham's black weekly publication, hears about the game, but the reporter agrees to protect McLendon by not publishing a story, and the game will remain a secret for more than half a century.

1956

North Carolina State loses a heartbreaker to Canisius, 79-78, in the NCAA Tournament's first-ever four-overtime game.

March 13

1990

Denver Nuggets coach Doug Moe, who played his college ball at the University of North Carolina, picks up his 600th career victory with Denver's 117-114 win over the Houston Rockets.

2006

Duke University lacrosse players host a team party at an off-campus house where a couple of exotic dancers are hired to perform. The next day, one of the strippers will tell Durham police three of the players forced her into a bathroom, where they beat and raped her—an accusation that will have wide-sweeping implications as the story plays out in the national media. In the wake of the allegations, the remainder of the team's season will be suspended and head coach Mike Pressler will be replaced. Evidence mounts, however, indicating a significant rush to ac-

58   ≡   *Instant Replay*

cuse by Durham District Attorney Mike Nifong, who will resign his office when ethics charges are levied against him, and he will ultimately be disbarred for "dishonesty, fraud, deceit and misrepresentation." The three lacrosse players charged in the incident—Reade Seligmann, Collin Finnerty and David Evans—will be exonerated on April 11, 2007, more than a year after the initial allegation. The accuser, Crystal Gale Mangum, will go on to write a book, *Last Dance for Grace: The Crystal Mangum Story*.

March 14

1906

In the state's second intercollegiate basketball game—and the first between future Atlantic Coast Conference teams—Wake Forest beats Trinity College (now Duke University), 24-10.

1942

Future Hall of Fame coach Sandra Kay Yow, who will win more than 700 games as the women's basketball coach at Elon College and North Carolina State University, is born in Gibsonville.

1969

Larry Johnson, who will become the Charlotte Hornets' No. 1 draft pick—and who will win the NBA's Rookie of the Year Award playing for the Hornets—is born in Tyler, Texas.

1980

Twenty-two members of USA Boxing—14 boxers and eight staff members—are among 87 people killed in a plane crash near Warsaw, Poland, due to mechanical failure. The team was en route to a competition in Poland. Among those killed is former High Point resident Joe Bland, who was a manager of the boxing team.

1994

Michael Jordan's novel attempt to play professional baseball loses some of its credibility when *Sports Illustrated*'s cover features a photograph of Jordan swinging at a pitch—and clearly whiffing—with the accompanying headline, "Bag It, Michael!" The subhead reads, "Jordan and The White Sox Are Embarrassing Baseball." The cover so angers Jordan that he will refuse to grant the magazine any more interviews.

March 15

1997

North Carolina beats Colorado, 73-56, in the NCAA East Regional Finals, in front of a Carolina-friendly crowd at Winston-Salem's Lawrence Joel Veterans Memorial Coliseum. The win gives Dean Smith his 877th coaching victory, putting him ahead of legendary Kentucky coach Adolph Rupp, and thus at the top of the career victory list for Division I coaches.

2011

Sidney Lowe, one of the heroes of the North Carolina State men's basketball program, resigns from his position as the Wolfpack's head coach after five disappointing seasons. Lowe starred on the 1983 State team that won an NCAA championship, but his coaching efforts leave fans—and, ultimately, N.C. State officials—frustrated. He steps down with an overall record of 86-78, an Atlantic Coast Conference record of only 25-55, and a dismal 3-13 mark against rivals Duke and North Carolina.

March 16

1969

Charles "Lefty" Driesell resigns as head coach of the Davidson Wildcats men's basketball team after compiling an impressive 176-65 record in nine seasons. Driesell earned Southern Conference Coach of the Year honors four straight years (1963-1966) and led the Wildcats to the NCAA Sweet 16 in 1966 and the Elite Eight in 1968 and 1969. Driesell, who played two seasons of college ball at Duke, will take the head coaching job at the University of Maryland, where he famously announces his intentions to make the Terrapins' basketball team "the UCLA of the East."

Coach Lefty Driesell
Courtesy of Davidson College Archives

1985
Crockett Park, an old, wooden stadium that's home to the minor-league Charlotte Orioles, is destroyed by a three-alarm fire. Investigators will determine arson to be the cause, and three juveniles will be implicated for igniting the blaze.

1987
Chicago Bulls guard—and former Tar Heel—Michael Jordan scores 23 consecutive points for the Bulls in a game against the Atlanta Hawks. He finishes the game with 61 points—one of four times he'll top the 60-point plateau in his NBA career.

1999
Bunn High School scores 68 runs in a girls' softball game against Weldon, a North Carolina state record. The game is called after two innings, with Bunn getting a 68-3 victory. Bunn's 45-run outburst in the second inning is also a state record.

> **Did You Know?**
> Back in the old days of girls' high-school basketball, when teams played six-on-six, it wasn't unusual for the star players to score dozens of points per game. And on a few occasions, they even topped the 100-point mark. For example, according to the N.C. High School Athletic Association, Melba Overcash of Landis High School scored 107 points against East Spencer in a 1949 game, Martha Ann Bowers of Norlina scored 107 against William R. Davie in 1955, and Beulah Thompson of New Hope scored 107 in a 1954 game. Also, Gayle Waldrop of Lowell scored 102 points against Sacred Heart in 1956, and Kay Wilson of Taylorsville scored 100 points against Marion in 1962.

March 17

1967
Unheralded Winston-Salem State College, led by senior scoring machine Earl "The Pearl" Monroe, captures the NCAA Division II national championship, defeating Southwest Missouri, 77-74. The title makes Winston-Salem State the first historically black college to win an NCAA championship. Monroe, who scored 34, 49, 29 and 23 points in the Rams' first four tournament games, pours in 40 points against Southwest Missouri, including 16 of the team's final 21 points and a pair of clutch free throws with 25 seconds left to seal the win. Monroe is a nearly unanimous choice for the Most Valuable Player award, while his

March 17 continued

coach—Clarence "Big House" Gaines—earns national Coach of the Year honors. The Rams finish their incredible season with a 31-1 record, having lost the season opener to High Point College and then running off 31 straight wins.

The 1966-1967 Winston-Salem State team
Courtesy of Winston-Salem State University Athletics

1972

Future women's soccer icon Mariel Margaret "Mia" Hamm, who will lead the University of North Carolina women's soccer team to four consecutive NCAA championships, is born in Selma, Alabama. She will come to be widely considered the greatest women's soccer player in history.

Mia Hamm
Courtesy of UNC Athletic Communications

1973

The Guilford College Quakers win the NAIA national championship in men's basketball, defeating Maryland-Eastern Shore in a 99-96 thriller for the title. Freshman Lloyd "World B." Free wins the Most Valuable Player award, and teammate M.L. Carr will join Free on the All-Tournament team. The *Greensboro Daily News* will welcome the champions home with this headline: "Quakers—The UCLA Of The NAIA."

The 1972-73 Guilford Quakers
Courtesy of Guilford College Athletics

2009

Former major-league baseball player and manager Whitey Lockman, a native of Lowell, dies at the age of 82. Lockman played from 1945 to 1960, during which he was an All-Star selection (1952) and a World Series champion (with the 1954 New York Giants).

2011

The 5th Quarter, a movie based on an inspirational true story surrounding the 2006 Wake Forest University football team, premieres in Winston-Salem, where much of the movie was filmed. Starring Ryan Merriman, Aidan Quinn and Andie MacDowell, *The 5th Quarter* is based on the true story of WFU linebacker Jon Abbate, who in 2006 dedicated his season to his younger brother, Luke, after Luke died in a car crash. The Demon Deacons went on to their most successful football season ever, finishing the regular season at 10-2, then defeating Georgia Tech in the ACC Championship Game and climaxing with an appearance in the Orange Bowl.

March 18

1920

Belus Smawley, a future All-American basketball player at Appalachian State, is born in Ellenboro in Rutherford County. Smawley will become a basketball pioneer, being credited by historians as one of the earliest players to employ the jump shot. He will develop the shot in the early 1930s, practicing in an old train depot with peach baskets nailed onto the walls. He will play and coach at Appalachian, leading the Mountaineers to postseason play in the 1943 season, before joining the NBA, where he will be one of the league's leading scorers. Following Smawley's death in 2003, his brother Fred will tell *The Charlotte Observer:* "He'd jump in the air, turn around and seem to hang there. You couldn't guard him. You couldn't keep him from shooting. He was a natural, I reckon. Just as natural as you ever saw. He didn't know he was making history."

Belus Smawley
Courtesy of ASU Athletics

1972

Former University of North Carolina basketball star Larry Miller, now playing for the American Basketball Association's Carolina Cougars, sets an ABA single-game scoring record with 67 points in the Cougars' 139-125 win over Memphis.

1978

Leon Spinks, who took up boxing as a Marine at Camp Lejeune, has his heavyweight title stripped for refusing to fight Ken Norton.

64 ≡ *Instant Replay*

1980
Duke University names little-known Army coach Mike Krzyzewski as its new head basketball coach, replacing Bill Foster, who resigned to take the head coaching job at the University of South Carolina. Duke officials prophetically describe their 33-year-old new coach as "the brightest young coaching talent in America." Krzyzewski had been head coach at the U.S. Military Academy for five years, where he led the Black Knights to three winning seasons and an overall record of 73-59. He will ultimately lead the Blue Devils to four NCAA championships.

March 19

1988
The North Carolina Tar Heels set an NCAA Tournament record with 36 assists in their second-round win over Loyola-Marymount, 123-97.

1995
Michael Jordan plays his first NBA game since retiring from the league 17 months earlier, wearing jersey No. 45 and scoring 19 points in the Chicago Bulls' 103-96 overtime loss to the Indiana Pacers. NBC broadcasts the game to an estimated 35 million viewers, making it the most-watched regular-season game in NBA history. The day before the game, Jordan had announced his return to the league with a memorable two-word press release: "I'm back."

March 20

1993
Duke's Grant Hill gets eight steals against the University of California-Berkeley, tying the NCAA Tournament record.

2011
Duke coach Mike Krzyzewski gets his 900th coaching win, a 73-71 nail-biter over Michigan that puts the Blue Devils in the Sweet 16 of the NCAA Tournament. The longtime Duke coach is only three wins shy of passing his former coach, Bobby Knight, as NCAA Division I's all-time winningest coach.

Did You Know?
Between 1960 and 1962, the boys' basketball team at Beaufort High School won 91 consecutive games, the seventh-longest streak in the nation.

March 21

1941
In its first trip to the NCAA Tournament, North Carolina sets a dubious tourney record—fewest points scored—when the Tar Heels lose to Pitt, 26-20, in the regional finals.

1945
Following a 36-hole playoff against his rival Sam Snead, golfer Byron Nelson wins the Charlotte Open by four strokes, his second straight PGA victory. He'll follow that up with consecutive wins at the Greensboro Open (eight strokes), the Durham Open (five strokes) and the next seven tournaments after those, amounting to an amazing 11-tournament winning streak—a record many feel will never be broken.

1964
After advancing to its first NCAA championship game, the Duke men's basketball team falls to UCLA, 98-83, becoming the first victim of UCLA Coach John Wooden's 10 NCAA titles in 12 years. The Blue Devils turn in a sloppy effort against the Bruins, committing 29 turnovers.

2003
UNC-Wilmington sharpshooter John Goldsberry goes 8-for-8 from the 3-point line in the Seahawks' first-round game of the NCAA Tournament against Maryland. Goldsberry's hot hand gives him the NCAA Tournament record for 3-point field-goal percentage—and he'll finish the game with 26 points—but Maryland narrowly escapes the upset bid with a 75-73 win.

> **Did You Know?**
> The University of North Carolina men's basketball team holds the NCAA record for consecutive 20-win seasons with 31, from 1971 to 2001.

March 22

1882
Future North Carolina governor O. Max Gardner is born in Shelby. In addition to serving as the state's 57th governor, Gardner will become the only person ever to captain the football teams of both N.C. State University and the University of North Carolina, attending N.C. State (then known as North Carolina A&M College) for his undergraduate studies

and then the University of North Carolina School of Law. While playing for UNC, he will be excused from playing in the game against his alma mater.

1926

Future major-leaguer Billy Goodman, who will win the 1950 American League batting crown with a hefty .354 average and finish his career with a solid .300 average, is born in Concord. Goodman will play most of his career with the Boston Red Sox and will be inducted into the Boston Red Sox Hall of Fame.

1969

Western Carolina University makes it all the way to the finals of the first-ever women's collegiate national basketball championship, but loses a laugher to West Chester State (Pennsylvania), 65-39. The Catamounts finish the season—the team's fourth—with a 14-3 record.

March 23

1957

The North Carolina Tar Heels beat Wilt Chamberlain and the Kansas Jayhawks, 54-53, in the only triple-overtime championship game in NCAA history. Ironically, UNC had advanced to the title game a day earlier by beating Michigan State, 74-70, *also in triple overtime.* Against

The 1956-57 Tar Heels
Courtesy of UNC Athletic Communications

March 23 continued

Kansas, the Tar Heels have to play all three overtime periods without their leading scorer, Lennie Rosenbluth, who fouls out in regulation. In the third overtime, Joe Quigg makes a pair of free throws with six seconds remaining to put Carolina ahead 54-53, then knocks away a pass intended for Chamberlain to clinch the win. With the win, Coach Frank McGuire's Tar Heels complete a perfect 32-0 season.

1974

North Carolina State, led by stars David Thompson and Tommy Burleson, snaps UCLA's streak of seven consecutive NCAA championships with a thrilling 80-77 double-overtime win over the Bruins in a national semifinal game at the Greensboro Coliseum. The Wolfpack, coached by Norm Sloan, overcomes an 11-point deficit in the second half and a 7-point deficit in the second overtime to defeat John Wooden's Bruins, led by Bill Walton and Keith Wilkes. Thompson finishes with 28 points and 10 rebounds, while Burleson scores 20 and grabs 14 rebounds. Point guard Monte Towe clinches the win by sinking a pair of free throws with 12 seconds remaining.

Tommy Burleson
Courtesy of N.C. State Athletics

2007

University of North Carolina student Jason Ray, who performs as the Tar Heels' mascot Ramses at basketball games, is struck by a car while in East Rutherford, New Jersey, for UNC's games in the NCAA East Regional. He will remain in critical condition before dying from his injuries three days later.

March 24

1891
Future major-league pitcher Ernie Shore is born in East Bend. Following a solid career from 1912 to 1920—including a 3-1 record for the Boston Red Sox in the 1915 and 1916 World Series—Shore will return to Forsyth County, where he will serve as sheriff for many years. In the 1950s, he will lead the effort to build a minor-league baseball park in Winston-Salem, a park that eventually will be named Ernie Shore Field and open in 1956.

1999
The Seattle Supersonics retire the No. 10 jersey of Raleigh native and former North Carolina State basketball star Nate McMillan, who played all 12 years of his NBA career with Seattle. Known for his all-around game, McMillan finished with career averages of 5.9 points, 6.1 assists and 1.9 steals per game. He retired from playing in 1998, but he stayed in the league as a coach.

2007
All-America point guard Anthony Atkinson of Barton College—a small liberal arts school in Wilson—spearheads one of the most stunning comebacks in college basketball history, scoring 10 points in the final 39 seconds to lead his Bulldogs to a 77-75 upset of NCAA Division II powerhouse Winona State in the national championship game. Winona State, the defending champion—which came into the game with a 57-game winning streak—appears poised to repeat as champions, taking a 74-67 lead with only 45 seconds remaining. Tournament personnel take the championship hats and T-shirts to the Winona State bench for their postgame celebration, but Atkinson has other ideas. The senior makes a spinning layup, two short jumpers and an acrobatic reverse layup—while Winona State can manage only a single free throw—leaving the game knotted at 75. On the final play of the game, with time winding down, Winona State races down the floor in hopes of hitting a game-winning basket; instead, Barton's Bobby Buffaloe steals the ball from behind and quickly passes it to Atkinson, who heads the other way and lays it in as time expires, capping the incredible comeback.

March 25

1918
Howard William Cohen is born in Winston-Salem. During his college years, Cohen will change his last name to Cosell, and he will go on to become one of the best-known and most outspoken sports journalists in

March 25 continued

history. At one point in his 30-year sports broadcasting career, Cosell will simultaneously be voted the most popular and the most disliked sportscaster in America. He will die in 1995, at age 77.

1974

North Carolina State, playing at the Greensboro Coliseum, wins its first NCAA championship with a 76-64 win over Marquette. After beating Goliath—the mighty UCLA Bruins—two days earlier, this game proves to be anticlimactic. The Wolfpack takes a 39-30 halftime lead, then goes up by as many as 19 points before settling for the 12-point win. State's David Thompson wins the tournament's Most Valuable Player honors.

David Thompson
Courtesy of N.C. State Athletics

1978

Duke's Jim Spanarkel sets the record for best free-throw percentage in a Final Four men's basketball game, shooting 12-for-12 in the Blue Devils' national semifinal matchup against Notre Dame. The Blue Devils' Christian Laettner will equal Spanarkel's mark in the championship game against Kansas on April 1, 1991.

1989

The Eagles of North Carolina Central University win the NCAA Division II national championship in Springfield, Massachusetts, destroying Southeast Missouri State, 73-46. The team finishes the season with a stellar 28-4 record.

March 26

1946
Oklahoma A&M becomes the NCAA Tournament's first two-time champion at the expense of North Carolina, defeating the Tar Heels 43-40 in the national championship game. A&M's Bob Kurland, a 7-footer, scores 23 points—including the first two dunks in NCAA Tournament history—to outshine UNC star John "Hook" Dillon.

1952
Kansas substitute guard Dean Smith plays the final 29 seconds of the Jayhawks' 80-63 win in the NCAA championship game. Ironically, Smith had gone to Kansas on an academic scholarship, but he made the basketball team under legendary Jayhawks head coach Phog Allen. Smith will go on to win two more NCAA titles—in 1982 and 1993—as head coach of the North Carolina Tar Heels.

March 27

1973
Minnesota Twins pitcher—and Williamston native—Jim Perry becomes the first player to use the "10 and 5 rule," allowing himself to be traded to the Detroit Tigers for a minor-league pitcher and cash. The rule mandates that players who have been in the majors for 10 years and with one club for five consecutive years cannot be traded without their consent.

1978
Playing for the NCAA title, Duke falls victim to one of the greatest individual performances in championship game history, as Kentucky's Jack "Goose" Givens scores a career-high 41 points to lead the Wildcats to a 94-88 victory over the Blue Devils. Says Duke captain Jim Spanarkel after the game, "Jack Givens played the best game I have ever seen anyone play."

March 28

1938
Sam Snead wins the inaugural Greater Greensboro Open, the first of his eight GGO titles, a record for most wins at a PGA Tour event. Snead's dominance at the GGO will inspire the Greensboro tourney to be nick-

March 28 continued

named "The Sam Snead Open." No other golfer has more than two wins at the tournament. When Snead wins his final GGO on April 4, 1965, he will become the oldest golfer ever to win a PGA tournament, at 52 years, 10 months, eight days.

1977

Al McGuire retires from coaching basketball after his Marquette Warriors knock off the University of North Carolina, 67-59, for the NCAA championship. McGuire won the title by beating two North Carolina schools back-to-back in the Final Four—UNC-Charlotte in the semifinals, followed by the Tar Heels in the championship game. McGuire, who will go on to become a successful sports commentator, began his head coaching career in North Carolina at Belmont Abbey College, where he coached from 1957 to 1964 and led the Crusaders to five postseason appearances. His overall record at Belmont Abbey was 109-64.

Coach Al McGuire
Courtesy of Belmont Abbey College Athletics

1990

Michael Jordan racks up a career-high 69 points in the Chicago Bulls' 117-113 overtime win over the Cleveland Cavaliers. It's the fourth time Jordan has scored 60 or more points in a game.

1992

Trailing Kentucky by a point with only 2.1 seconds remaining—and with a trip to the Final Four on the line—Duke's Grant Hill throws an 80-foot inbounds pass to teammate Christian Laettner, who dribbles once near the foul line, fakes right and spins left, then buries a 17-foot jump shot at the buzzer to give the Blue Devils a 104-103 overtime win. During the final half-minute of the game, the lead changes five times before Laettner's dramatic buzzer-beater gives Duke the NCAA East Regional championship and a trip to the Final Four. Laettner finishes with a perfect shooting night—10 for 10 field goals and 10 for 10 free throws for 31 points. *Sports Illustrated* will describe the instant classic as the greatest college basketball game of all time, and Duke will go on to win its second straight NCAA title.

March 29

1982

Dean Smith finally sheds his label as the best college basketball coach who's never won a national championship when his North Carolina Tar Heels defeat Georgetown, 63-62, in an NCAA title-game thriller at the New Orleans Superdome. The game goes back and forth throughout, with two former Gastonia high-school stars—Carolina's James Worthy and Georgetown's Eric "Sleepy" Floyd—playing major roles for their teams. The final moments are memorably surreal; after Floyd puts the Hoyas ahead, 62-61, with just over a minute to go, the Tar Heels take a timeout and then work the ball to freshman Michael Jordan, who swishes a jumper from the left wing with 17 seconds remaining. Georgetown quickly brings the ball upcourt, but Fred Brown mistakenly throws the ball to Worthy near the top of the key, allowing Carolina to preserve the win. Worthy finishes with 28 points and wins Most Outstanding Player honors.

2009

North Carolina defeats Oklahoma, 72-60, to advance to its NCAA-record 18th Final Four. UCLA has also made 18 Final Four appearances, but the Bruins' 1980 trip to the Final Four was later vacated by the NCAA for rules violations, giving UNC the record outright.

March 30

1981

The NCAA championship game between the Indiana Hoosiers and the North Carolina Tar Heels is nearly postponed following an afternoon assassination attempt of President Ronald Reagan. Less than an hour before game time, when the NCAA Tournament committee learns Reagan has come through surgery with flying colors and is out of danger, the decision finally is made to play. Later, though, it will be revealed that one of the committee's options was to cancel the game altogether and declare Indiana and UNC co-champions—an option that apparently received no support whatsoever. The Tar Heels lose, 63-50.

March 30 continued

1991

The underdog topples the undefeated as Duke upsets defending champion UNLV, 79-77, in the semifinals of the NCAA Tournament. With the win—which snaps UNLV's 45-game winning streak—the Blue Devils avenge their humiliating 30-point loss to the Runnin' Rebels in the 1990 NCAA championship game. Duke will go on to win its own title two days later.

1991

North Carolina head basketball coach Dean Smith becomes the only coach to ever get thrown out of a Final Four game, when he draws his second technical foul in the last minute of play during the Kansas Jayhawks' semifinal win over the Tar Heels. Smith apologizes for taking the attention away from the Jayhawks' win.

March 31

1986

The Duke Blue Devils come close to finally winning their first NCAA basketball title, but they fall in the championship game to Louisville, 72-69. The game, played in Dallas, Texas, concludes Duke coach Mike Krzyzewski's initial trip to the Final Four—the first of eleven such visits so far.

1994

The White Sox assign retired NBA star Michael Jordan—now attempting to play professional baseball—to the Birmingham Barons of the Class AA Southern League. In 127 games as an outfielder, Jordan will hit a paltry .202, with three home runs, 51 RBIs, 30 stolen bases and 11 errors.

1998

Wilmington native and former Duke University standout Quinten McCracken becomes the first official batter in the history of the Tampa Bay Devil Rays. At the end of the season, he will win the team's first-ever MVP award.

2001

The Duke men's basketball team overcomes a 22-point deficit against Maryland in the national semifinals, setting an NCAA record for the largest deficit overcome in a Final Four game. The Blue Devils trail 39-17 with 6:55 remaining in the first half, then storm back to claim a 94-84 win over the Terrapins.

APRIL

April 1

1979
Kannapolis native Dale Earnhardt wins the Southeastern 500 at Bristol International Speedway, the first of his 76 Winston Cup victories.

1991
Duke University wins its first NCAA title, knocking off Kansas, 72-65, at the Hoosier Dome in Indianapolis. Ironically, Kansas—led by future North Carolina coach Roy Williams—had defeated the Tar Heels in the other semifinal game, preventing a Duke-Carolina donnybrook for the national championship. In the title game, Christian Laettner leads the way with 18 points and 10 rebounds, while Final Four MVP Bobby Hurley adds 12 points and nine assists. The win allows Duke coach Mike Krzyzewski—making his fifth appearance in the Final Four since 1986—to finally get the monkey off his back and claim a championship.

April 1 continued

2003

Tar Heel basketball coach Matt Doherty resigns after a bumpy three-year ride in charge of the storied program. Hired in 2000 to replace Bill Guthridge, Doherty—who started on UNC's 1982 NCAA championship team—was named the 2001 AP National Coach of the Year, but the 2002-03 team had struggled all year and failed to make the NCAA Tournament. Questions about Doherty's ability to lead and his fiery demeanor with players—some who had threatened to leave the program if he was allowed to stay—led to his resignation.

2008

Brevard High School's Andrew Blackwell hits for the "home run cycle"—believed to be the only documented time that has occurred—by hitting a solo homer (6th inning), a two-run shot (7th inning), a three-run blast (1st inning) and a grand slam (5th inning) in Brevard's 16-7 win over Pisgah High School.

2010

North Carolina basketball star Deon Thompson plays in the 152nd game of his college career, setting a new NCAA record for most games played, when the Tar Heels play Dayton in the championship game of the NIT. He ends his career with a loss, though, as UNC falls, 79-68.

April 2

1907

Future major-leaguer and seven-time All-Star shortstop Luke Appling is born in High Point. Appling will play his entire major-league career—from 1930 to 1950—with the Chicago White Sox, winning a batting title in 1936 with his hefty .388 batting average. He will also earn the nickname "Old Aches and Pains," for his frequent complaints to his teammates about minor ailments such as a sore back or sprained finger.

1975

Greensboro native Bob McAdoo, who played college basketball for the University of North Carolina and now stars for the NBA's Buffalo Braves, wins the league MVP Award after finishing the season with a 34.5 points-per-game scoring average.

1990

Duke comes up empty in its quest for an NCAA championship, getting crushed in the title game by the UNLV Runnin' Rebels. The 103-73 final margin sets a record as the worst defeat in NCAA championship game history.

2001

Mike Krzyzewski's Duke Blue Devils win their third NCAA championship, defeating Arizona 82-72 at the Metrodome in Minneapolis. Four Blue Devils score in double figures—Mike Dunleavy with 21 points, Shane Battier with 18, Jason Williams with 16 and Carlos Boozer with 12—as Duke pulls away from Arizona for the win. Battier, an All-American senior and two-time national defensive player of the year, is named the tournament's Most Outstanding Player. Following the game, Battier—one of the most popular players in Duke history—says, "It's complete—all that's left for me is to ride off into the sunset on a white horse."

Shane Battier
Courtesy of Duke University Athletics

2007

Raleigh native Josh Hamilton, the first overall pick in the 1999 draft, makes his long-awaited major-league debut, pinch-hitting for the Cincinnati Reds against the Chicago Cubs. Hamilton had an up-and-down career in the minors, sidetracked by substance abuse problems, before finally getting the call to the big leagues. Ultimately, he will be traded to the Texas Rangers, where he will become an All-Star and win the 2010 American League MVP Award.

Did You Know?

At his home in Hertford, Hall of Fame pitcher Jim "Catfish" Hunter incorporated baseball bats into the construction of his staircase. Where most staircases have balusters supporting the handrail, Hunter had wooden baseball bats.

April 3

1899

The first Easter Monday baseball game is played in Raleigh, with North Carolina A&M (now known as N.C. State) defeating Mebane Military School, 5-4, in 11 innings. The game, always played in Raleigh on the Monday after Easter, and usually featuring cross-county rivals State and Wake Forest, will become an extremely popular annual tradition—so popular, in fact, that in 1935 the N.C. General Assembly will enact legislation declaring Easter Monday a state holiday, so that state employees can attend the baseball game. During its heyday, the game will draw thousands of spectators from all over the state. In 1956, however, when the game is rained out, it will not be rescheduled, and with Wake Forest moving to Winston-Salem—thus eliminating the county rivalry—interest in the game will wane. The birth of the Atlantic Coast Conference in 1953 will also contribute to declining interest in the Easter Monday game, and the 1955 contest will be the final one played. The Easter Monday holiday, however, will continue until 1987, when the Legislature will pass a bill moving the official Easter holiday from Easter Monday to Good Friday.

1924

In the first game ever played at McCormick Field in Asheville—an exhibition game between the Asheville Skylanders and the major-league Detroit Tigers—future Hall of Famer Ty Cobb swats a home run. The hometown Skylanders, however, will get the win, 18-14.

1948

The Yale University baseball team plays at North Carolina State and gets a banner day from its first baseman, George Bush, who goes three-for-four with a triple, a double, three RBIs and two runs scored. For good measure, the future president also steals a base in Yale's 9-6 win over the Wolfpack.

1994

In what has to be the most dramatic finish in NCAA women's basketball history, North Carolina's Charlotte Smith hits a 3-pointer at the buzzer to give the Tar Heels a 60-59 win over Louisiana Tech in the NCAA championship game. Smith makes the shot after UNC, trailing by two, gets possession on a jump ball with only 0.7 seconds on the clock. She finishes with 20 points and 23 rebounds—an NCAA Tournament record—and is named the Final Four's Most Outstanding Player. The Tar Heels complete their championship season with a 33-2 record.

1994

Former University of North Carolina at Charlotte basketball star Chad Kinch, 35, dies of AIDS-related complications at his home in New Jersey. As a freshman, Kinch started for the underdog UNC-Charlotte squad—led by Cedric "Cornbread" Maxwell—that went to the NCAA Final Four in 1977. Kinch had a very brief NBA career with the Cleveland Cavaliers and the Dallas Mavericks.

April 4

1950

In an odd exhibition baseball game believed to be the first of its kind, a mechanical pitching machine—rather than living, breathing, sweating pitchers—goes the distance on the mound for both teams. Wake Forest College, which has been using a pitching machine in practice for quite some time, gets an easy 8-0 victory over North Carolina State, whose players are hitting against a machine for the first time. Wake Forest collects 11 hits, including three home runs, while State manages only two hits. More than 600 spectators turn out to watch the game, which is played in Raleigh. Wake Forest's student newspaper, the *Old Gold and Black*, will even report on the unusual game, under the headline "Mechanical Pitcher Hurls Shutout Win."

1954

Rocky Mount native William H. "Blackie" Pitt enters his first NASCAR race, the Wilkes County 160, held at North Wilkesboro Speedway. Like several other drivers, Pitt will fail to even finish the race, but he'll turn things around before the end of the year, finishing 11th in the points standings and winning the inaugural NASCAR Rookie of the Year Award.

1965

Sam Snead, only one month shy of his 53rd birthday, wins the Greater Greensboro Open to become the oldest golfer ever to win a major PGA tournament. Snead, who won the National PGA Seniors title earlier this year, finishes 11 under par at the GGO, five strokes ahead of his nearest challengers. When told of his feat, Snead tells reporters, "I don't feel very old. In fact, right now I feel pretty young."

1968

Pistol Pete Maravich, who starred at Broughton High School in Raleigh, wraps up an NCAA single-season scoring record, finishing his sophomore year at Louisiana State University with a gaudy 43.8-point scoring average.

April 4 continued

1983

North Carolina State completes its improbable run to the NCAA championship game by upsetting the heavily favored Houston Cougars, 54-52, to win the title in Albuquerque, New Mexico. Houston had been nicknamed "Phi Slamma Jamma" for its high-flying, frequently dunking squad, but ironically, it's a Wolfpack dunk that seals the game when State's Lorenzo Charles grabs Dereck Whittenburg's errant shot—a desperation heave from 35 feet away—and slams it home at the buzzer. The Wolfpack had barely even made the NCAA Tournament, beginning its tourney run with 10 losses; no team had ever won the title with that many defeats. But head coach Jim Valvano's "Cardiac Pack" had won a series of heart-stoppers—their opponents had a habit of missing free throws down the stretch—to reach the championship game. State leads Houston 33-25 at halftime, but the Cougars go on a 17-2 run to open up a 42-35 lead, before State slowly creeps back into the game to set up the dramatic finish. Following the game, as Wolfpack players celebrate, Valvano is seen running frantically all over the court; he will later explain he was simply looking for someone to hug.

Courtesy of the Lew Powell Memorabilia Collection, North Carolina Collection, Wilson Library, UNC-Chapel Hill

1988

Former Greensboro prep star—and NCAA Player of the Year—Danny Manning scores 31 points to lead the Kansas Jayhawks to the NCAA title with an 83-79 upset win over Oklahoma. The team is coached by former University of North Carolina star Larry Brown, who will become the only coach in history to win both an NCAA championship and an NBA title (with the Detroit Pistons in 2004).

1994

President Bill Clinton attends the NCAA Final Four at the Charlotte Coliseum to watch his beloved Arkansas Razorbacks, marking the first time a sitting president has attended a Final Four. Arkansas defeats the home crowd favorite, the Duke Blue Devils, 76-72, to win the title.

2005

After a long, successful college coaching career, North Carolina's Roy Williams finally claims the one thing missing from his resume—an NCAA championship—as the Tar Heels defeat Illinois, 75-70, in St. Louis. Illinois misses an open 3-pointer late that would tie the game at 73, and UNC's Raymond Felton sinks a pair of free throws to clinch the victory. Sean May leads the way for Carolina with 26 points (on 10-of-11 shooting) and 10 rebounds, en route to winning Most Outstanding Player honors. The Tar Heels finish the season 33-4 as they claim UNC's fourth NCAA title, but this game will be remembered as the first championship for Williams, who had lost in two previous title games with Kansas. "The third championship was the charm," he says.

Roy Williams
Courtesy of UNC Athletic Communications

April 5

1915

Future North Carolina College for Negroes basketball coach John McLendon is born in Hiawatha, Kansas. McLendon will coach at the Durham college from 1941 to 1952, compiling a dominant 264-60 record. He will become the first coach in history to win three consecutive national championships, leading Tennessee State to the 1957, 1958 and 1959 NAIA titles. McLendon will then go on to become the first black coach at a predominantly white college when Cleveland State hires him in June 1966. Most fittingly, McLendon—who learned basketball from Dr. James Naismith as an undergraduate at Kansas University—will be inducted into the Naismith Memorial Basketball Hall of Fame.

1925

Babe Ruth staggers off a train in Asheville and faints in front of a crowd of spectators who have gathered to meet the famous New York Yankees slugger, prompting a New York sportswriter to famously describe Ruth's ailment as "the bellyache heard 'round the world." Teammates get a taxi and take the unconscious Ruth to Asheville's Battery

April 5 continued

Park Hotel for the night, where a doctor will tend to him until the following afternoon, when he will leave to return to New York. Meanwhile, with little official information being released, rumors will begin to circulate about Ruth's health, including one report that he has died in western North Carolina. Sportswriter W.O. McGeehan of the *New York Tribune* will describe Ruth's health scare as "the bellyache heard 'round the world," suggesting that an overdose of hot dogs, soda pop and beer was the culprit for Ruth's illness. Other reports will point a finger at everything from indigestion and an intestinal abscess to the flu and even venereal disease. Whatever the cause, Ruth will be hospitalized in New York for about seven weeks, before finally rejoining the Yankees on the field on June 1.

1959

Former Duke University golfer Art Wall Jr. shoots a final-round 66—including birdies on five of the last six holes—to pass 12 players, including defending champion Arnold Palmer, and win the Masters by a single stroke. In addition to the Masters, Wall will win three other tournaments in 1959 en route to being named the PGA Player of the Year.

Art Wall Jr.
Courtesy of Duke University Athletics

1993

The North Carolina Tar Heels win another NCAA championship at the Superdome in New Orleans—the site of their 1982 title—by knocking off the Michigan Wolverines and their "Fab Five," 77-71. UNC clinches coach Dean Smith's second championship when Michigan star Chris Webber unthinkingly calls a timeout in the game's closing seconds when the Wolverines, trailing 73-71, have no timeouts to call. The resulting technical foul gives the Tar Heels two free throws—which UNC star Donald Williams calmly sinks—and possession of the ball, essentially clinching the game for Carolina. Williams finishes with 25 points, including five three-pointers, en route to winning Most Outstanding Player honors.

1995

The Charlotte Hornets and Philadelphia 76ers combine to score an NBA record-low 19 points—11 for Charlotte, eight for Philly—in the second quarter of the Hornets' 84-66 win over the visiting 76ers. The Sixers' 66 points is also a franchise low.

2010

Duke survives a last-second halfcourt heave—which *barely* misses—to defeat underdog Butler University, 61-59, and win its fourth NCAA championship. The Blue Devils are led by Kyle Singler (19 points), Jon Scheyer (15) and Nolan Smith (13), but it's Butler star Gordon Hayward who nearly steals the show with his desperation shot at the buzzer. Duke finishes its stellar season at 35-5.

The 2009-2010 Blue Devils
Courtesy of Duke University Athletics

April 6

1958

Former Wake Forest University golfer Arnold Palmer, age 28, wins the Masters—the first of his seven major titles—by a single stroke over Doug Ford and Fred Hawkins. An eagle on the 13th hole of the final round helps propel him to the victory.

April 6 continued

1973

Hertford native Jim "Catfish" Hunter, pitching for the Oakland A's, gives up the first-ever home run by a designated hitter, the Minnesota Twins' Tony Oliva.

1987

In his return to boxing following an eye injury, Wilmington native Sugar Ray Leonard stuns the boxing world with a 12-round split decision over Marvelous Marvin Hagler to win the World Boxing Council's middleweight championship. The upset is Hagler's first loss in more than a decade.

1992

Duke overwhelms Michigan, 71-51, in the NCAA title game, becoming the first team to repeat as NCAA men's basketball champions since UCLA's string of titles from 1967 to 1973. Starting five freshmen, Michigan takes a 31-30 halftime lead, but Duke comes on strong in the second half to claim the runaway win. Christian Laettner scores 19 points and Grant Hill adds 18, but it's Duke's Bobby Hurley who wins Most Outstanding Player honors. The win gives coach Mike Krzyzewski his second national championship.

1996

Playing for the Charlotte Hornets, Robert Parish takes the court in his 1,561st game, passing Kareem Abdul-Jabbar to become the NBA's all-time leader in games played. Parish will finish his career with 1,611 games played, still the NBA record.

2009

North Carolina blows out Michigan State, 89-72, to win its fifth NCAA championship—and the second for head coach Roy Williams.

Tyler Hansbrough
Courtesy of UNC Athletic Communications

Carolina roars out to a quick 36-13 lead, holds a 55-34 halftime lead—setting a title-game record for most points at the half—and is never challenged in the second half. The Tar Heels are led by Ty Lawson's 21 points, Wayne Ellington's 19 and Tyler Hansbrough's 18. Lawson also sets an NCAA Tournament single-game record for steals with eight.

April 7

1979

Garry Ramey, a third-year student at St. Andrews Presbyterian College in Laurinburg, pulls off a rare athletic feat. In the morning, he travels with the St. Andrews tennis team to nearby Pembroke State University, where he wins both the number-one singles and number-one doubles matches. He then gets in a car and drives 85 miles to a track meet at Wingate College, where he proceeds to win the mile run, the 880-yard run and the three-mile run. Ramey's amazing day earns him a mention in *Sports Illustrated*—quite a coup for a small-school athlete.

1990

North Carolina State basketball coach Jim Valvano resigns in the wake of allegations of corruption spelled out in a book by Peter Golenbock titled *Personal Fouls*. Valvano was cleared of breaking any academic rules, but some of his players were found to have sold game tickets and shoes—both violations of NCAA regulations—and committed other irregularities. Les Robinson will take over as basketball coach, and Valvano will become a popular sports commentator.

> **Did You Know?**
> Golfer Chuck Merriam of South Mecklenburg High School won three straight individual state titles between 1963 and 1965.

April 8

1920

During an exhibition game between the New York Yankees and the Brooklyn Dodgers—played at the Old Fairgrounds in Winston-Salem—Babe Ruth wallops a ball farther than the sportswriters accompanying the Yankees have ever seen. Ironically, the hit is ruled a ground-rule double rather than a home run because it lands among a

April 8 continued

throng of spectators gathered at the makeshift baseball field, but it seems certain it would've been a home run otherwise. Sportswriter Sid Mercer of the *New York Globe* will write: "The experts finally agreed that Ruth's hit carried at least 600 feet and bounded at least 50 feet farther. This gives Babe a new record as nobody else has ever batted a ball anywhere near that distance. It is certainly a record that will stand for all time in Winston-Salem."

1926

The great Babe Ruth gives some 4,000 Charlotte baseball fans a thrill by swatting a seventh-inning home run during a spring training exhibition game against the Brooklyn Robins (later the Brooklyn Dodgers). *The Charlotte Observer* will describe the scene this way: "Ruth had previously singled, but that only whetted the appetite of the hungry mob. They had come from miles around to see Babe Ruth knock a home run. Nothing else would satisfy them. The Bambino took his stout stand at the plate. With the air tense with excitement, he slammed one of Williams' fast ones out of the park, bringing home Paschal and Gehrig ahead of him. Immediately after the smash of the Bam, the crowds began to file out of the grandstand. Everybody was happy."

1946

Future major-league pitcher James Augustus "Catfish" Hunter is born in Hertford. Hunter's stellar 15-year career with the Oakland Athletics and the New York Yankees will include eight All-Star selections, five World Series championships, a Cy Young Award, a perfect game and induction into the National Baseball Hall of Fame.

1948

Asheville's McCormick Field hosts its first integrated baseball game when the minor-league Asheville Tourists play an exhibition game against Jackie Robinson and the Brooklyn Dodgers. Robinson, who broke the major-league color barrier in 1947, draws scattered boos but mostly cheers from the crowd of about 10,000, despite going hitless in the game.

1988

Former Wake Forest golfer Curtis Strange aces the par-3 No. 12 during the second round of the Masters.

1994

Michael Jordan's professional baseball debut with the minor-league Birmingham Barons draws a Hoover, Alabama crowd of more than 10,000, but the former University of North Carolina and Chicago Bulls star goes 0-for-3. The Barons lose to the Chattanooga Lookouts, 10-3.

1996
The Charlotte Hornets stun the Chicago Bulls, 98-97, to snap Chicago's NBA record 44-game home winning streak. Only three nights earlier in Charlotte, the Bulls had crushed the Hornets by 34 points.

2006
The Denver Nuggets' Julius Hodge, who starred for the N.C. State Wolfpack, is shot after leaving a nightclub when another vehicle pulls alongside his on the highway and fires several shots. He comes within minutes of bleeding to death, but will recover and return to playing basketball.

2011
Tampa Bay Rays slugger Manny Ramirez, who played most of his minor-league career in North Carolina, retires after testing positive for performance-enhancing drugs. Rather than face a 100-game suspension, the 38-year-old Ramirez—one of the game's greatest hitters—decides to walk away, finishing his career with 555 home runs. Ramirez made his professional debut with the Burlington Indians in 1991, being named the Appalachian League's Most Valuable Player. He played the 1992 season with the Kinston Indians and much of the 1993 season with the Charlotte Knights, where he was named Minor League Player of the Year by *Baseball America*.

April 9

1947
In a preseason minor-league baseball game against Raleigh, Rocco Marchegiano of the Goldsboro Goldbugs plays left field and goes 0-for-1 at the plate. Soon after his brief tryout with the Goldbugs, he will give up his dream of becoming a professional baseball player—realizing he doesn't have the skills to play at that level—and instead will turn his attention to boxing under a different name, Rocky Marciano. Not a bad decision, considering he will go on to win the heavyweight title and retire undefeated—the only heavyweight champ to do so.

1962
Former Wake Forest golfer Arnold Palmer wins his third green jacket at the Masters, beating Gary Player and Dow Finsterwald in the tournament's first three-way playoff. Palmer fires a 68 in the 18-hole playoff, three strokes up on Player and nine strokes ahead of Finsterwald.

April 9 continued

1978

In an attempt to clinch the NBA scoring title on the last day of the season, the Denver Nuggets' David Thompson—a Shelby native and former N.C. State star—pours in a career-high 73 points (including an NBA-record 31 in one quarter and 53 in the first half) in an afternoon game against the Detroit Pistons. The Nuggets lose, 139-137, but Thompson's 73-point outburst sets an NBA record for guards, and seemingly locks up the season scoring title. That night, however, San Antonio's George Gervin—needing 59 points to steal the title from Thompson—scores 63 (including 33 in one quarter to top Thompson's record from earlier in the day). Thus, Thompson loses the scoring title in the closest race ever, 27.22 points per game to 27.15 points per game.

1980

Only two days before the start of their season, minor-league baseball's Durham Bulls discover their uniforms have been stolen. The Bulls, part of the Atlanta Braves' farm system, decide to wear their road uniforms for home games, and Hank Aaron, the director of the Braves' minor-league system, sends the team a set of used Braves uniforms to wear on the road.

1989

Dennis Burlingame, a 19-year-old pitcher making his debut with the minor-league Durham Bulls, throws what is believed to be the only opening-day perfect game in professional baseball history. He accomplishes the feat in a seven-inning, 4-0 win over the Frederick Keys on the Carolina League's opening day. (The game is only seven innings because it's the first game of a doubleheader.) Burlingame had been drafted by the Atlanta Braves, but he'll never make it to the majors, despite his perfect game.

2001

Former major-league baseball star Willie Stargell, 61, dies in Wilmington—where he will also be buried—following complications related to a stroke. One of the game's most affable players, Stargell played the 1961 season with the minor-league Asheville Tourists—batting .289 and smacking 22 home runs—before moving on to a Hall of Fame career with the Pittsburgh Pirates.

2011

Former University of North Carolina basketball star Ty Lawson, now with the Denver Nuggets, becomes the first player in NBA history to make each of his first 10 three-point attempts in a game. He finally misses when he heaves a running 28-footer just before the end of the third quarter—a shot the Nuggets didn't even need in their blowout win over the Minnesota Timberwolves—to finish the game 10-for-11 from the three-point line. Lawson's previous career high for three-pointers in a game was three.

April 10

1960
Arnold Palmer collects his second green jacket, shooting birdies on the final two holes to claim a one-stroke victory over Ken Venturi at the Masters golf tournament.

April 11

1954
Billy Joe Patton, an amateur golfer from Morganton, nails a hole-in-one on the par-3 sixth hole during the final round of the 1954 Masters, en route to winning the award for the amateur with the lowest score. In fact, Patton nearly wins the tournament, leading during the final round before a double bogey on the 13th hole steals his momentum. Even with that double bogey, Patton misses making an 18-hole playoff with Sam Snead and Ben Hogan by a single stroke.

1969
Davidson College hires former University of North Carolina and ABA star—and first-time head coach—Larry Brown to replace Lefty Driesell as coach of the men's basketball team. Davidson interviews others for the job—including a young head coach at Army named Bobby Knight—but ultimately picks the 28-year-old Brown, who had been an assistant under UNC's Dean Smith before joining the ABA. On July 2, before he even coaches a single game, Brown will change his mind and resign. He will end up coaching the ABA's Carolina Cougars instead. Ultimately, Brown will have a long, successful coaching career at the college and professional level, becoming the only coach in history to win an NCAA championship (with Kansas in 1988) and an NBA title (with the Detroit Pistons in 2004). Meanwhile, Davidson will replace Brown with Terry Holland, who played and coached under Driesell and who later will have a successful stint coaching the University of Virginia.

1976
Fort Bragg native Raymond Floyd easily wins the Masters golf tournament, finishing eight strokes ahead of runner-up Ben Crenshaw. It will be the only time Floyd gets to don the famed green jacket.

April 11 continued

1981

Michael Jordan, a product of Laney High School in Wilmington, sinks a pair of free throws with 11 seconds remaining to give the underdog East team a 96-95 upset win in the McDonald's All-American High School Basketball Game. Jordan finishes with a game-high 30 points, which will remain the annual all-star game's scoring record until 1999.

1999

The New Jersey Nets retire the No. 52 jersey of Rocky Mount native Buck Williams. During his 17-year NBA career with the Nets, the Portland Trailblazers and the New York Knicks, Williams scored 16,784 points and grabbed 13,017 rebounds. He made three All-Star teams and won the NBA's Rookie of the Year honors in 1982.

April 12

1964

Arnold Palmer becomes the first golfer to win the Masters four times. He finishes at 12 under par, six strokes ahead of Dave Marr and Jack Nicklaus.

Arnold Palmer
Courtesy of Wake Forest Media Relations

1966

Atlanta Braves pitcher—and Cherryville native—Tony Cloninger pitches the first major-league game ever played in Atlanta. He pitches all 13 innings, but loses to the Pittsburgh Pirates, 3-2.

1981
Charlotte native Larry Littleton makes his major-league debut with the Cleveland Indians. Unfortunately, in his brief, 26-game career, he will tie the major-league record for at-bats without a hit by a non-pitcher, with 23. He will, however, get one RBI in the books.

1998
Goldsboro native Mark O'Meara sinks a 20-foot birdie putt on the final hole to win the Masters by a single stroke over David Duval and Fred Couples. O'Meara finishes at nine under par.

2006
Duke basketball star J.J. Redick wins the Sullivan Award—the annual honor given to the nation's top amateur athlete—becoming the first men's basketball player since UCLA's Bill Walton in 1973 to win the award.

April 13

1954
Greensboro native and former North Carolina A&T State University baseball star Tom Alston makes his major-league debut, becoming the first black player to appear in a St. Louis Cardinals uniform. Seven years earlier, St. Louis had threatened to strike when Jackie Robinson integrated the major leagues. Despite being a groundbreaker, Alston will not last long in the majors, playing only three seasons with the Cardinals and finishing with a .244 career batting average.

1961
Charlotte native Charlie Sifford, the first African-American to earn a PGA Tour card, finds his name at the top of the leaderboard after firing a three-under-par 68 in the opening round of the Greater Greensboro Open. Sifford, 38, will struggle through the rest of the tournament, though—in part because of racial taunts from the gallery—and he'll finish tied for fourth.

2007
Brandi Ingram of West Stokes High School steals 10 bases—a state high-school softball record—in a 22-0 win over Atkins.

April 14

1996

Raymond Floyd, a 53-year-old Fort Bragg native and former University of North Carolina golfer, aces the par-3 sixteenth hole during the final round of the Masters.

2003

One week after leading Kansas to the NCAA title game, Roy Williams returns to the University of North Carolina—his alma mater—to replace Matt Doherty as men's head basketball coach. Williams spent ten years as an assistant coach at UNC under Dean Smith before a 15-year stint as the head coach at Kansas.

April 15

1984

Durham native John Lucas, playing for the San Antonio Spurs, chalks up 14 assists in the second quarter, an NBA record for one period, against the Denver Nuggets. He finishes the game with 24 assists.

2005

The Central Cabarrus High School girls' softball team, ranked No. 4 in the nation, clobbers West Charlotte, 55-0, in only two innings of play. The lopsided score will earn Central Cabarrus coach Monte Sherrill a two-game suspension. School officials reportedly had warned Sherrill the previous year about running up the score against inferior opponents.

April 16

1915

Ralph Overton "Razor" Ledbetter puts his colorful nickname in the annals of major-league baseball, pitching a single inning—the only one of his career—for the Detroit Tigers in a home game against the Cleveland Indians. The 20-year-old Burke County native gives up a hit but allows no runs, giving him a career earned-run average of 0.00. He will return to the minors for several more seasons, including stints with the Charlotte Hornets and the Durham Bulls.

1987
Michael Jordan becomes the first NBA player in nearly a quarter-century to score 3,000 points in a season. Wilt Chamberlain was the last to reach the milestone, doing so in 1962-63.

1996
Defense takes a back seat to offense as Greenville's D.H. Conley and Jacksonville's White Oak combine for 67 runs in a girls' high-school softball game, with D.H. Conley winning, 41-26. The game sets a state record for combined scoring output and at one point is tied for ninth-most combined runs in the nation.

2004
Golf superstar Tiger Woods concludes four days of training with the U.S. Army Special Operations Command at Fort Bragg, an endeavor he undertook to better relate to the experiences of his father, retired Lt. Col. Earl Woods, who trained at Fort Bragg in 1963. Following the intense training, Woods wraps up his visit by hosting a junior golf clinic.

April 17

1995
Rocky Mount native Buck Williams of the Portland Trailblazers snares 12 rebounds against Seattle, making him only the eighth player in NBA history to record 12,000 rebounds and 15,000 points in his career.

2011
Wake Forest golfer Cheyenne Woods, the niece of Tiger Woods, turns in a Tiger-esque performance on the final day of the Atlantic Coast Conference women's golf championship. Woods fires a 3-under 68 and finishes the three-day tournament with a 5-under 208 total, good enough to win the individual title. Woods is the only competitor to finish the tourney under par, and her closest competitor finishes seven strokes behind her.

April 18

1955
Whitey Lockman, a native of Lowell in Gaston County, caps off an unusual feat as he and three of his San Francisco Giants teammates hit

April 18 continued

for the cycle in the fourth inning of a game against the Pittsburgh Pirates. All of the hits come against reliever Al Grunwald in his major-league debut—a single by Don Mueller, a double by Monte Irvin, a triple by Willie Mays and then a home run for Lockman. The Giants win, 12-3.

April 19

1915

Oxford native Lee "Specs" Meadows makes his major-league debut as a pitcher for the St. Louis Cardinals. One of the earliest major-leaguers to wear glasses in the field—thus earning the nickname "Specs"—Meadows will play 15 seasons in the big leagues, compiling a 188-180 career record.

1986

Atlanta guard Spud Webb, who starred at North Carolina State, records 18 assists in a playoff game against the Detroit Pistons, an NBA record for rookies. The Hawks win, 137-125.

1998

Michael Jordan notches his NBA-record 10th scoring title, scoring 44 points against the New York Knicks to finish the season with an average of 28.7 points per game.

> **Did You Know?**
>
> In 1999, East Davidson High School shortstop Neil Thompson homered in nine consecutive games, tying a national record and earning himself a mention in *Sports Illustrated*. He finished the season with 14 homers—including six in the playoffs—in leading the Golden Eagles to a 23-9 record and a state 2A championship.

April 20

1986

Michael Jordan torches the Boston Celtics for an NBA playoff-record 63 points—breaking Elgin Baylor's 24-year-old record of 61 points for the Los Angeles Lakers—but the Bulls lose, 135-131, in double overtime of their Eastern Conference first-round playoff game at the Boston Garden. Playing in only the second playoff game of his career—against a team considered to be one of the greatest of all time—Jordan shoots 22 of 41 from the field and 19 of 21 from the free-throw line. Following the game, Boston's Larry Bird shakes his head and says, "He is the most exciting, awesome player in the game today. I think it's just God disguised as Michael Jordan."

April 21

1951

Gil Coan, a former Minor League Player of the Year—and a native of Monroe—ties a major-league record held by only a handful of players when he triples twice in the same inning for the Washington Senators.

1970

Chris Cawthon of Fayetteville 71st High School sets a national record by drawing eight walks in a baseball game against Fayetteville Cape Fear.

1993

Bear Grass High School in Williamston draws 31 walks in a game against Buxton's Cape Hatteras High School, setting a state high-school baseball record that is also the second-most walks drawn in the nation.

2009

Master Yogi Berra, a dog that entertains fans at Greensboro Grasshoppers minor-league games, becomes the first canine ever to be ejected from a professional baseball game. Umpire Jason Hutchings throws Yogi out between the third and fourth innings of a game against the Asheville Tourists, after Yogi fetches a ball in deep center field and then stops to poop on the center-field grass. The incident draws national media attention, including a mention in *Sports Illustrated*. Grasshoppers general manager Donald Moore defends Yogi, saying, "When you gotta go, you gotta go."

April 22

1948

The Martinsville A's and North Carolina's Burlington Bees light up the scoreboard in the seventh inning of their minor-league game against one another, scoring a combined 20 runs (11 for the A's and 9 for the Bees).

April 22 continued

1965

A new season of professional baseball begins at Thomasville's Finch Field with a beanball for the ages—and then, ironically, a beanball that wins the game. Before the hometown Hi-Toms play the Shelby Rebels, Thomasville Mayor Tom Johnson throws the ceremonial first pitch, failing to notice that the reigning Miss North Carolina—a Thomasville gal named Sharon Finch, who made a few pregame remarks to the crowd of more than 7,000—was still standing near home plate, having been detained by a TV reporter. Alas, Johnson's pitch goes astray and strikes Miss North Carolina squarely on her chin. As people rush to assist her and Johnson apologizes profusely, Finch responds in memorable beauty-queen fashion, telling him, "Well, that's all right, Mr. Mayor, but I'm sure glad you're not our regular pitcher."

Just as the game began with a beanball, it later ends with one. With the score tied 4-4, the Hi-Toms load the bases in the bottom of the ninth inning, and Shelby reliever Art Groza's first pitch to Terry Dooley hits him in the head, sending him to first base and forcing home the winning run for the Hi-Toms.

The first beanball, of course, will make more headlines than the second one. *Sports Illustrated* will declare the mayor to be "in last place in the first-ball league," while *The Sporting News* will put the mayor's wild pitch on its list of "The 32 Biggest Bloopers of the 1965 Baseball Season."

1987

The NBA officially grants an expansion franchise to Charlotte entrepreneur George Shinn, along with franchises being awarded to Miami, Orlando and Minneapolis. Six months earlier, a skeptical Phoenix newspaper columnist covering an NBA owners' meeting had predicted "the only franchise Charlotte gets will have golden arches," but Charlotte wins the league over and will begin play in the 1988 season. The Hornets will play 14 seasons in Charlotte before moving to New Orleans.

Courtesy of the Lew Powell Memorabilia Collection, North Carolina Collection, Wilson Library, UNC-Chapel Hill

1994

The Carolina Panthers break ground on their new stadium in downtown Charlotte. The open-air stadium, which will have a seating capacity of nearly 74,000, will open in the summer of 1996.

1995

The Carolina Panthers select quarterback Kerry Collins of Penn State as the team's first draft choice in franchise history, taking him with the fifth overall pick. Collins will play three seasons with the Panthers, leading them to the NFC Championship Game in his second season. The Panthers will lose that game to the Green Bay Packers, 30-13.

April 23

1944

Cecil Washington "Turkey" Tyson, a native of Elm City in Wilson County, makes an ever-so-brief appearance in the major leagues, pinch-hitting for the Philadelphia Phillies. The 29-year-old rookie makes an out. He will play several more seasons of minor-league ball, but will not make it back up to the majors.

1952

San Francisco Giants rookie pitcher—and Huntersville native—Hoyt Wilhelm gets his career off to a terrific start by smacking a home run in his first major-league at-bat. Over the rest of his career, though—spanning 1,070 games in 21 seasons—Wilhelm will never homer again.

Hoyt Wilhelm (front row, far right)
with the 1947 Mooresville Moors
Courtesy of Chris Holaday

1995

Winston-Salem native Howard Cosell, one of the best-known and most outspoken sportscasters of all time, dies of a heart embolism in Manhattan, at the age of 77. Cosell, whose family moved to Brooklyn when he was young, was best-known for his 14 seasons as a broadcaster on ABC's "Monday Night Football."

April 23 continued

2004

Kymberly Lamm of Southern Nash High School wallops three grand slams in a game against Nash Central, tying the national high-school record for grand slams in a softball game.

April 24

1902

The Durham Tobacconists—the forerunner of the Durham Bulls—take the field for the first time, playing an exhibition game against Trinity College (now Duke University). The team will be renamed the Bulls 11 years later and, except for 1971-1980, when there's no minor-league baseball in the city, they will continue to play in Durham up to the present day.

1967

Philadelphia 76ers reserve forward Billy Cunningham, who played college basketball at the University of North Carolina, scores 13 points in a furious fourth-quarter comeback, leading the 76ers to a 125-122 win over San Francisco for the NBA championship. It's the first title won by someone other than the Boston Celtics since 1958.

April 25

1932

George "Meadowlark" Lemon, the future "Clown Prince of Basketball" for the world-famous Harlem Globetrotters, is born in Wilmington. Lemon will join the Globetrotters in 1955 and go on to become arguably the most famous Globetrotter of all time.

1943

Winston-Salem native Rufe Gentry, a pitcher for the minor-league Buffalo Bisons, pitches an 11-inning no-hitter to defeat the Newark Bears, 1-0. Gentry will finish the season with 20 wins and a stellar 2.65 earned-run average, good enough to get him promoted to the major leagues, where he'll pitch parts of five seasons for the Detroit Tigers, compiling a 13-17 record.

1976

Future Wake Forest University basketball star Timothy Theodore "Tim" Duncan is born in the U.S. Virgin Islands. Duncan, who will be a competitive swimmer before taking up basketball in the ninth grade, will have a stellar career with the Demon Deacons, earning several national Player of the Year honors during his senior season (1996-97). He will win three straight Defensive Player of the Year awards and end his college career as the number-two shot blocker in NCAA history. After being the top pick in the 1997 NBA Draft—taken by the San Antonio Spurs—he'll win Rookie of the Year honors. He'll win four NBA titles with the Spurs and win the NBA Finals Most Valuable Player award three of those times. He'll also win the league's overall MVP award twice and will be a 13-time NBA All-Star.

Tim Duncan
Courtesy of Wake Forest Media Relations

1989
Girls' soccer player Leigh Murray of East Forsyth High School records 10 assists in a game against Carver High School, a national record. She will finish her career in 1989 with 153 assists, also first in the nation.

2008
Emma Comer, a softball pitcher for Central Davidson High School, pitches a rare perfect doubleheader—back-to-back perfect games on the same day—against Lexington. Several high-school pitchers have pitched consecutive perfect games, but she's the only one to do it in a doubleheader.

Did You Know?
In the 1994 and 1995 high-school baseball seasons, Shawn Gallagher of New Hanover High School put together a very Dimaggio-like hitting streak, getting a hit in 51 consecutive games. The streak tied a national high-school record at the time, but it has since been surpassed.

April 26

1950

Basketball standout Harold Hunter of North Carolina College at Durham (now North Carolina Central University) becomes the first black player to sign an NBA contract, signing with the Washington Capitols. Hunter was drafted the day before—along with another black player, Earl Lloyd of West Virginia State—but Hunter's college coach, John McLendon, arranged for Hunter to sign before Lloyd, so he would be the first African-American to sign. Hunter will be cut from the team during training camp and will never play in the NBA, but he will have a successful coaching career at Tennessee State University.

Harold Hunter
Courtesy of NCCU Archives and Records

2001

Timothy Midgett of Cape Hatteras High School steals nine bases in a game against Creswell High School, a state baseball record.

2006

Durham Bulls star Delmon Young, the reigning Minor League Player of the Year, draws a 50-game suspension for throwing his bat at the umpire—the harshest suspension in the 123-year history of the International League. After being called out on strikes in the first inning, Young argues the call and gets ejected for refusing to leave the batter's box. After being ejected, he underhandedly tosses his bat at the umpire, which will earn him the suspension, plus 50 hours of probation. He will also lose about $145,000 in salary.

April 27

1916
Future Hall of Fame major-leaguer Enos "Country" Slaughter is born in Roxboro. Slaughter will play 19 seasons in the big leagues, including stints from 1938 to 1942 and 1946 to 1953 with the St. Louis Cardinals (he'll miss three seasons when he serves in the military). His impressive career will end with 169 home runs, more than 2,300 hits and a .300 lifetime batting average. He'll be selected for the All-Star team 10 times and win four World Series championships. Slaughter will be inducted into the National Baseball Hall of Fame in 1985, and the Cardinals will retire his No. 9 jersey in 1996.

1929
Graham native Clise Dudley, a rookie relief pitcher for the Brooklyn Robins, becomes only the second player in major-league history to hit a home run on the first major-league pitch thrown to him. During the rest of his five-year big-league career, Dudley will hit only two more round-trippers.

1998
Former Wake Forest star Tim Duncan—now with the NBA's San Antonio Spurs—wins the league's Rookie of the Year award, receiving 113 of a possible 116 votes. Duncan averaged 21.1 points, 11.9 rebounds, 2.7 assists and 2.51 blocked shots per game, while shooting nearly 55 percent from the field.

2003
Philadelphia Phillies pitcher—and Gastonia native—Kevin Millwood throws a no-hitter against the San Francisco Giants, getting a 1-0 win. The 28-year-old right-hander needs only 108 pitches to accomplish the feat, which is the first Philadelphia no-hitter in a dozen years.

2005
A 26-inning marathon, the longest high-school girls' softball game in North Carolina history, finally ends, with Ashe County defeating North Surry, 2-0. The game was played over three days, with play having to be suspended on April 22 and again on April 25. Ashe County's Kayla Richardson pitches the entire game—26 shutout innings—recording 40 strikeouts.

Did You Know?
Who said soccer has to be low-scoring? The boys' soccer team at Hickory High School averaged 9.3 goals per game during the 1988 season, the all-time top scoring average in the nation.

April 28

1988
Edward Gerald of St. Paul's High School in Robeson County sets a state and national record by hitting five doubles in a game against Lumberton's Magnolia High School.

1993
Former North Carolina State basketball coach Jim Valvano, who led the Wolfpack to the 1983 NCAA title, dies after a yearlong battle with cancer. His gravestone in Raleigh's Oakwood Cemetery will read, "Take time every day to laugh, to think, to cry."

Jim Valvano
Courtesy of N.C. State Athletics

1995
Shawn Gallagher of New Hanover High School in Wilmington slams five home runs—a North Carolina high-school state record—in a 16-4 win over Southern Wayne. Earlier that season, Gallagher had another monster game, hitting four homers against Jordan High School in Durham.

2011
With the number-one overall pick in the NFL Draft, the Carolina Panthers select quarterback Cam Newton of Auburn University. As a senior at Auburn, Newton won the AP Player of the Year Award and the Heisman Trophy while leading the Tigers to an NCAA championship.

April 29

1931
Cleveland Indians pitcher—and Greensboro native—Wes Ferrell pitches a no-hitter against the St. Louis Browns, striking out eight in the Indians' 9-0 win. He comes up big offensively, too, with a homer, a double and four runs batted in. Ferrell's older brother, Rick, who plays for the Browns, comes closest to getting a hit, reaching base on an error.

1951
Future NASCAR legend Dale Earnhardt Sr. is born in Kannapolis. He will follow in his father Ralph's footsteps as a racecar driver, running his first Winston Cup race in 1975. Earnhardt, nicknamed "The Intimidator," will win 76 races and seven season championships, but his marvelous career will end in tragedy when he dies in a wreck during the final lap of the 2001 Daytona 500, at age 49.

1993
Boston Celtics star Reggie Lewis collapses during a playoff game against the Charlotte Hornets. He will subsequently be warned that he has a severe form of heart disease that could kill him if he keeps playing basketball, but he chooses to keep playing. On July 27—less than three months after collapsing against Charlotte—the 27-year-old will die during an off-season basketball practice.

2006
North Carolina State defensive end Mario Williams, a native of Richlands in Onslow County, becomes the first player in Atlantic Coast Conference history to be taken as the number-one overall pick in the NFL Draft, when he's selected by the Houston Texans. Williams, a.k.a. "Super Mario," left school a year early to make himself available for the draft. He will become a Pro Bowl defensive standout for the Texans.

April 30

1850
Benjamin Wesley Rippay, who will become baseball's first big-time slugger in the late 19th century, is born in Alamance County. Playing under the name Charley Jones, he will star in the National Association—the first professional baseball league—and then in the newly established major leagues. Through the major leagues' first nine seasons, Jones will be the leading home run hitter, despite missing two of those seasons (1881 and 1882) when he was blackballed from baseball be-

April 30 continued

cause of a salary dispute. His best overall season will be the 1879 season with the Boston Red Caps, when he'll lead the league in homers (nine), RBI's (62) and runs scored (85). He'll hit 10 homers in 1883—after his two-year absence from the sport—but then his numbers will tail off, and he'll finish his career with 56 home runs.

1937

Former Duke University star Clarence "Ace" Parker, making his major-league debut with the Philadelphia Athletics, hits a home run in his very first at-bat.

1988

Gastonia native Sleepy Floyd scores 42 points and teammate Hakeem Olajuwon scores 41 to lead the Houston Rockets to a 119-108 win over the Dallas Mavericks in Game 2 of their Western Conference first-round playoff series. Their offensive show is only the second time in NBA history that two teammates score 40 or more points in a playoff game.

Did You Know?

The girls' soccer team at Myers Park High School in Charlotte once scored 26 goals in a single game, a state record. Defensively, the girls' soccer teams at Sanderson High School in Raleigh (1991) and High Point Central High School (1998) hold the record for stinginess, giving up only three goals the entire season. High Point's season included an amazing run of 21 consecutive shutouts.

MAY

May 1

1930
Lexington golfer Dr. Reynolds Shoaf gets an unintentional birdie when his drive strikes a bird in mid-flight—approximately 150 yards from where he hit the ball—during a round of golf at the Forsyth Country Club course near Winston-Salem. The bird apparently dies instantly and flutters to the ground. The other three members of Shoaf's foursome vouch for his unbelievable story, which will earn him a mention in *Ripley's Believe It Or Not.*

1959
Floyd Patterson, a native of Waco, North Carolina, successfully defends his heavyweight boxing title with an 11th-round knockout of Brian London.

May 1 continued

1988

Former Tar Heel Michael Jordan becomes the first NBA player to score 50 or more points in consecutive playoff games when he lights up the Cleveland Cavaliers for 55 points to lead his Chicago Bulls to a 106-101 win in Game 2 of their first-round playoff series. Three days earlier, Jordan scored 50 in Chicago's 104-93 win.

May 2

1876

Alamance County native Charley Jones, playing for the Cincinnati Reds, hits what may be the first home run in National League history. His homer is one of two hit on this day in the league, and it's uncertain which one is hit first.

1964

The Minnesota Twins go back-to-back-to-back-to-back to become only the third team in major-league history to hit four consecutive home runs in an inning. The four players all have ties to North Carolina: Tony Oliva played for the Charlotte Hornets in 1962, Bob Allison and Harmon Killebrew played for the Hornets in 1956, and Mount Holly native Jimmie Hall played for the Kinston Eagles and the Wilson Tobs in 1957 and the Hornets in 1958.

May 3

1974

The NBA expansion New Orleans Jazz acquire Atlanta's Pete Maravich, who played basketball at Broughton High School in Raleigh, for a veritable king's ransom—first-round draft picks in 1974 and 1975, second-round picks in 1975 and 1976, and a couple of expansion draft selections. Maravich will shine for the Jazz, making the All-NBA first team in 1976 and 1977, and leading the league in scoring in the 1976-77 season with 31.1 points per game.

1999

Carolina Hurricanes defenseman Steve Chiasson dies in a single-vehicle crash near his home in Raleigh, while driving home from a team party after the Hurricanes were eliminated from the playoffs.

May 4

1980
Duke University introduces its new men's basketball coach, little-known former Army coach Mike Krzyzewski. Duke's student newspaper, *The Chronicle*, will announce Coach K's hiring with this headline: "Krzyzewski: This Is Not A Typo."

May 5

1969
Wilmington native and former North Carolina Central star Sam Jones ends his 12-year NBA career—all of those years with the Boston Celtics—by winning his 10th NBA championship, as the Celtics defeat the Los Angeles Lakers, 108-106, in Game 7 of the NBA Finals. Only Jones' teammate, Bill Russell, has more NBA titles, with 11. Jones scored more than 15,000 points in his illustrious career, making five NBA All-Star teams. He will be named one of the 50 greatest players in NBA history and will be enshrined in the Basketball Hall of Fame in 1984.

Sam Jones
Courtesy of NCCU Archives and Records

1986
College and NBA legend Pete Maravich is inducted into the Naismith Memorial Basketball Hall of Fame.

May 5 continued

1993

Alonzo Mourning sinks a 20-foot jump shot with 0.4 seconds left to give the Charlotte Hornets a 3-1 series win over the Boston Celtics in the first round of the NBA's Eastern Conference playoffs. Following the game, which is played in Charlotte, Celtics star forward Kevin McHale—one of the greatest ever to play the game—announces his retirement.

Did You Know?

Girls' softball pitcher Crystal Cox of Central Cabarrus High School won 54 straight games in 2000 and 2001, the seventh-longest win streak in the nation. Her career from 1999 to 2002 included 79 shutouts, 37 no-hitters, five consecutive no-hitters and 17 perfect games. Also, during the 2001 season, Central Cabarrus allowed only seven runs all season, and only two of them were earned runs. A few years later, between 2004 and 2006, Central Cabarrus reeled off 83 straight victories, the fifth-longest winning streak in the nation.

May 6

1982

Williamston native Gaylord Perry of the Seattle Mariners becomes only the 15th member of baseball's elite 300-win club, picking up a 7-3 win over the New York Yankees.

1985

Chris Paul, who will star at Wake Forest and go on to win the 2006 NBA Rookie of the Year, is born in Winston-Salem.

1985

Former University of North Carolina basketball star Billy Cunningham—who also played for the Carolina Cougars of the ABA—is inducted into the Naismith Memorial Basketball Hall of Fame. Cunningham, who was nicknamed "The Kangaroo Kid" for his jumping ability, was an All-American in college, a five-time NBA All-Star with the Philadelphia 76ers, and a successful coach who led the 76ers to the 1983 NBA title.

1996

Shelby native David Thompson, the former N.C. State hoops phenom who led the Wolfpack to an NCAA title in 1974, is enshrined in the Naismith Memorial Basketball Hall of Fame.

1997
Peter Karmanos, owner of the Hartford Whalers, announces the team will relocate to Raleigh, giving North Carolina its first NHL franchise. The team will play its first two seasons in Greensboro while Raleigh's RBC Center is completed, then make Raleigh its permanent home.

1998
Offensive juggernaut Michael Jordan, formerly of Wilmington, shows he can play on both ends of the court by becoming the first player in NBA history to be named to the league's All-Defensive first team nine times.

May 7

1968
In a pitching duel for the ages, Garland High School's Larry Smith records 27 strikeouts in a 14-inning state-playoff game. That would be pretty amazing, if it weren't for Smith's counterpart—E.V. Spell of Clement High School—who strikes out 33 batters to lead Clement to a 1-0 win. Spell's 33 strikeouts are a North Carolina high-school record, as are the combined 60 strikeouts in the game.

1989
Michael Jordan nails "The Shot," a buzzer-beating jumper over the Cleveland Cavaliers' Craig Ehlo, to give the Chicago Bulls a 101-100 victory over the Cavs and a 3-2 win in their best-of-five series in the first round of the NBA Playoffs. The dramatic shot will become one of the most replayed highlights in NBA history.

May 8

1953
The Atlantic Coast Conference is founded in Greensboro with seven charter members: Clemson, Duke, Maryland, North Carolina, North Carolina State, South Carolina and Wake Forest.

1957
Future Super Bowl-winning coach—and North Carolina State football star—Bill Cowher is born in Crafton, Pennsylvania. For the Wolfpack, Cowher will be a starting linebacker, team captain and team Most Valuable Player his senior year. He will graduate in 1979 with a

May 8 continued

bachelor's degree in education, then play in the NFL from 1979 to 1984 before launching a successful coaching career in the league. As a head coach, he will lead the Pittsburgh Steelers to a Super Bowl title in 2006 and will win NFL Coach of the Year awards in 1992 and 2004.

1968

Hertford native Jim "Catfish" Hunter throws a rare perfect game, retiring all 27 Minnesota batters he faces, as the Oakland Athletics blank the Twins 4-0. The 22-year-old pitching phenom notches 11 strikeouts as he becomes the first American League pitcher since 1922 to throw a regular-season perfect game. Hunter, a respectable hitter, also goes three-for-four at the plate, with a double and three runs batted in.

1973

When Chicago Cubs manager—and Gaston County native—Whitey Lockman is ejected in the 11th inning of a game against the San Diego Padres, it allows his temporary replacement, Ernie Banks, to technically become the first black to manage a major-league team.

May 9

1982

World welterweight champ Sugar Ray Leonard, a Wilmington native, undergoes a two-hour operation at Johns Hopkins Hospital in Baltimore to repair a partially detached retina in his left eye.

2009

Former Duke University assistant basketball coach Chuck Daly dies in Jupiter, Florida, at the age of 78. Daly assisted Duke head coach Vic Bubas from 1964 to 1969 and went on to an outstanding NBA coaching career, leading the Detroit Pistons to consecutive championships in 1989 and 1990. He also coached the U.S. men's basketball team—the original "Dream Team"—to a gold medal at the 1992 Summer Olympics in Barcelona, Spain.

2010

Oakland A's reserve catcher—and Raleigh native—Landon Powell becomes a part of history when he fills in behind the plate for regular catcher Kurt Suzuki, who is injured. With Powell calling the pitches, A's starter Dallas Braden throws only the 19th perfect game in major-league history.

May 10

1970
Huntersville native Hoyt Wilhelm, pitching for the Atlanta Braves against the St. Louis Cardinals, becomes the first major-league pitcher to appear in 1,000 games.

1987
Gastonia native Eric "Sleepy" Floyd of Golden State sets two NBA playoff records—29 points in the fourth quarter and 39 points in the second half—as the Warriors beat the Los Angeles Lakers, 129-121, in Game 4 of the Western Conference Semifinals. He finishes the game with 51 points.

1993
Former NBA center Walt Bellamy, a native of New Bern, is inducted into the Naismith Memorial Basketball Hall of Fame. Bellamy starred at Indiana University, where he averaged more than 20 points and more than 15 rebounds per game, and started on the 1960 U.S. Olympic team that won a gold medal in Rome. As a pro, he was selected by the Chicago Packers as the number-one overall pick in the 1961 NBA Draft and earned NBA Rookie of the Year honors, racking up 31.6 points per game and 19 rebounds per game during his debut season. He was an NBA All-Star four times during his stellar 14-year career, and he retired from the league with nearly 21,000 career points.

2007
Dale Earnhardt Jr. announces he will leave his father's company, Dale Earnhardt Inc., to drive for another team in 2008. Earnhardt says his decision is based on his desire to win a Sprint Cup Championship. About a month later, he will announce he has signed a five-year contract with Hendrick Motorsports of Concord.

May 11

1915
In his final major competition, held in Memphis, Tennessee, two-time world champion trapshooter George Lyon of Durham hits 147 out of 150 targets, despite being in poor health. He will die eight months later of tuberculosis. In addition to his world titles in 1911 and 1912, Lyon coached the U.S. trapshooting team to a gold medal in the 1912 Olympics at Stockholm.

May 11 continued

1984

After 27 months of retirement, Sugar Ray Leonard returns to the ring and gets a ninth-round technical knockout of Kevin Howard. Despite Leonard's win, Howard puts the former champ on the canvas in the fourth round—for the first time in Leonard's career—and after the fight, he shocks the boxing world by retiring again.

Courtesy of the Lew Powell Memorabilia Collection, North Carolina Collection, Wilson Library, UNC-Chapel HIll

1995

The NBA fines the Chicago Bulls $25,000 for allowing Michael Jordan to wear his old No. 23 jersey in the Bulls' playoff series against the Orlando Magic. Since his return to the league after retiring to play baseball, Jordan had been wearing No. 45, because 23 had already been retired. He ultimately had decided he was more comfortable wearing 23, and the Bulls had agreed to support his decision.

2000

Former Duke star Elton Brand of the Chicago Bulls shares NBA Rookie of the Year honors for the 1999-2000 season with Steve Francis of the Houston Rockets, with each player receiving 58 of a possible 121 votes. Brand, who was the consensus National Player of the Year at Duke and the top overall pick in the 1999 NBA Draft, averaged about 20 points and 10 rebounds per game in his rookie year.

2001

Former Tar Heel Vince Carter, now with the NBA's Toronto Raptors, makes eight three-pointers in a half during a 102-78 playoff win over the Philadelphia 76ers. Carter's hot shooting breaks the previous record of six three-pointers made in a half of a playoff game.

May 12

1951
Future NBA coaching legend George Karl, who will play his college basketball at the University of North Carolina, is born in Penn Hills, Pennsylvania.

1964
East Rowan High School pitcher Phil Robbins throws a no-hitter so dominant that his opponents, Monroe High, fail to even hit a ball into fair territory. The lefty strikes out 19 of the 21 batters he faces in the seven-inning game, while one batter draws a walk but is picked off, and another batter makes an out on a pop foul. The game is one of three no-hitters Robbins will throw for East Rowan, after which he'll play college ball at Gardner-Webb.

1977
Vern Benson, a Granite Quarry native who played collegiately at Catawba College and now coaches with the Atlanta Braves, manages his one and only major-league game under the most unusual of circumstances. After the Braves started their season 8-21, including a 16-game losing streak, team owner Ted Turner fired manager Dave Bristol and managed the team himself, despite having no baseball experience. That lasted only one game—a loss—before baseball commissioner Bowie Kuhn ordered Turner out of the dugout, citing the rule that prohibits players and managers from owning a share of a team. So Benson steps in as interim manager for one game before Bristol is rehired for the rest of the season. The Braves win, and Benson will end his managerial career with a 1.000 winning percentage.

1992
USA Basketball adds Clyde Drexler and Duke star Christian Laettner to the much-heralded "Dream Team" for the 1992 Olympics. Laettner, whose college career ended a month earlier with the Blue Devils' second consecutive NCAA championship, will be the only college player on the gold medal-winning "Dream Team," which will come to be regarded by many as the greatest sports team ever assembled. Laettner, who will go on to play 13 seasons in the NBA, was an All-American and the 1992 National Player of the Year at Duke. He's the only player ever to start in four Final Fours, and he's the NCAA Tournament's all-time leading scorer, with 407 points. His No. 32 jersey at Duke will be retired.

Christian Laettner
Courtesy of Duke University Athletics

May 13

2002
The University of North Carolina baseball team completes a three-game sweep of Duke. With the wins and resulting points, the Tar Heels win the inaugural Carlyle Cup, an award based on head-to-head competition between the two rivals.

2011
The Methodist University women's golf team wins its 14th straight NCAA Division III national championship. Since 1986, the team has won 24 national team titles, and Methodist golfers have won the individual championship 15 times. Meanwhile, the Methodist men's golf team has won 10 national team titles and nine individual championships.

May 14

1981
Kinston native and former University of North Carolina at Charlotte star Cedric "Cornbread" Maxwell wins the NBA Finals MVP Award after leading the Boston Celtics to the NBA championship over the Houston Rockets.

2004
Mia Hamm, who became a national soccer star playing for the University of North Carolina, announces her retirement from international soccer, explaining that she hopes to start a family with her husband, Nomar Garciaparra. Her retirement will take effect after the 2004 Athens Olympics in August.

May 15

1960
Chicago Cubs pitcher—and Winston-Salem native—Don Cardwell pitches a no-hitter against the St. Louis Cardinals, only two days after coming to the Cubs in a trade with the Philadelphia Phillies. It's the first no-hitter ever thrown by a pitcher making his first start with a new team. Cardwell gets the first batter out, walks the next one, and then retires 26 straight batters for the no-hitter.

1966

The Rocky Mount Leafs, playing a Carolina League doubleheader against the Greensboro Yankees, stun the hometown Yankees with a pair of no-hitters from pitching roommates Dick Drago and Darrell Clark. The Leafs win the games 5-0 and 2-0.

1990

Earl "The Pearl" Monroe, who starred at Winston-Salem State University and led the Rams to the NCAA Division II national championship in 1967, then went on to an outstanding career in the NBA, is inducted into the Naismith Memorial Basketball Hall of Fame.

Earl Monroe
Courtesy of Winston-Salem State University Athletics

May 16

1953

One of the most bizarre events in NASCAR history happens at Hickory Motor Speedway, when driver Tim Flock wins the 200-lap Grand National race with a rhesus monkey—yes, a monkey!—riding shotgun as his co-driver. The monkey, named Jocko Flocko, becomes the only monkey ever to win a NASCAR race—a wacky distinction that's certain never to be taken away.

Jocko initially rode with Flock—wearing his own little driving uniform and riding in a specially designed seat—as a publicity stunt suggested by car owner Ted Chester, who had bought Jocko at a pet shop. "I thought Ted had been hittin' the jug too much," Flock will tell biographer Larry Fielden years later. "He couldn't be serious. But the more I got to thinking about it, the more I liked it. Jocko Flocko could race with me anytime—if he proved he could handle the Grand National Circuit."

May 16 continued

During that era, drivers often had mechanics riding with them so they could fix the racecars when necessary, but Flock didn't know how NASCAR officials would feel about a monkey riding with him, so he simply didn't tell them. Jocko's first race was at a dirt track in Charlotte, where he and Flock finished fourth. Following the race, Jocko mingled with spectators in the grandstands and instantly became a fan favorite.

Altogether, Jocko will ride in eight races with Flock, the final one the Raleigh 300 on May 30, two weeks after his historic win at Hickory Motor Speedway. Flock's explanation of Jocko's retirement: "Back then the cars had a trap door that we could pull open with a chain to check our tire wear. Well, during the Raleigh 300, Jocko got loose from his seat and stuck his head through the trap door, and he went berserk! Listen, it was hard enough to drive those heavy old cars back then under normal circumstances, but with a crazed monkey clawing you at the same time, it becomes nearly impossible! I had to come into the pits to put him out and ended up third. The pit stop cost me second place and a $600 difference in my paycheck. Jocko was retired immediately. I had to get that monkey off my back!"

Tim Flock and Jocko
Courtesy of Frances Flock

1957

Future N.C. State University cross-country star Joan Benoit-Samuelson, who will win All-America honors while running for the Wolfpack, is born in Cape Elizabeth, Maine. She will also win two Boston Marathons and the gold medal in the first women's Olympic marathon in 1984.

1985
Former University of North Carolina standout Michael Jordan, now a Chicago Bull, earns NBA Rookie of the Year honors with his eye-popping 28.2-point scoring average, to go along with 6.5 rebounds, 5.9 assists and 2.4 steals per game.

1992
Charlotte Motor Speedway becomes the first non-short track to have night racing, when it hosts The Winston All-Star Race under the lights. Davey Allison gets the win, beating Kyle Petty to the checkered flag by less than half a car length.

May 17

1912
Clarence "Ace" Parker, a future All-American tailback at Duke University, is born in Portsmouth, Virginia. Parker, who will also become a baseball standout at Duke, will go on to play major-league baseball and star in the National Football League. He will be named the NFL's Most Valuable Player in 1940 and will be inducted into the Pro Football Hall of Fame in 1972.

Ace Parker
Courtesy of Duke University Athletics

1956
Future boxing legend Ray Charles "Sugar Ray" Leonard is born in Wilmington. In addition to an Olympic gold medal, world titles and induction into the International Boxing Hall of Fame, Leonard will become the first boxer to earn more than $100 million in purses.

May 17 continued

1966

Future North Carolina high-school basketball phenom Danny Manning, who will lead Greensboro's Page High School to a state championship before moving to Kansas for his senior season, is born in Hattiesburg, Mississippi. Manning will go on to lead the University of Kansas to an NCAA title in 1988 and win the John R. Wooden Award as college basketball's most outstanding player.

1987

Kannapolis native Dale Earnhardt survives his famous "Pass in the Grass" during the 1987 running of The Winston at Charlotte Motor Speedway. When Earnhardt collides with Bill Elliott and is forced into the grass, he keeps his foot on the gas and maintains control of his car, still holding the lead when he returns to the track. Earnhardt goes on to win the race.

1995

Former Duke star Grant Hill, now of the Detroit Pistons, shares NBA Rookie of the Year honors with Jason Kidd of Dallas.

May 18

1922

Future major-leaguer Gil Coan, who will play 11 seasons in the big leagues, is born in Monroe. In 1945, he will be named the Minor League Player of the Year by *The Sporting News*. Two years later, as an outfielder for the Washington Senators, Coan will get 21 hits in 42 at-bats for a stellar batting average of .500, the highest average of any player with 30 or more at-bats in a season. In 1951, Coan will perform the unusual feat of hitting two triples in the same inning.

1998

Michael Jordan wins his fifth and final NBA Most Valuable Player award, tying him for second-most league MVP awards with Bill Russell. (Kareem Abdul-Jabbar won the award six times.)

May 19

1981

Franklinton native Jim Bibby, a pitcher for the Pittsburgh Pirates, throws a near-perfect game against the Atlanta Braves. After giving up a lead-off single, Bibby retires 27 straight batters—the equivalent of a perfect game—as the Pirates win, 5-0.

May 20

1996
Michael Jordan receives 109 out of 113 first-place votes—an NBA record 96.5 percent—to win the league's 1995-96 Most Valuable Player award, the fourth time he's won the award. His season stats include 30.4 points per game, 6.6 rebounds, 4.3 assists and 2.2 steals.

2000
More than a hundred racing fans are injured, some of them seriously, when a pedestrian bridge at Lowe's Motor Speedway collapses following a NASCAR all-star race. As the fans are crossing from the speedway to a nearby parking lot, the walkway collapses and falls about 25 feet onto a Concord highway.

May 21

1923
Clarence "Big House" Gaines is born in Paducah, Kentucky. In 47 years of coaching men's basketball at Winston-Salem State University, Gaines will win 828 games en route to the Basketball Hall of Fame.

Clarence "Big House" Gaines
Courtesy of Winston-Salem State University Athletics

May 21 continued

1981

Future major-league All-Star Josh Hamilton is born in Raleigh. His major-league career will be delayed by substance abuse problems, but he'll go on to become a star for the Texas Rangers. In addition to becoming a three-time All-Star (as of this writing), Hamilton will win the American League batting title and the American League's Most Valuable Player award, both in 2010.

May 22

1975

Former Gardner-Webb basketball star Artis Gilmore scores 28 points and grabs a playoff-record 31 rebounds to lead the Kentucky Colonels to a 110-105 win over the Indiana Pacers, giving the Colonels the ABA championship. Gilmore also snares MVP honors for the championship series.

1995

"Strike Out Domestic Violence Night" seems like a good idea, but the promotion takes an ironic twist when the host Durham Bulls engage in a nasty, half-hour brawl with the visiting Winston-Salem Warthogs after the Warthogs pitcher hits three Bulls batters by only the third inning. One player winds up in the hospital with a broken jaw and five missing teeth. The donnybrook results in the ejection of 10 players, and the president of the Carolina League will hand down $6,000 in fines and 124 days of suspensions.

1999

Mia Hamm scores her 109th goal to break the all-time international goal record for women's soccer. The milestone comes in a game against Brazil in Orlando, Florida.

May 23

1991

Philadelphia Phillies pitcher Tommy Greene—a Lumberton native who played baseball at Whiteville High School—fires a no-hitter, defeating the Montreal Expos, 2-0, in Montreal. Greene, who is only pitching because of an injury to regular starter Danny Cox, strikes out 10 en route to the no-hitter. When Greene played for Whiteville (1982-85), he threw nine no-hitters, a state high-school record.

2010

The new NASCAR Hall of Fame, located in Charlotte, inducts its historic first class. In addition to NASCAR founder Bill France Sr. and longtime NASCAR president Bill France Jr., the class includes North Carolina racing legends Richard Petty, Dale Earnhardt and Junior Johnson.

Junior Johnson (left) with
driver Cale Yarborough
Courtesy of North Carolina State Archives

May 24

1964

Glenn "Fireball" Roberts, one of NASCAR's most popular and most successful drivers, suffers second- and third-degree burns over 80 percent of his body in a fiery crash during the seventh lap of the World 600 at Charlotte Motor Speedway. When Ned Jarrett and Junior Johnson collide, Roberts crashes trying to avoid them, causing his car to slam backwards into a retaining wall, flip over and burst into flames. He will be airlifted to a Charlotte hospital in critical condition and will die about six weeks later of complications from his injuries.

1979

Future seven-time NBA All-Star Tracy McGrady—who will play his senior year of high-school basketball at Mount Zion Christian Academy in Durham—is born in Bartow, Florida.

May 24 continued

2000

Greensboro native Bob McAdoo, who played a season at the University of North Carolina—and was a first-team All-American—before leaving for the NBA, is elected to the Naismith Memorial Basketball Hall of Fame. McAdoo enjoyed a stellar professional career, winning the 1973 NBA Rookie of the Year Award and the 1975 Most Valuable Player Award, both as a member of the Buffalo Braves. He was voted an NBA All-Star five times and won three consecutive NBA scoring titles in his second, third and fourth seasons in the league. McAdoo was also popular with fans, leading the league in fan voting for the 1975 All-Star Game.

<u>May 25</u>

1975

Kannapolis native Dale Earnhardt makes his Winston Cup debut, driving in the World 600 at the Charlotte Motor Speedway. He finishes 22nd.

1975

Al Attles, a former college basketball star at North Carolina A&T, becomes only the second black coach (after Bill Russell) to win an NBA championship, when his Golden State Warriors defeat the Washington Bullets 96-95 to complete a four-game sweep.

<u>May 26</u>

1959

Former Winston-Salem Cardinals pitcher Harvey Haddix, now with the Pittsburgh Pirates, pitches an amazing 12 perfect innings—and 12 1/3 no-hit innings—before finally giving up a run to the Milwaukee Braves in the bottom of the 13th. In spite of Haddix losing the game, many will still call it the greatest game ever pitched. Haddix had shown signs of greatness while in Winston-Salem, once striking out 19 batters in a game against the Durham Bulls.

1999

Former Tar Heel Vince Carter, now with the Toronto Raptors, is named the 1998-99 NBA Rookie of the Year. During his rookie season, he averaged 18.3 points, 5.7 rebounds, 3.0 assists, 1.5 blocked shots and 1.1 steals per game.

122 ≡ *Instant Replay*

Did You Know?

In 1968, East Rowan High School pitcher Randy Benson went an entire season without giving up any earned runs, joining a list of only 27 pitchers in the history of high-school baseball to accomplish the feat. He went on to mediocre success in the minor leagues, but never made the majors.

May 27

1960
Clint Courtney of the Baltimore Orioles becomes the first catcher to use an oversized mitt, designed by his manager Paul Richards specifically for catching knuckleballs thrown by Orioles pitcher—and Huntersville native—Hoyt Wilhelm. The mitt apparently works, as Wilhelm pitches the entire game with no wild pitches or passed balls, and he gets a 3-2 win over the New York Yankees.

May 28

1960
Former University of North Carolina track star Jim Beatty breaks the American mile record, running it in 3:58 at the California Relays in Modesto, California.

1982
Durham Bulls manager Bobby Dews unleashes one of the most entertaining tantrums ever seen at a baseball game. During a heated argument with the umpires, Dews pulls up second base and hurls it into the stands, then removes his jersey and powders his underarms with the rosin bag before kicking it into the air.

1987
Charlotte O's pitcher Bob Milacki pitches an astounding 11 1/3 innings of no-hit baseball against Chattanooga before finally surrendering a hit. He ends up pitching 13 of the game's 14 innings and notches a 2-1 win.

2002
The Carolina Hurricanes earn their first trip to the Stanley Cup Finals when they defeat Toronto, 2-1—in an overtime thriller—in Game 6

May 28 continued

of the Eastern Conference Finals to claim the franchise's first conference championship. The Canes will win the first game of the Stanley Cup Finals over the Detroit Red Wings, but then drop four straight games to lose the series.

May 29

1951

The Cleveland Indians sign high-school star pitcher Billy Joe Davidson of Marion, paying him a bonus somewhere between $100,000 and $150,000. Despite beliefs that the lanky lefthander is the best Indians pitching prospect since Hall of Famer Bob Feller, Davidson will never play a game in the major leagues. He will compile only a 51-39 record in the minors before having his career completely derailed by a basketball injury.

1989

Longtime Western Carolina University football coach and athletic director Bob Waters dies of amyotrophic lateral sclerosis—better known as Lou Gehrig's disease—after a six-year battle against the disease. Waters, who had been football coach at WCU since 1969, had continued to coach even as his illness progressed, until he was forced to step down in March 1989, just a couple of months before his death at age 50. In 1988, the field at WCU's Whitmire Stadium was named Bob Waters Field in his honor.

Coach Bob Waters
Courtesy of WCU/Mark Haskett

> **Did You Know?**
>
> In one of the most noted sporting events of the 19th century, more than 60,000 spectators showed up at the Union Race Course in Long Island, New York, to watch the fastest horse in the North take on the fastest horse in the South—which happened to be Sir Henry, a 4-year-old stallion from North Carolina that was trained by Lemuel Long of Halifax County. The race, held on May 27, 1823, was the deciding race in a best-of-three challenge competition between the horse from the North, American Eclipse, and Sir Henry. Surprisingly, Sir Henry had won the first race over the favored American Eclipse, but had lost the second one. In the tight deciding race, American Eclipse eventually pulled away and won by three lengths.

May 30

1964

Greensboro racecar driver Eddie Sachs dies in a fiery crash on the second lap of the Indianapolis 500. The crash occurs when Dave MacDonald, in his first Indy 500, loses control of his car and slams into a wall, igniting a horrific fire. As his car slides back across the track, Sachs is unable to avoid broadsiding the car, which triggers another massive explosion, resulting in Sachs' death. MacDonald also dies in the crash.

1967

Hertford's Jim "Catfish" Hunter of the Kansas City Athletics hits the first of his six major-league home runs during a game against the Washington Senators. Ironically, a fellow North Carolinian—Statesville native Barry Moore—surrenders the long ball to Hunter.

May 31

1964

Williamston native Gaylord Perry, who will develop a widely known reputation as a pitcher who illegally doctors the baseball—but who will still make the Hall of Fame—throws his first illegal pitch, a spitball. Pitching for the San Francisco Giants in the second game of a doubleheader at Shea Stadium against the New York Mets, he enters the game in the bottom of the 13th inning, with the game tied 6-6 and runners on first and second. When a fight breaks out in the stands near the Mets' dugout—and everyone stops to watch—Perry fires a wad of saliva at the

May 31 continued

baseball. Years later, in his autobiography, *Me and the Spitter: An Autobiographical Confession*, Perry will write, "Using the fight as a cover, I held the ball up to my mouth and spit right on her, just like I read Burleigh Grimes used to do. Nobody saw me do it."

Gaylord Perry
Courtesy of Chris Holaday

2003
Bombing suspect Eric Rudolph is arrested in Murphy and will be charged in the infamous Centennial Olympic Park bombing in Atlanta, which occurred on July 27, 1996, during the 1996 Summer Olympics. The violent explosion killed one spectator, wounded 111 others and cast a dark shadow over the Olympics. Rudolph will agree to a plea bargain that allows him to escape the death penalty but will keep him in prison for the rest of his life.

2008
Mount Olive College wins the 2008 NCAA Division II Baseball National Championship with a 6-2 win over Ouachita Baptist.

2008
Red Sox slugger Manny Ramirez, whose minor-league career included stints with the Burlington Indians, Kinston Indians and Charlotte Knights, blasts his 500th major-league home run, a shot over the right-field wall at Camden Yards in Baltimore. He is the 24th major-leaguer to reach the 500-homer milestone.

JUNE

June 1

1997
Former Tar Heel Michael Jordan drains a last-second 20-foot jumper to give the Chicago Bulls a dramatic Game One win over the Utah Jazz in the 1997 NBA Finals.

2006
The Carolina Hurricanes defeat Buffalo, 4-2, in Game 7 of the Eastern Conference Finals to advance to the Stanley Cup Finals for only the second time in franchise history.

June 2

1951
The minor-league Tarboro Athletics record professional baseball's biggest inning in 1951, racking up 24 runs in a single inning against the

June 2 continued

hapless Wilson Tobs. An amazing 25 batters come to the plate before the first out is recorded, and Tarboro goes on to get the lopsided win, 31-4.

1951

During a game against the Durham Bulls, visiting Danville's shortstop Mike Romello hits the umpire after being called out for leaving third base too early. A judge who happens to be at the game arrests Romello on the spot, and he will later be fined $25 for the assault.

1960

Future NASCAR driver Kyle Petty—son of Richard Petty and grandson of Lee Petty—is born in Randleman. He will win in his very first start—an ARCA race at Daytona in 1979—and go on to record eight career victories. Despite the success of his father and grandfather, Kyle will become the first Petty to win $1 million in a season, accomplishing the feat in 1992.

Kyle Petty
Courtesy of High Point Enterprise/*Sonny Hedgecock*

1990

Competing in the NCAA Track & Field Championships, held on the campus of Duke University, University of Wisconsin track star Suzy Favor wins the 800 meters and 1,500 meters, giving her an NCAA-record nine individual titles.

1999

The Tampa Bay Devil Rays use their number-one draft pick to select Raleigh prep star Josh Hamilton. It's the first time a high-school player has been the overall first pick since 1993, when Alex Rodriguez was chosen first. Hamilton would receive a nearly $4 million signing bonus, but the blue-chip prospect's career would be derailed by a drug addiction; he would not make his major-league debut until April 2, 2007, with the Cincinnati Reds.

June 3

1911

Will Robinson, who will become the first black head coach of an NCAA Division I men's basketball program, is born in Wadesboro. In 1970, at the age of 60, Robinson will be hired to coach at Illinois State University, finally breaking the color barrier for Division I head basketball coaches.

1943

William John "Billy" Cunningham, who will star in basketball for the North Carolina Tar Heels and later for the ABA's Carolina Cougars, is born in Brooklyn, New York. Cunningham's impressive leaping ability will earn him the nickname "The Kangaroo Kid."

1955

Duke University sprinter Dave Sime, who had come to Duke to play baseball, sets a world record in the 220-yard dash, running it in 20 seconds flat at an AAU championship meet in Stockton, California. Dubbed "Superman in Spikes" by *Sports Illustrated*, Sime will hold six world records in sprinting and hurdling at one point during the mid-1950s. University of North Carolina sprinter Rand Bailey will tell the *Raleigh News & Observer*, "You don't exactly feel like you're stopping or standing still when Sime zooms by you. It's more like you're being sucked backwards. It's a strange feeling." At the 1960 Olympics, Sime will lose the 100-yard dash in a photo finish, earning a silver medal. He will also anchor the U.S. 4 x 100 relay team, which will appear to set a world record, but a bad baton exchange will result in the team's disqualification.

1991

The New York Yankees select 19-year-old Brien Taylor of Beaufort with the number-one overall pick in the 1991 Major League Baseball Draft. With a 98-mph fastball, the left-handed pitcher is expected to become a star for the Yankees; instead, he will become only the second player ever to be the number-one overall pick and never make it to the major leagues. After signing for $1.55 million, Taylor will begin working his way up through the minors, but in December 1993 he'll dislocate his left shoulder in a fistfight, and he'll never again be the dominating pitcher he once was. Taylor will struggle a few more years in the minors before finally retiring in 2000, never having made it to the big leagues.

June 3 continued

1992

Michael Jordan sets an NBA Finals record with his six three-pointers and 35 points in the first half, leading the Chicago Bulls to a 122-89 victory over Portland in Game 1. After making his sixth three-pointer of the first half, Jordan famously shrugs, as if to say, "Looks like everything's going in tonight."

1998

San Diego businessman Richard Esquinas announces publication of a book in which he claims to have won more than $1 million in golf bets from Michael Jordan—an amount that they negotiated down to $300,000. Jordan will acknowledge losing bets to Esquinas, but will deny he has a gambling addiction. The NBA will investigate, but will find no violations of league rules on Jordan's part.

2006

Morgan Childers of Kings Mountain High School strikes out 24 batters, a state record for high-school girls' softball in North Carolina, in a game against Southwestern Randolph.

June 4

1986

Kathy Ormsby, a 21-year-old distance runner for North Carolina State University—and one of the favorites to win the 10,000 meters at the NCAA track and field championships in Indianapolis—shocks the nation with a bizarre apparent suicide attempt during the race. Only six weeks earlier, Ormsby had set an NCAA record in the 10,000 meters, but something snaps inside her during this race. At about the 6,500-meter mark—running in fourth place but only a few strides behind the three frontrunners—the Rockingham native suddenly veers off the track, ducks under a railing, sprints up into the stands and runs right out of the stadium. She keeps running to a nearby bridge, where she hurls herself over the side and plunges to the ground about 35 feet below. In addition to a broken rib and collapsed lung, she suffers a fractured vertebra that will render her paralyzed from the waist down. Ormsby's actions—which even she will have trouble explaining—stun those who know her. At Richmond High School in Rockingham, she was her class valedictorian, a star athlete and, by all accounts, a highly respected young woman who seemed to have everything going for her. Following a period of rehabilitation, Ormsby will become an occupational therapist, though she will remain paralyzed.

June 5

1949

Major-league baseball commissioner Happy Chandler lifts a ban he had imposed on players who defected to the Mexican League—among them, Denton native Max Lanier, a pitcher for the St. Louis Cardinals, who had jumped to the Mexican League in 1946 for more money. Lanier had tried to return to the Cardinals in 1948, alleging his Mexican League contract had been broken, but Chandler's ban prohibited his return. In response, Lanier filed suit against the major leagues, but when Chandler lifts the ban, he will drop his suit and return to the Cardinals.

1991

In Game 2 of the NBA Finals between the Chicago Bulls and the Los Angeles Lakers, Michael Jordan provides another highlight for the ages. Driving down the lane for a dunk with his right hand, Jordan spots a defender out of the corner of his right eye and acrobatically switches the ball to his left hand in midair, then lays it in on the left side of the rim. "It was just instinct to change hands," Jordan will explain later. "It was just one of those creative things. Sometimes you never know what's going to happen."

June 6

1939

Tarboro native Burgess Whitehead is one of five New York Giants to homer in a single inning, a major-league record.

June 7

1938

Lenoir native Johnny Allen, pitching for the Cleveland Indians against the Boston Red Sox, angrily storms off the mound after being ordered by the umpire to cut off his dangling sweatshirt sleeve, which the ump deems to be a distraction to batters. Allen refuses and does not return to the game, and the controversial shirt eventually will wind up in the Hall of Fame.

June 7 continued

1941

Famed ex-convict Edwin "Alabama" Pitts—whose efforts to play professional baseball after his release from prison sparked a national debate on the merits of prison rehabilitation—dies after being stabbed during an altercation at a Valdese roadhouse. Pitts, whose short-lived career in the minor leagues had brought him to North Carolina, is stabbed by a jealous boyfriend after Pitts attempted to cut in and dance with the man's date. Though his injury does not appear to be life-threatening, the 31-year-old Pitts dies a couple of hours later.

In 1930, at age 19, Pitts was convicted of armed robbery and sentenced to 8-16 years at New York's famed Sing Sing Correctional Facility, a maximum-security prison. The young man excelled in athletics at Sing Sing, particularly football and baseball, capturing the interest of professional teams and prompting the *Los Angeles Times* to label Pitts "the most prominent jailbird athlete in America." About two weeks before his June 1935 release from prison (his sentence had been shortened for good behavior), Pitts signed a minor-league contract with the Albany Senators, but minor-league officials—notably Durham judge William Bramham, then president of the National Association of Professional Baseball Leagues, which governed the minors—refused to approve the contract, arguing that allowing Pitts to play was "against the best interests of the game." The ruling sparked a heated national debate on the merits of prison rehab, as numerous journalists, baseball players, managers and fans lobbied for Pitts to be given a chance, until finally baseball commissioner Kenesaw Mountain Landis overturned the ruling, giving Pitts a chance to play.

After a so-so season with Albany—and then a brief, unsuccessful foray into professional football—Pitts came to North Carolina in 1936 and played for a string of minor-league teams across the state: the Charlotte Hornets, the Winston-Salem Twins, the Gastonia Spinners, the Valdese Textiles and the Hickory Rebels. At the time of his death, Pitts had been playing for a Valdese mill team. As a testament to Pitts' popularity as a player—despite his decidedly mediocre results on the field—an estimated 5,000 people will attend his funeral.

1995

Former Tar Heel Kenny Smith, now with the Houston Rockets, sets the NBA Finals records for most three-pointers in a game (seven) and in a quarter (five), to lead the Rockets to a 120-118 overtime win against Orlando in Game 1.

June 8

1961

Milwaukee Braves third-baseman Eddie Mathews, whose professional baseball career began in the minors with the High

Point-Thomasville Hi-Toms, blasts a two-run homer in the seventh inning of a game against the Cincinnati Reds, igniting the first barrage of four-straight-homers-in-an-inning in major-league history. Following Mathews' homer, teammates Hank Aaron, Joe Adcock and Frank Thomas do likewise. Mathews hits two homers for the game, but the Braves still lose, 10-8.

1964
Jim Hunter, a promising baseball pitcher from Hertford, signs with the Kansas City A's. The following year, A's owner Charles O. Finley, thinking his new pitcher needs a catchy nickname, dubs him "Catfish," a nickname that will become better known than Hunter's given name. The young pitcher will go on to a Hall of Fame career.

June 9

1992
Future University of North Carolina basketball and track star Marion Jones of Thousand Oaks, California, sets a new high-school record for the 100-meter dash with 11.14 seconds, breaking her previous mark of 11.17.

June 10

1880
Alamance County native Charley Jones, playing for the Boston Red Caps, becomes the first major-leaguer to hit two home runs in an inning, accomplishing the feat in the eighth inning of a 19-3 rout of the Buffalo Bisons.

1946
Sixty-eight-year-old Jack Johnson, one of the greatest boxers of all time, dies in a car crash near Franklinton, reportedly as he's driving angrily away from a diner that refused to serve him because he's black.

1988
Racing at the New Asheville Speedway in Asheville, driver Shawna Robinson wins the AC Delco 100, a Dash Series race, becoming the first woman ever to win a NASCAR touring event.

June 11

1946
Pitcher Bill Kennedy strikes out an astonishing 24 of the 27 batters he retires, leading his minor-league Rocky Mount Rocks to a 2-0 win over the Goldsboro Goldbugs.

1953
The minor-league Winston-Salem Cardinals score 17 runs in a single inning against the Reidsville Luckies.

1973
Kernersville native Kemp Wicker, a former New York Yankees pitcher who played alongside Lou Gehrig, dies of amyotrophic lateral sclerosis—ironically, the same ailment that killed Gehrig and is now commonly referred to as Lou Gehrig's disease.

1988
Bull Durham, a minor-league baseball comedy in which many of the scenes were filmed at the old Durham Athletic Park, premieres at the Carolina Theatre in downtown Durham. Produced by Durham native Thom Mount, the movie will be a box-office success and help spark a nationwide revival of minor-league baseball. In the movie, Kevin Costner stars as Crash Davis, a character whose name was inspired by real-life player Lawrence "Crash" Davis. The real Davis grew up in Gastonia, played college ball at Duke University, and played in the minors for the Durham Bulls, the Reidsville Luckies and the Raleigh Capitals. *Bull Durham* will make Davis a minor celebrity until his 2001 death in Greensboro.

The real Crash Davis
Courtesy of Chris Holaday

134 ≡ Instant Replay

1997

In what will come to be known as "The Flu Game," a physically drained Michael Jordan battles flu-like symptoms all night, but still scores 38 points to lead the Chicago Bulls to a thrilling 90-88 win over the Utah Jazz in Game 5 of the NBA Finals. His 15-point fourth quarter includes the final dagger—a game-winning 3-pointer with 25 seconds remaining, giving the Bulls a 3-2 series lead. Jordan's teammate Scottie Pippen will say after the game, "I didn't even think he would be able to put his uniform on."

June 12

1976

Future NBA star Antawn Jamison—who will play his high-school ball in Charlotte and his college ball at North Carolina—is born in Shreveport, Louisiana. At UNC, Jamison will win national Player of the Year honors in 1998 and eventually have his No. 33 jersey retired.

1984

Kinston native Cedric "Cornbread" Maxwell scores 24 points to lead the Boston Celtics to a 111-102 win over their arch rival, the Los Angeles Lakers, in a dramatic Game 7 showdown in the NBA Finals, giving Boston its 15th NBA title.

1991

Michael Jordan racks up 30 points and 10 assists to lead Chicago to a 108-101 win over the Lakers, giving the Bulls their first NBA championship with a 4-1 series win in the NBA Finals. Jordan also wins the Finals MVP honors.

June 13

1975

Major-league pitcher Gaylord Perry, a Williamston native, proves to be a hot commodity when the Cleveland Indians trade him to the Texas Rangers for three pitchers—Jim Bibby, Jackie Brown and Rick Waits—plus approximately $100,000. In three-plus seasons with the Rangers, Perry will post a 48-43 record with an earned run average of 3.26.

June 14

1959
Richard Petty takes the checkered flag at Atlanta's Lakewood Speedway and heads to Victory Lane with what he thinks is his first career win. But wait! The second-place finisher—who drove another lap after Petty finished—protests that Petty finished one lap too soon. After a thorough review, the sanctioning body agrees and strips the trophy from Petty, awarding it instead to the second-place finisher, who just happens to be ... Petty's father, veteran racer Lee Petty. Years later, the elder Petty will say, "I would have protested even if it was my mother."

1964
Walter Maxwell of Charlotte catches the largest tiger shark ever landed—1,780 pounds—while fishing from the pier at Cherry Grove, South Carolina. His catch tops the previous world-record tiger shark by more than 350 pounds. Two years later, he'll catch a 1,150-pound tiger shark at Oak Island, the largest tiger shark caught in North Carolina.

1992
Michael Jordan becomes the first player to win the NBA Finals MVP in consecutive years, after leading Chicago to a 97-93 win over Portland, giving the Bulls their second straight NBA title.

1998
Michael Jordan does it again, winning his sixth NBA Finals MVP in leading the Bulls to their sixth NBA championship in eight seasons with a heart-stopping 87-86 win over the Utah Jazz. With his team down by a point and time running out, Jordan swipes the ball from Utah's Karl Malone on the defensive end, brings the ball to the other end and nails a game-winning 20-foot jump shot over Utah's Byron Russell. This will be Jordan's final shot as a Chicago Bull.

June 15

1938
Former Durham Bulls pitcher Johnny Vander Meer, now pitching for the Cincinnati Reds, fires his second consecutive no-hitter, a 6-0 win over the Brooklyn Dodgers, to become the first and only major-leaguer to accomplish the feat. Vander Meer's first no-hitter came four days earlier in a 3-0 victory over Boston. The young pitcher's potential was evident when he played for Durham, where he was named the Minor League Player of the Year in 1936.

1986

Fort Bragg native Raymond Floyd shoots a final-day 66 to become the oldest winner of a U.S. Open, at 43 years, 9 months and 11 days. The win is Floyd's 20th career win on the PGA Tour and his fourth major title.

June 16

1955

Wake Forest wins the College World Series to claim North Carolina's only NCAA Division I baseball championship. Making their second appearance in the CWS (the first came in 1949, when they finished second), the Demon Deacons clinch the title with a thrilling 7-6 win over Western Michigan. The squad goes 5-1 in the CWS, including three shutout wins, en route to the championship.

The 1955 Wake Forest baseball team
Courtesy of Wake Forest Media Relations

1991

Atlanta Braves outfielder Otis Nixon, a native of Columbus County, steals six bases in a single game, setting a National League record and tying the major-league record. Nixon will end his 17-year major-league career with 620 stolen bases, placing him among the top 20 base-stealers of all time.

1993

Michael Jordan scores 55 points in Game 4 of the NBA Finals, tying the second-highest scoring output in NBA Finals history. Jordan's Chicago Bulls win the game, 111-105, over the Phoenix Suns.

June 16 continued

2011

The North Carolina General Assembly adopts stock car racing as the official sport of the Tar Heel State.

June 17

1940

Future football Hall of Famer Bobby Bell is born in Shelby. He will make the College Football Hall of Fame after starring at the University of Minnesota—where he'll win the 1962 Outland Trophy as the nation's most outstanding lineman—and then be inducted into the Pro Football Hall of Fame after a stellar career with the Kansas City Chiefs.

June 18

1922

Dobson native Clement Manly Llewellyn makes his major-league debut—and, ironically, his major-league farewell—pitching a single inning for the New York Yankees. Though he gives up only one hit and surrenders no runs, he'll never pitch in the majors again.

1948

Ernie Sawyer, an 18-year-old pitcher for the minor-league New Bern Bears, pitches an 11-inning no-hitter, shutting out Rocky Mount for a 1-0 win.

1960

Former Wake Forest golfer Arnold Palmer pulls off what will become the most famous come-from-behind win in PGA history, shooting a final-round 65 to erase a 7-stroke deficit and win the U.S. Open at Cherry Hills Country Club in Denver. Palmer finds himself seven strokes behind leader Mike Souchak at the start of the day, but he birdies the first four holes and keeps charging throughout the day, finishing two strokes ahead of 20-year-old amateur Jack Nicklaus to claim what will be the only U.S. Open win of his career.

1999

Fayetteville hosts a boxing series for the aged—er, ages—when former heavyweight champions Larry Holmes, now a 49-year-old grandfather, and 46-year-old James "Bonecrusher" Smith, a Duplin County native, step into the ring. Holmes wins in the eighth round when his powerful jabs force Smith to throw in the towel. In the evening's undercard, two more former champions—41-year-old Tim Witherspoon and 40-year-old Greg Page—do battle, with Page getting the victory after seven rounds.

June 19

1949

In the first NASCAR Strictly Stock race, held at the old Charlotte Speedway, driver Jim Roper gets the win under unusual circumstances. Roper, who had learned about the race when he read about it in a comic book, drove all the way from Kansas—some 1,000 miles—in the car he would compete in. Roper actually finishes second in the 200-lap event, three laps behind apparent winner Glenn Dunnaway, but Dunnaway's car is disqualified for using illegal "bootlegger" springs, giving the win—and the $2,000 first prize—to Roper.

1960

Little-known journeyman racer Joe Lee Johnson wins the inaugural World 600 at Charlotte Motor Speedway, upsetting a host of better-known drivers. In fact, the outcome is so surprising that many NASCAR fans believe the race was won by *Junior* Johnson, not Joe Lee. North Carolina's racing Pettys, Lee and Richard, are both disqualified for improperly entering the pits.

1966

Arnold Palmer uncharacteristically blows a seven-stroke lead on the back nine of the U.S. Open's final round, allowing Billy Casper to draw even and force an 18-hole playoff the next day. Casper will win the playoff by four strokes, and *Sports Illustrated* will proclaim Palmer's epic collapse to be "one of the great debacles of modern times, comparable to the Italian retreat at Caporetto, the Edsel car and Liz Taylor's *Cleopatra.*"

1984

The Chicago Bulls select Michael Jordan with the third overall pick in the NBA Draft, behind Hakeem Olajuwon (Houston Rockets) and Sam Bowie (Portland Trailblazers). Bulls general manager Rod Thorn assesses his young guard from North Carolina like this: "We wish Jordan were 7-feet, but he isn't. There just wasn't a center available. What can you do? Jordan isn't going to turn this franchise around. I wouldn't ask him to. He's a very good offensive player, but not an overpowering offensive player." Jordan, of course, will prove Thorn wrong, becoming not just a very good offensive player but an overpowering offensive player who will, indeed, turn the Chicago franchise around and lead the Bulls

June 19 continued

to six NBA titles, in the process establishing himself as arguably the greatest basketball player ever.

Michael Jordan
Courtesy of UNC Athletic Communications

1995

Former Boston Celtics player M.L. Carr, a Wallace native who played college ball at Guilford College—and who has zero coaching experience—accepts the Celtics' head coaching job. "It's an open question as to whether M.L. can coach," Celtics chairman of the board Paul Gaston says at a news conference. "I think we're all going to have fun finding out." While the fun part may be open to debate, Carr's coaching ability is not—he'll go 33-49 in his first season, then follow that up with a record of 15-67, the worst record in Celtics history. He'll be replaced after those two miserable seasons.

M.L. Carr
Courtesy of Guilford College Athletics

2006

North Carolina claims its first major professional sports championship when the Carolina Hurricanes win the coveted Stanley Cup, defeating the Edmonton Oilers, 3-1, in Game 7 of the Stanley Cup Finals. Playing at the RBC Center in Raleigh, the Hurricanes lead 2-1 late in the game, forcing the Oilers to pull their goalie for an additional offensive player, in an attempt to score the tying goal. With 1:01 remaining, Justin Williams scores into the empty net to give the Canes a 3-1 lead, virtually sealing the win for Carolina. Cam Ward, the Hurricanes' rookie goalie, wins the Conn Smythe Trophy as the Most Valuable Player in the playoffs.

The Hurricanes win the Stanley Cup
Courtesy of the Carolina Hurricanes/Gregg Forwerck

Did You Know?

Many sports fans know Richard Petty holds the record for the most Winston Cup victories in a career, with 200, but he also holds the record for the most second-place finishes, with 158. Furthermore, he holds the record for most consecutive wins (10) and most consecutive second-place finishes (4).

June 20

1960

Cleveland County's Floyd Patterson reclaims his heavyweight boxing title in dramatic fashion, knocking out Swedish fighter Ingemar Johansson in the fifth round. The win makes Patterson the first boxer to win a heavyweight championship twice.

June 20 continued

1965

Jay Dahl, a 19-year-old pitcher for the minor-league Salisbury Astros—and former major-leaguer—dies in a late-night car wreck in Salisbury, making him the youngest at death of any current or former major-leaguer. Dahl was only 17 when he started a game on Sept. 27, 1963 for the Houston Colt .45s (now the Astros); he was yanked after giving up seven runs in less than three innings. He would never play again in the majors, but after recovering from a back injury, he would try again in the minors, playing for the Statesville Colts, the Durham Bulls and Salisbury, the team he was with when he died. No player who has played in the major leagues has died at a younger age than Dahl, who was still more than five months shy of his 20th birthday.

1980

Wilmington-born boxer Sugar Ray Leonard loses for the first time as a professional, dropping a close but unanimous decision—and his World Boxing Council welterweight title—to Roberto Duran. Leonard will regain the title from Duran five months later, in a beating that forces Duran to proclaim to the referee "*No más* (no more)."

2011

The Florida Marlins name Elon resident Jack McKeon interim manager for the remainder of the season. At 80, McKeon—who managed the Marlins from 2003 to 2005—becomes the second-oldest manager in major-league history, behind only Connie Mack.

June 21

1988

Gastonia native and former University of North Carolina star James Worthy records the first triple-double of his career as he leads the Los Angeles Lakers to a 108-105 Game 7 win over Detroit in the NBA Finals. Worthy—aka "Big Game James"—finishes with 36 points, 16 rebounds and 10 assists.

2010

The apparent winner of the 52nd Annual Big Rock Blue Marlin Fishing Tournament—a Hatteras-based boat named *Citation*, which landed a record-setting 883-pound blue marlin the previous week—is disqualified when it's discovered one of the crew members had failed to purchase the required North Carolina fishing license to compete in the tournament. His lack of a license—a mere $15 purchase—costs the ironically named *Citation* $912,825 in prize money, as well as first place and a spot in the tournament record books. The second-place finisher—a

Cape Carteret-based boat named *Carnivore*—becomes the winner with its 528-pound blue marlin.

June 22

1974

Wake Forest freshman golfer Curtis Strange—who will go on to an outstanding professional career—dramatically eagles the final hole of the NCAA golf championship, simultaneously clinching the team title for WFU and the individual medal for himself. Strange drains a 7-foot putt on the 540-yard, par-5 18th hole, giving him a one-stroke edge for the individual championship and the Demon Deacons a two-stroke lead for the team trophy.

Curtis Strange
Courtesy of Wake Forest Media Relations

1988

The Charlotte Hornets select 5-foot-3 point guard Muggsy Bogues, the shortest player in NBA history, in the expansion draft. The former Wake Forest star will play 14 seasons in the league, 10 of them with the Hornets, where he will lead the team in assists and steals, and become one of the most popular players in Hornets history.

1998

Michael Jordan appears on the cover of *Time* magazine—one of the few athletes to be so honored—after leading his Chicago Bulls to their second championship "three-peat."

June 23

1917

Yadkin County native Ernie Shore, a pitcher for the Boston Red Sox, pitches a rare perfect game against the Washington Senators. Or does he? Shore, who was born in East Bend and played college ball at Guilford College, comes in to pitch in the first inning when starter Babe Ruth walks the leadoff batter and then gets himself ejected for arguing with—and taking a swing at—the umpire. The runner gets thrown out trying to steal second, and then Shore mows down 26 straight batters to get a 4-0 win at Fenway Park. While it's not a traditional perfect game—Shore didn't start the game, after all, so it wasn't a complete game—baseball officials will debate the issue and ultimately credit Shore with a perfect game, making him the only reliever in major-league history to pitch a perfect game.

Red Sox pitchers; Ernie Shore is on the left, Babe Ruth on the right

Courtesy of Forsyth County Public Library Photograph Collection

1970

Tom McMillen, widely regarded as the top high-school basketball player in the country, notifies North Carolina head coach Dean Smith he'll play for the Tar Heels. A couple of months later, however, McMillen will famously change his mind and commit to the University of Maryland—coached by former Davidson coach Charles "Lefty" Driesell—where he will become an All-American, then play in the NBA and get elected to Congress.

2005
Former Wake Forest star Tim Duncan is named Most Valuable Player of the NBA Finals after his San Antonio Spurs defeat the Detroit Pistons in seven games. In the deciding game, Duncan scores 25 points and grabs 11 rebounds to lead the Spurs to an 81-74 win.

2007
Drew Weaver, a 20-year-old High Point native, becomes the first American to win the British Amateur golf tournament since 1979, earning an invitation to the British Open in July and to the 2008 Masters. Weaver, a junior at Virginia Tech University, dedicates his victory to the 32 victims of a mass shooting on the Virginia Tech campus two months earlier.

2011
Former Duke University basketball star Kyrie Irving is the number-one overall pick in the 2011 NBA Draft, going to the Cleveland Cavaliers. Irving left Duke after his freshman season to enter the draft.

June 24

1946
Southpaw pitcher Bill Kennedy of the minor-league Rocky Mount Leafs baffles Goldsboro, striking out an incredible 24 batters. Kennedy will finish the season 28-3, with an earned-run average of 1.03. He'll make it to the major leagues in 1948, but will prove to be a disappointment, striking out only 256 batters over eight seasons.

1988
The minor-league Burlington Indians lose to the visiting Bluefield Orioles, 3-2, in a 27-inning marathon at Burlington Athletic Stadium that's believed to be the longest continuous professional game in baseball history. The teams battle for 8 hours, 16 minutes, until the game mercifully ends at 3:27 a.m., only nine minutes shy of the longest game ever (an 8-hour, 25-minute minor-league game that was suspended and continued later). By the time the game ends, the crowd of more than 2,200 has dwindled down to a few dozen.

2010
With the number-one overall pick in the 2010 NBA Draft, the Washington Wizards select University of Kentucky point guard—and Raleigh native—John Wall. After playing his high-school ball in Garner and then

June 24 continued

at Raleigh's Word of God Christian Academy, Wall played only a year at Kentucky before declaring himself eligible for the draft.

2010

On the famed grass courts of Wimbledon, Greensboro native John Isner wins the longest professional tennis match in history, defeating Nicolas Mahut of France 6-4, 3-6, 6-7, 7-6, 70-68. Wimbledon's quirk of not playing a fifth-set tiebreaker causes the match to keep going ... and going ... and going. The grueling match finally comes to an end after 11 hours, 5 minutes of play spread over three days, with the marathon fifth set alone lasting 8 hours, 11 minutes. The two competitors play 980 points—711 of them in the final set—and Isner sets a record for aces with 112, easily eclipsing the previous mark of 78. Finally, Isner hits a backhand winner down the line to break Mahut's serve and win the first-round match. "You know," Isner tells the crowd moments after his historic win, "it stinks someone had to lose."

June 25

1993

Greensboro native Fred "Curly" Neal, a basketball star at Johnson C. Smith University in Charlotte, is inducted into the "Harlem Globetrotters Legends Ring," a select group of honorees who have made major contributions to the Globetrotters through their athletic ability, showmanship, crowd appeal and humanitarianism. Neal was one of the most popular Globetrotters of all time, playing in more than 6,000 games in 97 countries with the team between 1963 and 1985. Known for his shaved head, his infectious smile and his magical dribbling ability, Neal is one of only five Globetrotters—including fellow North Carolina native Meadowlark Lemon—to have his jersey retired.

Curly Neal
Courtesy of Harlem Globetrotters International Inc.

1997

The San Antonio Spurs select Tim Duncan from Wake Forest with the number-one overall pick in the 1997 NBA Draft, held at the Charlotte Coliseum. Duncan will earn Rookie of the Year and become a perennial All-Star, and exactly two years after being drafted, he will earn the NBA Finals Most Valuable Player award as he leads the Spurs to the first of their four NBA championships.

June 26

1959

Heavyweight champion Floyd Patterson, a Cleveland County native, loses his title to challenger Ingemar Johansson, getting knocked to the canvas a staggering seven times in the third round.

1991

With the overall first pick in the 1991 NBA Draft, the Charlotte Hornets select forward Larry Johnson of UNLV. Johnson will go on to win NBA Rookie of the Year honors and become a two-time All-Star for the Hornets.

1996

With the 13th pick in the 1996 NBA Draft, the Charlotte Hornets take 17-year-old high-school prodigy Kobe Bryant. The future superstar will never put on a Hornets uniform, though, because his selection is part of a draft deal with the Los Angeles Lakers, to whom Bryant will be traded for center Vlade Divac.

1999

More than 7,000 athletes from around the world converge on Raleigh's Carter-Finley Stadium for the opening ceremonies of the 1999 Special Olympics World Summer Games. Over the next week in Raleigh, Durham and Chapel Hill, the Special Olympians will compete in 19 sports for medals.

June 27

1988

Boxer Michael Spinks, who trained at Camp Lejeune before hitting the big time, gets knocked out by Mike Tyson, suffering the only loss of his professional boxing career.

June 27 continued

2001

Michael Jordan, team president of the Washington Wizards, convinces his organization to draft high-schooler Kwame Brown, making the Wizards the first team to ever choose a high-school prospect with the number-one overall pick in the draft. The pick doesn't pan out—as Brown will bounce from one NBA team to another—but he will be reunited with Jordan when he signs with Jordan's Charlotte Bobcats in 2010.

2011

Former N.C. State basketball star Lorenzo Charles, 47, dies in an afternoon bus crash on Interstate 40 in Raleigh. Charles made the last-second, game-winning dunk to give the Wolfpack the 1983 NCAA championship.

June 28

1964

Future major-leaguer Mark Grace, who will enjoy a 16-year career in the big leagues—most of those years with the Chicago Cubs—is born in Winston-Salem. Grace will earn the distinction of getting more hits during the 1990s (1,754) than any other player.

1988

The Los Angeles Clippers select former Greensboro prep star Danny Manning with the first overall pick in the 1988 NBA Draft. During his long career, Manning will become a two-time All-Star and win the league's Sixth Man of the Year award in 1998.

1988

The Charlotte Hornets select former University of Kentucky star Rex Chapman with the eighth overall pick in the NBA Draft. Chapman will become the first player ever signed in Hornets history, and he will become a fan favorite, averaging nearly 17 points a game during his first season.

2005

The New York Knicks sign former University of North Carolina star Larry Brown to a five-year coaching deal worth a reported $50 to $60 million, making him the NBA's highest-paid coach. However, he will be fired after a disastrous first season.

June 29

1905

Fayetteville native Archibald "Moonlight" Graham, an outfielder for the New York Giants, makes a brief debut—and farewell—appearance in the majors that will earn him posthumous fame decades later. Graham gets into a game against Brooklyn in the bottom of the eighth inning, playing right field. In the top of the ninth, he's on deck when the final out is made; he returns to the field for the bottom of the ninth, but he doesn't get a chance to bat. The game turns out to be his only appearance in a major-league game, as he will return to the minors for three seasons before giving up baseball and enjoying a long career as a small-town doctor in Chisholm, Minnesota. In 1982, ten years after Graham's death, he will be incorporated as a character in author W.P. Kinsella's book *Shoeless Joe*. In 1989, the novel will be made into the popular Kevin Costner movie *Field of Dreams*, and the unusual tale of Moonlight Graham will become well-known across the nation.

A Moonlight Graham baseball card
Courtesy of the Lew Powell Memorabilia Collection, North Carolina Collection, Wilson Library, UNC-Chapel Hill

1982

The Los Angeles Lakers select University of North Carolina star James Worthy—who just led the Tar Heels to an NCAA championship—with the overall number-one pick in the 1982 NBA Draft. Worthy, who left school after his junior year to enter the draft, will play his entire career with the Lakers, becoming a seven-time All-Star and a three-time NBA champion.

June 29 continued

1989

The NBA levels a lifetime ban against Hickory native Chris Washburn of the Atlanta Hawks for violating the league's substance-abuse policy by failing three drug tests in three years. Washburn, who played college ball at North Carolina State University and was selected third overall in the 1986 NBA Draft, will be widely considered to be one of the biggest busts in NBA history.

> **Did You Know?**
>
> North Carolina has hosted the PGA Championship only twice in the prestigious golf tournament's nearly 100-year history. The 1936 PGA was held at Pinehurst Resort on its famed No. 2 course, and was won by Denny Shute. In 1974, Lee Trevino won the PGA Championship held at Tanglewood Country Club in Clemmons. North Carolina's next PGA Championship will be hosted by Charlotte's Quail Hollow Club in 2017.

June 30

1951

Future High Point College basketball star Orlando "Tubby" Smith, who will play for the Panthers from 1969 to 1973, is born in Scotland, Maryland. Though he will have a solid playing career at High Point, Smith will distinguish himself more as a college coach, earning several Coach of the Year honors and leading the Kentucky Wildcats to an NCAA title in 1998.

1999

Duke University star Elton Brand becomes the number-one overall pick in the 1999 NBA Draft when he's chosen by the Chicago Bulls. Brand is one of four Blue Devils selected in the top 14 picks, along with Trajan Langdon (No. 11), Corey Maggette (No. 13) and William Avery (No. 14). The former Naismith College Player of the Year will share NBA Rookie of the Year honors with Houston Rockets guard Steve Francis.

JULY

July 1

1946

New head basketball coach Everett Case begins his duties at North Carolina State. Case will become the winningest coach in Wolfpack history, compiling a record of 377-134 over 18 seasons. During one stretch of his tenure at State, from 1946 to 1955, he'll win nine consecutive conference titles—six in a row in the Southern Conference, and then the first three titles of the newly formed Atlantic Coast Conference. He will earn three ACC Coach of the Year awards and will lead the Wolfpack to a third-place finish in the 1950 NCAA Tournament. Case will be posthu-

July 1 continued

mously inducted into the Naismith Memorial Basketball Hall of Fame in 1982.

Everett Case
Courtesy of N.C. State Athletics

1970
Cincinnati Reds second baseman—and Charlotte native—Tommy Helms christens Cincinnati's new Riverfront Stadium by being the first to hit a home run in the ballpark. Ironically, it will be his only homer of the season and one of only 34 in his entire 14-season career.

July 2

1937
Richard Lee Petty, who will become "The King" of NASCAR with his record 200 wins—including seven Daytona 500s—is born in Level Cross.

1964
Racing pioneer Glenn "Fireball" Roberts, only 35 years old, dies from complications of severe burns suffered about six weeks earlier in a fiery crash during the World 600 at the Charlotte Motor Speedway. His tragic death will prompt new NASCAR regulations requiring drivers to wear fire-retardant uniforms.

1973
Pitcher Robert Galasso of the minor-league Asheville Tourists sets a dubious Southern League record, walking 12 batters in a single game.

July 3

1953

Vic Seixas, a former All-American tennis player at the University of North Carolina, wins the men's singles title at Wimbledon, defeating unheralded Danish player Kurt Nielsen 9-7, 6-3, 6-4. Seixas, who graduated from UNC in 1949, came into the tournament as the No. 2 seed. He will win numerous other titles in his tennis career, including the U.S. National (now the U.S. Open) in 1954, and will serve three times as captain of the U.S. Davis Cup team. He will be inducted into the International Tennis Hall of Fame in 1971.

Vic Seixas
Courtesy of UNC Athletic Communications

1965

Former University of North Carolina at Greensboro golfer Carol Mann wins the U.S. Women's Open Golf Championship. Mann, who turned pro in 1960, will collect 38 wins on the LPGA Tour, including two majors—the 1964 Western Open and the '65 U.S. Women's Open. She will be inducted into the World Golf Hall of Fame in 1977.

1966

Atlanta Braves pitcher Tony Cloninger, a Cherryville native, becomes the first National League player—and the only pitcher in either league—to hit two grand slams in a game, leading the Braves to a 17-3 win over the San Francisco Giants at Candlestick Park. After getting his grand slams in the first and fourth innings, Cloninger nearly gets a chance at another one late in the game. With two runners on base and Cloninger on deck, some of the hometown Giants fans begin chanting "Put him on! Put him on!," so Cloninger would come to bat with the bases loaded. Instead, the batter strikes out, denying Cloninger the

July 3 continued

chance to make even greater history. He will finish the game with nine RBI's, a major-league record for pitchers.

1973

For the only time in their major-league careers, Williamston brothers Gaylord and Jim Perry pitch against one another, Gaylord pitching for the Indians and Jim for the Tigers. Neither finishes the game, but Gaylord takes the 5-4 loss.

Gaylord and Jim Perry
Courtesy of North Carolina State Archives

July 4

1862

Union prisoners in the POW camp at Salisbury celebrate the Fourth of July with a baseball game. Baseball at the prison will be depicted in a famous lithograph by Otto Boetticher. It was during the Civil War era that baseball gained its popularity in North Carolina.

1942

Future major-league infielder and manager Hal Lanier, whose accomplishments will include being named the 1986 National League Manager of the Year for the Houston Astros, is born in Denton. He is the son of major-league pitcher Max Lanier, who is also a Denton native.

1947

Future college basketball coach Bobby Cremins is born in the Bronx, New York. At age 27, Cremins will become the youngest head basketball coach in NCAA Division I when he's named to lead the program at Appalachian State University. His success at ASU will help him land his most famous coaching job, at Georgia Tech.

1984

Randolph County's Richard Petty gets his historic 200th win—the final win of his legendary racing career—when he takes the checkered flag in the Firecracker 400 at Daytona International Speedway, edging out Cale Yarborough for the win. With President Ronald Reagan on hand, the race marks the first time a sitting president has attended a NASCAR race. Following the race, the president will join Petty and his family in Victory Lane.

July 5

1945

Eighteen-year-old New York Giants rookie—and Gaston County native—Whitey Lockman joins a select club of baseball players, hitting a home run in his first major-league at-bat. He becomes the youngest player ever to accomplish the feat. Lockman will go on to hit 114 homers in his 15-year career.

July 6

1933

North Carolina-born brothers Rick and Wes Ferrell, both of the American League, participate in major-league baseball's first-ever All-Star Game at Comiskey Park in Chicago. Rick catches the entire game for the American League, but Wes—a good-hitting pitcher—doesn't get into the game. The American League wins, 4-2.

1957

Former Wilmington resident Althea Gibson becomes the first black tennis player to claim a championship at Wimbledon, knocking off Darlene Hard 6-3, 6-2 to win the women's singles title. In 1946, at the age of 19, South Carolina native Gibson moved to Wilmington. There she trained with Hubert Eaton, a gifted black tennis player who was nationally ranked in—and once served as president of—the American Tennis Association, the governing body of tennis for African-Americans at that

July 6 continued

time. In addition to Wimbledon, where she will win again in 1958, Gibson will also become the first black to win the U.S. Open, claiming the women's singles title in 1957 and 1958. Following her career in tennis, she will become the first African-American to join the Ladies Professional Golf Association, doing so in 1964. Her best finish on the LPGA Tour will be a tie for second. In 1971, Gibson will be inducted into the International Tennis Hall of Fame, and in 2009 her former hometown of Wilmington will name its new tennis complex the Althea Gibson Tennis Center. She will die in 2003, at age 76.

2000

Former Carolina Panthers running back Fred Lane, who was recently traded to the Indianapolis Colts but still living in Charlotte, is shot and killed by his wife Deidra during an alleged domestic dispute in their home. She will plead guilty to voluntary manslaughter and serve about six years at the Raleigh Correctional Center for Women before being released.

> **Did You Know?**
>
> When it comes to unusual athletic feats, it's hard to top—or even understand, for that matter—the one accomplished by 17-year-old Johnny Pearce of Zebulon. In 1930, Pearce swam 2½ miles with a lighted pipe in his mouth—apparently just to prove it could be done.

July 7

1999

The Colorado Rockies score for their 15th consecutive inning, tying a 1903 major-league record, before Philadelphia Phillies pitcher Curt Schilling finally brings the streak to an end. Schilling, who will be a six-time All-Star and dominant postseason performer, played part of his minor-league career in North Carolina, pitching for the Greensboro Hornets in 1987 and the Charlotte Knights in 1988.

July 8

1970

San Francisco Giants third baseman—and Hookerton native—Jim Ray Hart performs the rare feat of hitting for the cycle, collecting a single, a double, a triple and a home run in the same game.

July 9

2003

Randall Simon, a former Durham Bull now playing for the Pittsburgh Pirates, finds trouble when he playfully assaults a young woman in a sausage costume during the traditional "Sausage Race" at a Milwaukee Brewers home game. In the race, four contestants wearing sausage costumes have a footrace, but it turns ugly when Simon leans over the dugout railing and jokingly hits one of the contestants with his bat, causing her to fall in the path of another runner. She suffers only minor injuries, but Simon will be questioned by police and fined $432 for disorderly conduct. He will also be suspended by major-league baseball for three games.

July 10

1920

Tris Speaker's streak of 11 consecutive hits, a major-league record, is finally snapped by Washington Senators pitcher—and Graham native—Tom Zachary.

July 11

1944

Lou Hudson, a future six-time NBA All-Star with the Atlanta Hawks franchise, is born in Greensboro. Hudson, nicknamed "Sweet Lou," will have his jersey retired by the Hawks and by the University of Minnesota, where he'll play his college ball.

1945

Poor second baseman Owen Friend of the minor-league Raleigh Capitals discovers just how human it is to err, committing five errors in a single game.

1964

Charlotte Hornets pitcher Hal Stowe pulls off an extremely rare feat—winning a game without throwing a single pitch. The left-handed pitcher enters the game against the Asheville Tourists in the top of the ninth inning with two outs, a runner at first, and the score tied, 5-5. Before even throwing a pitch, Stowe fires a strike to first base to pick off the runner, ending the inning; when the Hornets score a run in the bottom

July 11 continued

of the ninth, Stowe gets credit for the 6-5 win, despite never throwing a pitch.

1996

The Charlotte Hornets trade 17-year-old high-school phenom Kobe Bryant, whom they had drafted two weeks earlier, to the Los Angeles Lakers for center Vlade Divac. The Hornets will enjoy a successful season with Divac in the fold, but Bryant will become one of the greatest players in NBA history, leading the Lakers to five NBA championships.

July 12

1894

Future major-leaguer Lee "Specs" Meadows is born in Oxford. During his solid career from 1915 to 1929, Meadows was one of the first players—and possibly the first pitcher—to wear glasses on the field, earning him the nickname "Specs."

1973

Maryland University head basketball coach Charles "Lefty" Driesell—who played college ball at Duke University and coached for a decade at Davidson College—saves the lives of at least 10 children from burning buildings in Bethany Beach, Delaware. While surf fishing around midnight, Driesell sees flames shooting from a townhouse complex behind him and rushes to the scene, where he breaks down a door and begins helping children to safety. The fire destroys four buildings, but there are no injuries—thanks in large part to Driesell's courageous action. The NCAA will award Driesell its Award of Valor, given to coaches, administrators and current or former athletes who put themselves at risk to avert or minimize a potential disaster.

1994

Rocky Mount native Walter "Buck" Leonard, a star of the Negro National League's Homestead Grays, serves as an honorary captain for major-league baseball's 1994 All-Star Game. The game is played in Pittsburgh, hometown of the Grays, and the 86-year-old Leonard appears in a Grays uniform.

2009

BassPack, the fishing club at North Carolina State University, wins its second bass fishing national collegiate championship in three years, earning first place at the 2009 Under Armour College Bass National Championship. BassPack beats 60 other collegiate teams to win the three-day competition, held on the Arkansas River in North Little Rock, Arkansas.

July 13

1954

Future basketball Hall of Famer David "Skywalker" Thompson, who will popularize the game's alley-oop play at North Carolina State, is born in Shelby. Thompson and teammate Monte Towe may not be the first to perform the alley-oop in college basketball, but they certainly will perfect it and popularize it in the college game during Thompson's career with the Wolfpack. The All-American Thompson will lead State to an NCAA title in 1974 and win national Player of the Year honors in 1975, before moving on to an outstanding professional career in the ABA and NBA. He will be enshrined in the Basketball Hall of Fame in 1996.

1986

Heisman Trophy winner Bo Jackson, now pursuing a career in baseball, hits his first professional home run at Crockett Park in Charlotte. Playing for the minor-league Memphis Chicks, Jackson gets the milestone homer off of the Charlotte O's on a hard drive that clears the left-field fence—and breaks his bat in the process. Within a couple of months, the famous two-sport athlete will be making his major-league debut for the Kansas City Royals, and the following year he'll debut with the NFL's Los Angeles Raiders. In 1990, he'll become the first athlete to play in major-league baseball's All-Star Game and the NFL Pro Bowl.

July 14

1967

The Houston Astros' Eddie Mathews, whose professional baseball career began in the minors as a member of the High Point/Thomasville Hi-Toms, becomes only the seventh member of the prestigious 500-homer club, knocking No. 500 off of Giants ace Juan Marichal at Candlestick Park.

2008

At major-league baseball's annual All-Star Game festivities, being held at Yankee Stadium, Raleigh native Josh Hamilton sets a Home Run Derby record with 28 homers in the first round. The previous record was 24. Hamilton, representing the Texas Rangers, will lose in the finals to Justin Morneau of the Minnesota Twins.

July 14 continued

2008

Longtime college basketball commentator Billy Packer, who played college ball at Wake Forest, parts ways with CBS after 27 years. Though he was thought of as a bit of a curmudgeon and an occasional lightning rod for controversy, his knowledge of the game was indisputable, and he held the distinction of calling 34 consecutive Final Fours, dating back to 1975, when he worked for NBC. He also won an Emmy Award for Outstanding Sports Personality/Analyst in 1993. At Wake Forest, he led his team to two Atlantic Coast Conference titles and to the 1962 Final Four. Packer also was an assistant coach for Wake Forest, under Bones McKinney, before he began his broadcasting career.

Billy Packer (34) in his playing days
Courtesy of Wake Forest Media Relations

July 15

1961

Former Wake Forest golfer Arnold Palmer wins the British Open at England's Royal Birkdale course.

2008

North Carolina-based track coach Trevor Graham receives a lifetime ban from the U.S. Anti-Doping Agency for his role in a widespread doping scandal that involves a number of his elite athletes, including well-known sprinters Marion Jones, Tim Montgomery and Justin Gatlin. Graham is a St. Augustine's College graduate whose Raleigh-based Sprint Capitol USA was an elite training team until a number of his athletes were implicated in the use of performance-enhancing drugs. In May 2008, he was convicted of lying to federal investigators about his connection to an admitted steroids dealer, and was sentenced to one year of house arrest. It was also Graham who instigated the notorious BALCO scandal of 2003 when he anonymously sent a syringe containing the then-undetectable designer steroid THG—a.k.a. "The Clear"—to the U.S. Anti-Doping Agency. That led to a widespread investigation focusing on a number of well-known athletes, including major-league baseball home run king Barry Bonds.

July 16

1945

Tough-luck pitcher Claude Crocker of the minor-league Burlington Bees pitches a no-hitter—the first in Carolina League history—but still loses the game, 1-0, to the Greensboro Patriots. The Patriots score the winning run off the Caroleen native on a walk, an error on a bunt, and a wild pitch.

1971

A thrilling race turns bizarre during a Pan Africa-United States dual track meet at Duke University's Wallace Wade Stadium. American Steve Prefontaine—who will help spark America's running craze of the 1970s—is running neck-and-neck with little-known Ethiopian Mirus Ifter in the 5,000-meter race with two laps to go. Suddenly, on the next-to-last lap, Ifter inexplicably sprints out to a large lead, but as the gun sounds announcing the final lap, he slows and stops, raising his arms in the air as if he has won. A bewildered Prefontaine keeps running and completes the final lap to win the race. Post-race interviews indicate the Ethiopian lost count of how many laps he had run.

July 17

1945

Durham Bulls pitcher Wallace Mitchell pitches 18 innings in a marathon game against the Martinsville Athletics. He might be able to keep going, but the game is called because of curfew.

2010

The family of University of North Carolina basketball legend Dean Smith releases a letter acknowledging that the 79-year-old former coach has "a progressive neurocognitive disorder," confirming rumors that had been swirling about his health.

July 18

1927
Detroit Tigers pitcher Sam Gibson, a native of King, gives up Ty Cobb's historic 4,000th career hit.

1987
New York Yankees first baseman Don Mattingly, a former Greensboro Hornet, homers in his eighth consecutive game, tying a major-league record. Mattingly played for the minor-league Hornets, a Yankees farm team, in 1980.

July 19

1930
Charlotte Hornets All-Star pitcher Jim Mooney, pitching at Augusta, Georgia in the South Atlantic League's first-ever night game, strikes out an amazing 23 batters, though some observers will credit his feat to a poor lighting system that made it difficult for batters to see the ball. Mooney will make his major-league debut with the New York Giants.

1933
North Carolina brothers Rick and Wes Ferrell become the first brothers in major-league history to homer in the same game when playing on opposing teams. Rick, playing for the Boston Red Sox, actually hits his homer off of his brother, who is pitching for the Cleveland Indians.

1982
Luke Appling, a 75-year-old baseball Hall of Famer from High Point, hits a leadoff home run—a 250-foot dinger over the shortened left-field fence at Washington's RFK Stadium—in the inaugural Old-Timers' All-Star Classic. Appling, who played his entire career for the Chicago White Sox, shuffles around the bases as a crowd of approximately 29,000 gives him a standing ovation. Even Hall of Fame pitcher Warren Spahn, who gave up the homer, applauds Appling.

1998
Goldsboro native Mark O'Meara wins the British Open—his second major golf championship of the year—defeating fellow American Brian Watts in a four-hole playoff.

July 20

1888

Future legendary minor-league pitcher Jesse Morgan "Rube" Eldridge, who will win 312 games in the minors, is born in Elkin. Eldridge will develop a reputation for devoting as much attention to moonshine and horseplay as he does baseball—his best pitch will be the "barleycorn fadeaway"—but his performances on the mound will speak for themselves. He'll pitch both ends of more than a hundred doubleheaders, racking up wins for teams from the likes of Greensboro, High Point, Raleigh and Charlotte. Despite his pitching prowess, Eldridge—who likely embellished his reputation for the attention it got him—will turn down a number of opportunities to advance and possibly even pitch in the majors, explaining that "I don't want to play anywhere I can't walk home." After retiring from professional baseball at age 37, he'll do some barnstorming with semi-pro teams, finally pitching his final game at age 63. Eldridge will die in 1968, at the age of 80.

Rube Eldridge
Courtesy of Dwight Davis

1969

Light-hitting San Francisco Giants pitcher Gaylord Perry, a Williamston native, hits the first home run of his major-league career, fulfilling a prophetic statement he or his manager supposedly made years earlier. One version of the story is that one day in 1962, as the rookie Perry took batting practice for the San Francisco Giants, a sportswriter told Giants manager Alvin Dark, "This Perry kid's going to hit some home runs for you." To which Dark laughingly replied, "Let me tell you something—there'll be a man on the moon before Gaylord Perry hits a home run." The other version of the story is that around 1963, Perry himself made the comment, "They'll put a man on the moon before I hit a home run." Sure enough, on July 20, 1969—less than 30 minutes after Apollo 11's historic touchdown on the moon—Perry connects for his first home run in a game played at San Francisco's Candlestick Park against the Los Angeles Dodgers. Perry will finish his career with six home runs, but none more memorable than this one.

Did You Know?

Denton native Max Lanier, a successful major-league pitcher in the 1940s, was born righthanded, but he switched and became a lefty after breaking his right arm.

July 21

1991

Gaylord Perry, one of major-league baseball's winningest pitchers, is elected to the Baseball Hall of Fame. In a career that spanned from 1962 to 1983, Perry won 314 games and recorded 3,534 strikeouts, which will place him eighth among career strikeout leaders. He was the first pitcher to win the prestigious Cy Young Award in both leagues—the American League in 1972 and the National League in 1978—and he was voted onto five All-Star teams.

July 22

1963

Sonny Liston knocks out former champion—and Cleveland County native—Floyd Patterson in the first round to retain the world heavyweight championship, denying Patterson's attempt to win the title for a record third time. He will continue trying to regain the title—unsuccessfully—and will retire in 1972, at the age of 37.

1997

A groundbreaking ceremony is held for the new Raleigh Entertainment and Sports Arena, located next to Carter-Finley Stadium. The facility, which will become the RBC Center, will be the home arena for North Carolina State men's basketball and for the Carolina Hurricanes of the NHL.

July 23

2005

Angler Derek Williams pulls in a world-record hogfish (21 pounds, 6 ounces) at Frying Pan Shoals.

July 24

1939

Walt Bellamy, who will excel on the basketball court in college, at the Olympics and in the NBA, is born in New Bern. Bellamy will star at Indiana University, earning All-America honors in his junior and senior years, and help lead the U.S. men's basketball team to a gold medal at the 1960 Summer Olympics in Rome. After being taken by the Chicago Packers as the top overall pick in the 1961 NBA Draft, Bellamy will earn NBA Rookie of the Year honors in 1962 (averaging 31.6 points per game, second only to Wilt Chamberlain among NBA rookies). He will become a four-time NBA All-Star and be inducted into the Naismith Memorial Basketball Hall of Fame in 1993.

1968

Chicago White Sox pitcher Hoyt Wilhelm, a Huntersville native, makes his 907th career appearance in a major-league game. Wilhelm breaks the immortal Cy Young's record for appearances, but Chicago loses the game to the Oakland A's, 2-1.

1983

Following the infamous "pine tar incident"—in which Kansas City Royals slugger George Brett's apparent home run against the New York Yankees is disallowed because of excessive pine tar on his bat—Royals pitcher Gaylord Perry is ejected for trying to hide the evidence, sneakily giving the bat to a bat boy to hide in the clubhouse. The ruling will be overturned upon protest, and the Royals will come away with a controversial win.

July 25

1926

Future major-league player and manager Whitey Lockman is born in the Gaston County town of Lowell. Lockman's 15-year playing career in the majors will include such highlights as hitting a double to set up Bobby Thomson's famous "Shot Heard 'Round the World" home run in 1951, hitting a home run of his own in the 1951 World Series, being named an All-Star in 1952, and winning a World Series with the New York Giants in 1954.

July 26

1975

Brian Dowling, the former Yale quarterback who was the inspiration for cartoonist Garry Trudeau's B.D. character in the "Doonesbury" comic strip, starts at quarterback for the Charlotte Hornets of the World Football League. The Hornets, formerly the struggling New York Stars, moved to Charlotte in the middle of the 1974 season and played there

July 26 continued

until the middle of the 1975 season, when the league folded. Dowling, who was cut by three NFL teams, would do no better in the WFL, throwing far more interceptions than touchdowns.

1987

Hertford native Jim "Catfish" Hunter, a star pitcher for the Kansas City and Oakland Athletics and the New York Yankees, is elected into the National Baseball Hall of Fame. Highlights of Hunter's 15-year career include a perfect game in 1968, the American League Cy Young Award in 1974, and World Series championships in 1972, 1973, 1974, 1977 and 1978. He was also an eight-time All-Star, and *The Sporting News* named him Pitcher of the Year in 1974. He won 20 or more games in a season for five consecutive seasons between 1971 and 1975.

2007

Wake Forest University basketball coach Skip Prosser dies at age 56 of a massive heart attack suffered in his office. Prosser is the only coach in NCAA history to take three separate schools to the NCAA Tournament in his first year coaching the teams, accomplishing the feat at Loyola University, Xavier University and Wake Forest. In six years with the Demon Deacons, Prosser compiled a 126-68 record and earned Atlantic Coast Conference Coach of the Year honors in 2003.

Skip Prosser
Courtesy of Wake Forest Media Relations

2008

Former East Carolina University running back Chris Johnson, a first-round draft pick of the Tennessee Titans, signs a five-year, $12 million contract with the Titans. Johnson, who finished his college career as the Pirates' all-time leader in touchdowns and all-purpose yards, will pay big dividends for Tennessee, earning Pro Bowl selections in each of his first three seasons and winning the NFL Offensive Player of the Year Award in 2009.

Chris Johnson
Courtesy of ECU Athletic Media Relations

July 27

1964

High Point's Luke Appling is inducted into the National Baseball Hall of Fame. Appling played his entire career with the Chicago White Sox (1930-1950) and was a seven-time All-Star. In 1936, his .388 batting average earned him an American League batting title—the first ever won in the league by a shortstop—and he won another batting title in 1943. He ended his playing career with a .310 batting average, and the White Sox retired his No. 4 jersey.

1965

Jim "Catfish" Hunter gets his first major-league win, a victory over the Boston Red Sox at Fenway Park.

1976

Team USA defeats Yugoslavia, 95-74, to win the gold medal in men's basketball at the 1976 Summer Olympics in Montreal. Coached by Dean Smith of the North Carolina Tar Heels, the team features Tar Heel players Phil Ford, Walter Davis, Mitch Kupchak and Tom LaGarde, as well as Duke's Tate Armstrong and N.C. State's Kenny Carr.

July 27 continued

1983

Gaylord Perry, now with the Kansas City Royals, becomes only the fourth pitcher to record 3,500 strikeouts, reaching the milestone in a 5-4 win over the Cleveland Indians.

> **Did You Know?**
>
> The most popular sport in colonial North Carolina was horse racing, and the state's best-known, most successful racehorse was a thoroughbred named Sir Archie. Though born in Virginia in 1805, Sir Archie spent 25 of his 28 years in North Carolina, during which he established himself as one of the greatest thoroughbreds of all time. Sir Archie was purchased by Warren County native William Ransom Johnson, who was deemed to be the nation's first great horse trainer. Johnson described Sir Archie as "the best horse I have ever seen." By the time the horse was 3 years old, there were scarcely any other horse owners willing to put their best against the celebrated Sir Archie. As amazing as he was racing, though, Sir Archie's most remarkable contribution to the sport was probably as a sire. Many of the greatest racehorses in history are descendants of Sir Archie, including the likes of War Admiral, Whirlaway, Secretariat, Seattle Slew, Affirmed, Man O'War and Seabiscuit. The state of North Carolina honored Sir Archie with a State Highway Historical Marker in 1974, and he was inducted into the National Museum of Racing and Hall of Fame in 1955. Incidentally, Sir Archie's one-time owner, William Ransom Johnson, was also a Hall of Fame inductee in 1986.

July 28

1943

The University of North Carolina Pre-Flight School Cloudbusters, a baseball team made up of men in the Navy's Pre-Flight School at UNC—including Boston Red Sox slugger Ted Williams and Boston Braves pitcher Johnny Sain—plays a war-benefit game at Yankee Stadium against a combined team of New York Yankees and Cleveland Indians. The combined squad includes retired Yankees outfielder Babe Ruth, who draws a walk as a pinch hitter. The service team from UNC wins, 8-5.

1985

North Carolina natives Enos "Country" Slaughter and Hoyt Wilhelm go into the National Baseball Hall of Fame together. Slaughter, a native of Roxboro, played 19 seasons in the majors, most of those years with the St. Louis Cardinals. He made 10 All-Star teams and played for four World Series champions. Slaughter will die in Durham in 2002, at the age of 86. Wilhelm, a Huntersville native, played in the majors from 1952 to 1972, earning eight selections as an All-Star and playing on one World Series championship team. The knuckleballer was the first pitcher to record 200 saves in his career and the first to appear in 1,000 games. He was also one of the oldest players in the majors, pitching until just shy of his 50th birthday. Wilhelm will die in 2002, at the age of 80.

2002

Pitcher Rick Cercy of the minor-league Carolina Mudcats takes a walk on the wild side, plunking four batters in a single inning—including three in a row—in a 16-4 loss to the Greenville Braves.

July 29

1940

In what will be the final fight of his career, former world heavyweight boxing champion Jack Dempsey—now 45 years old and out of shape—scores a second-round knockout before a crowd of about 6,500 at Charlotte's Memorial Stadium. His overmatched opponent? Little-known Ellis Bashara, a small-time pro wrestler formerly known as The Purple Flash. The abbreviated fight is the third and final one in Dempsey's pitiful comeback attempt. Four days later, apparently recognizing that he's only tarnishing his image, Dempsey will announce that the comeback is over.

1984

Nancy Hogshead, who swam collegiately at Duke University, wins a gold medal in the 100-meter freestyle at the 1984 Summer Olympics in Los Angeles. She finishes in a dead heat—the first in Olympic swimming history—with U.S. teammate Carrie Steinseifer, meaning they had identical times and are both awarded gold medals.

1995

The Carolina Panthers win their very first game, an exhibition match-up against fellow expansion team the Jacksonville Jaguars, 20-14. The game is the annual Pro Football Hall of Fame Game, played the weekend of the Hall of Fame's induction ceremonies in Canton, Ohio.

Did You Know?

Meredith College has its own synchronized swimming team. They're called the Aqua Angels.

July 30

1973
Franklinton native Jim Bibby throws a no-hitter—the first in Texas Rangers history—against the Oakland A's. Bibby gives up six walks but strikes out 13 in recording the 6-0 win.

1992
Gastonia native Mel Stewart wins a gold medal in the 200-meter butterfly—and sets an Olympic record in the process—at the 1992 Summer Olympics in Barcelona, Spain. Stewart will also win a gold medal in the 4 x 100-meter individual medley, and a bronze medal in the 4 x 200-meter freestyle.

1994
In his 354th professional at-bat, former North Carolina basketball star Michael Jordan—now giving baseball a try—finally belts his first home run for the Birmingham Barons, a minor-league affiliate of the Chicago White Sox.

July 31

1976
Wilmington-born boxer Sugar Ray Leonard, fighting as a light welterweight, wins a gold medal in the Summer Olympics at Montreal, having won all six of his bouts by a 5-0 decision.

AUGUST

August 1

1950
Future Hall of Famer Roy Williams, who will lead the University of North Carolina men's basketball team to NCAA championships in 2005 and 2009, is born in Marion.

2007
Cincinnati Reds second baseman Brandon Phillips, a Raleigh native, pulls off the rare feat of stealing two bases on a single pitch in a game against the Washington Nationals. The Nationals employ an extreme defensive shift to pitch to the Reds' left-handed pull hitter Adam Dunn—meaning the third baseman is closer to second base than he is to third—which allows Phillips to steal second and keep on going to third, where there's no one covering the bag.

August 2

1936

Harry Williamson, a 23-year-old High Point native and former University of North Carolina track star, becomes North Carolina's first Olympian, competing in the 800-meter run at the 1936 Summer Olympics in Berlin, Germany. Williamson will win both his qualifying and semifinal heats, but he will finish a disappointing sixth place in the finals on Aug. 4, with a time of 1:55.8. Had he run the 1:53.1 that he ran in the semifinals, it would've been good enough to earn him a silver medal behind fellow U.S. runner John Woodruff, who will win the gold. In fact, only three weeks earlier, Williamson had run the 800 in 1:51.3, which would've been good enough to win the gold in Berlin. "I've always contended that I should've won that race," he will tell a *High Point Enterprise* reporter decades later. Only days after the Olympics, Williamson and three teammates—competing at the British Empire Games in London—will set a world record in the two-mile relay. Following that race, he'll return to High Point for a nice reception and then give up competitive running.

Harry Williamson (3), just after handing the baton to John Woodruff (4) in the two-mile relay at the 1936 British Empire Games
From the Author's Collection

1952

Cleveland County native Floyd Patterson wins the gold medal in boxing's middleweight division at the 1952 Summer Olympics in Helsinki, Finland, scoring a first-round knockout over Romania's Vasile Tita in the finals.

172 ≡ Instant Replay

August 3

1982
Goldsboro native Clyde King, who played collegiate baseball at the University of North Carolina, becomes the manager of the New York Yankees—the third manager of the season for fickle Yankees owner George Steinbrenner. Bob Lemon, who started the season by going 6-8, was replaced by Gene Michael, who went 44-42. King will post a 29-33 record to finish out the season.

1996
Former Duke University basketball star Grant Hill wins a gold medal at the 1996 Summer Olympics as a member of the U.S. men's basketball team.

2005
Muggsy Bogues, former basketball star for the Wake Forest Demon Deacons and the Charlotte Hornets, is named head coach of the WNBA's Charlotte Sting. Ironically, at 5-foot-3, Bogues is shorter than every woman on the team. He will remain coach until the team folds in January 2007.

2007
Statesville native Chris Cole wins the gold medal in the skateboard street finals at X Games 13. Cole also won the gold in 2006 and won the bronze in 2005.

August 4

1961
Goldsboro native George Altman becomes the first player to hit two home runs in the same game off of Dodgers pitcher Sandy Koufax, a future Hall of Famer who is widely considered to be one of the greatest pitchers in major-league history.

August 5

1954
Future college basketball All-American Susan Yow—the younger sister of legendary N.C. State women's basketball coach Kay Yow—is

August 5 continued

born in Gibsonville. She will earn All-America honors at Elon College and N.C. State, before going on to a successful coaching career, including winning a gold medal at the 1988 Olympics in Seoul, Korea as an assistant coach of the U.S. women's team.

1961

University of North Carolina chancellor William Aycock names assistant basketball coach Dean Smith the team's new head coach. The 30-year-old Smith replaces Frank McGuire, who stepped down in the wake of recruiting violations. Aycock will later say of Smith: "When Frank McGuire got in trouble with the NCAA, he sent Dean to me to deal with the charges. Over a period of several months, he and I worked on preparing a response, and I got to know him well. Frank wouldn't have hired him if Dean didn't know a lot about basketball. But I also discovered he was a person of great character. It took me about 15 minutes to decide to appoint him."

1967

Seven-foot-tall Richard Sligh, who played college football at North Carolina College at Durham (now North Carolina Central University), plays in his first NFL game—an exhibition game between his Oakland Raiders and the San Diego Chargers—officially becoming the tallest player in NFL history (and its only 7-footer). A 300-pound defensive tackle, Sligh will play in eight games for the Raiders—and even play in Super Bowl II against the Green Bay Packers—but his NFL career will only last one season. Sligh will die on Dec. 23, 2008, at the age of 64.

Richard Sligh (77) towers over his North Carolina College at Durham teammates
Courtesy of NCCU Archives and Records

1984

Former N.C. State cross-country runner Joan Benoit captures the gold in the first women's marathon ever run during Olympic competition, in Los Angeles. Benoit, who spent three semesters with the Wolfpack, finishes the race in 2:24.52, some 400 meters ahead of runner-up Grete Waitz of Norway.

1993

North Carolina authorities find James Jordan's stripped 1993 Lexus near Fayetteville. In the days to follow, a badly decomposed body that had been found in a South Carolina swamp Aug. 3 will be identified as James Jordan, the father of former UNC basketball phenom Michael Jordan. Eventually, investigators will determine Jordan was murdered near Lumberton on July 23, 1993, by two local teenagers who stole the car. The teens, Daniel Green and Larry Martin Demery, will be convicted and sentenced to life in prison.

2008

Using his granddaughter's hot-pink Barbie fishing rod, Wilkes County fisherman David Hayes lands a 21-pound, 1-ounce channel catfish—a North Carolina state record. The previous record was 18 pounds, 5 ounces. Fishing in a pond behind his house with his 3-year-old granddaughter, Alyssa, Hayes holds her 2-foot rod while she goes to the bathroom, and that's when the monster catfish takes the bait. It takes Hayes about 25 minutes to finally land the fish, which is 32 inches long—longer than the rod used to catch it. A biologist with the N.C. Wildlife Resources Commission will verify the catch and later tell a reporter, "If you would have told anybody that you could catch a fish like that on this rod, they'd have laughed at you."

August 6

1959

Baltimore Orioles reliever—and Huntersville native—Hoyt Wilhelm nearly pitches a rare "no-hitter" in relief against the Chicago White Sox. Wilhelm enters the game at the beginning of the ninth inning and holds Chicago hitless for 8 2/3 innings before finally giving up a hit in the 17th inning.

August 7

1976

Three boxers with North Carolina connections win gold medals at the 1976 Summer Olympics in Montreal. Brothers Michael and Leon

August 7 continued

Spinks, who trained at Camp Lejeune, win in the middleweight and light heavyweight divisions, respectively, and Wilmington native Sugar Ray Leonard wins the light welterweight division.

2000

The Los Angeles Lakers promote former University of North Carolina All-American Mitch Kupchak to executive vice president of basketball operations, succeeding longtime executive Jerry West.

August 8

1982

Fort Bragg native Raymond Floyd, who played golf collegiately at North Carolina, wins his second PGA Championship with a 3-stroke victory over former Wake Forest golf standout Lanny Wadkins.

1992

The American "Dream Team," widely considered to be the most dominant Olympic men's basketball team ever assembled, wins the gold medal in Barcelona, Spain, with a 117-85 rout over Croatia. The juggernaut—which defeats its eight opponents by an average of 44 points—features 11 NBA All-Stars, including former North Carolina star Michael Jordan, and only one collegiate star, Duke's Christian Laettner. Jordan scores 22 points in the championship game, en route to his second gold medal.

August 9

1943

Future heavyweight boxing champion Ken Norton is born in Jacksonville, Illinois. As a Marine, Norton will take up boxing at Camp Lejeune and will win North Carolina's amateur Golden Gloves competition before going on to become the world heavyweight champion.

1963

Only one loss shy of tying major-league baseball's record of 19 straight losses, New York Mets pitcher—and Durham native—Roger Craig attempts to avoid the dubious distinction by conjuring up a reverse jinx, changing his uniform number to unlucky 13. Jinx or not, Craig gets the improbable win when teammate Jim Hickman pinch-hits for him with two outs in the bottom of the ninth—and hits a walk-off grand slam. The Mets defeat the Cubs, 7-3, and Craig keeps his name out of the record book.

2000
NASCAR pioneer Herb Thomas, a native of the Olivia township in Harnett County, dies at age 77 in Sanford. One of the most successful drivers of the 1950s, Thomas won Grand National championships in 1951 and 1953—becoming the first two-time series champion—and finished his career with 48 victories. He was inducted into the International Motorsports Hall of Fame in 1994 and named one of NASCAR's 50 Greatest Drivers in 1998.

August 10

1911
Future Chicago White Sox outfielder Taft Shedron "Taffy" Wright, who will set an American League record in 1941 by getting at least one RBI in 13 straight games, is born in Tabor City.

1916
Future major-leaguer Buddy Lewis is born in Gastonia. A solid hitter, Lewis will lead the American League in triples in 1939, with 18.

1984
Former North Carolina star Michael Jordan leads the U.S. men's basketball team to a gold medal at the 1984 Summer Olympics in Los Angeles, securing the medal with a 96-65 rout of Spain. Jordan's Tar Heel teammate, Sam Perkins, also picks up a gold medal.

2010
Former Olympic gold-medalist sprinter Antonio Pettigrew—who was subsequently stripped of his medal after admitting he had used performance-enhancing drugs—is found dead in the back seat of his locked car in Chatham County. An autopsy on the 42-year-old Pettigrew—an assistant track coach at the University of North Carolina—will rule his death a suicide. A 400-meter specialist, Pettigrew was a four-time NCAA Division II champion in that event while a student at St. Augustine's College in Raleigh, and he won a gold medal at the 1991 World Championships. At the 2000 Summer Olympics in Sydney, Australia, he won a gold medal as part of the 4 x 400-meter relay team, but the International Olympic Committee subsequently stripped the team of its medals after Pettigrew admitted in 2008 that he had used performance-enhancing drugs.

August 11

1950

University of North Carolina star halfback Charlie "Choo-Choo" Justice wins the Most Valuable Player award in the 1950 College All-Star Game, leading the college team to a 17-7 upset win over the defending NFL champions, the Philadelphia Eagles. Justice runs for 133 yards—48 yards more than the entire Eagles team—and scores a touchdown in the win.

Charlie "Choo-Choo" Justice
Courtesy of UNC Athletic Communications

1974

Richard Petty survives a mass sabotage attempt at Talladega Superspeedway and wins the Talladega 500. At least 16 racecars, possibly more, had been tampered with the night before the race—slashed tires, cut fuel lines, sand in gas tanks—but the culprit was never found. On Petty's famed No. 43, someone had tampered with the front-end alignment, but his crew fixed it and he won the race.

August 12

1910

The minor-league Fayetteville Highlanders acquire first baseman—and future Olympic decathlon and pentathlon gold medalist—Jim Thorpe from the Rocky Mount Railroaders. He will play in only 16 games for the Highlanders, though, before being hit in the head by a catcher's throw while trying to steal second, forcing him to miss the rest of the season. In addition to his gold medals at the 1912 Olympics, Thorpe will also play major-league baseball and professional football.

1973

Lenoir native Larry Smith, the 1972 NASCAR Winston Cup Rookie of the Year, dies in a single-car crash on the 14th lap of the Talladega 500. It is rumored, but never confirmed, that Smith had ripped the inner lining out of his driver's helmet—to accommodate his long hair—and the lack of that lining could have resulted in the massive head injuries that killed the 31-year-old driver.

1978

Cherryville native Jack Tatum—an Oakland Raiders defensive back nicknamed "The Assassin"—ends the promising career of New England receiver Darryl Stingley with a ferocious hit as the 26-year-old receiver leaps to catch a pass during an NFL preseason game in Oakland. The hit damages Stingley's spinal cord, paralyzing him from the chest down for the rest of his life.

1984

Durham native Rick Ferrell is inducted into the National Baseball Hall of Fame by the Veterans Committee.

1988

Only a day after the dedication of the new Charlotte Coliseum, the facility's multimillion-dollar scoreboard crashes to the coliseum floor, destroying both the scoreboard and the basketball court it lands on. The accident occurs as officials are repositioning the scoreboard for an exhibition basketball game that night, but an alternate floor will be brought from nearby Independence Arena in time for the game.

August 13

1961

The Western North Carolina 500, a Grand National event held at the old Asheville-Weaverville Speedway in the Flat Creek community, is called off at just past the halfway point because the track is crumbling, throwing chunks of asphalt at the drivers' cars and even into the grandstands. Junior Johnson survives the difficult track conditions and wins the race, despite a busted windshield. "I had a hole right in front of my face, where a chunk of asphalt had come up," Johnson will tell a reporter years later. "I was driving, leaning all the way away from that hole,

August 13 continued

because I was afraid a rock or something would come through there and knock my head off."

August 14

1955

The minor-league Greensboro Patriots sign the team's first black player—legendary Negro leagues and major-league pitcher Satchel Paige, now age 48—but he will never throw a pitch for the Patriots. Though he is scheduled to pitch a home game against the Reidsville Luckies three days after the signing—a game that will quickly sell out—the director of the Phillies' farm system (which includes the Luckies) will protest, calling Paige's appearance "a travesty of the game." The National Association of Professional Baseball Leagues will rule that Paige can play only in exhibition games, but not in the Reidsville game. Ultimately, Hurricane Diane will wash out the game anyway, and the Patriots will decide to release him. Ironically, 11 years later, the seemingly immortal Paige—now pitching for the Peninsula Pilots—will finally play his last game, against the Greensboro Patriots. He'll pitch two innings, giving up two runs in the first and none in the second, and then leave the game, never to pitch again.

1977

Twenty-seven-year-old Lanny Wadkins, who played his collegiate golf at Wake Forest, pars the third hole of a sudden-death playoff with Gene Littler to win his first PGA Championship at Pebble Beach. Wadkins overcomes a five-stroke deficit on the final nine holes of regulation to force sudden death, then stays strong to grab the win.

Lanny Wadkins
Courtesy of Wake Forest Media Relations

August 15

1936
The U.S. 4 x 800-meter relay team, featuring High Point native Harry Williamson, sets a world record at a competition in London, England. The team's time of 7:35.8 eclipses the previous record, set in 1929, by about six seconds.

1969
Future NFL wide receiver Yancey Thigpen is born in Tarboro. Following a stellar career at Winston-Salem State University, Thigpen will go on to a solid NFL career, earning two All-Pro selections and playing in two Super Bowls. In 1998, the Tennessee Oilers will sign Thigpen to a five-year, $21 million contract, making him the highest-paid receiver in the league at the time.

August 16

1954
The debut issue of *Sports Illustrated* is published, with the inaugural cover featuring a photo of Braves slugger Eddie Mathews, whose professional baseball career began with the minor-league Hi-Toms of High Point/Thomasville.

1992
Taylorsville's Harry Gant wins the Champion 400 at Michigan International Speedway. At 52 years, 219 days, he becomes the oldest driver ever to win a Winston Cup race.

Harry Gant
Courtesy of High Point Enterprise/*Sonny Hedgecock*

August 17

1997

Charlotte native Davis Love III, who played his collegiate golf at the University of North Carolina, wins the only major tournament title of his professional career, the PGA Championship. Love finishes 11 under par, five strokes ahead of runner-up Justin Leonard.

Davis Love III
Courtesy of UNC Athletic Communications

2008

For only the sixth time in major-league history, a player is intentionally walked with the bases loaded when the Tampa Bay Rays walk Raleigh native Josh Hamilton of the Texas Rangers. The unorthodox move comes in the bottom of the ninth inning, with the Rays leading 7-3, bringing Marlon Byrd to the plate. The move works, as the Rays win, 7-4. Rays manager Joe Maddon will explain his thinking: "We didn't want Hamilton to hit a home run. He's got 28, and Marlon Byrd's got 8."

Did You Know?

Steve Streater may have been better-known for his football exploits—he starred for the North Carolina Tar Heels and signed with the Washington Redskins before being paralyzed in an automobile accident—but he may have been an even better baseball pitcher, at least in high school. That's probably what they would tell you at Sylva-Webster High School, where in 1977 he tied a national record by winning 23 games in a season. He finished his high-school career with 61 wins—also a national record at the time—including eight no-hitters. He still holds the state record in both categories, as well as for throwing 12 shutouts in a single season.

August 18

1943
Shelby native Rogers Hornsby McKee—who was named for Hall of Famer Rogers Hornsby—makes his major-league debut with the Philadelphia Phillies as a 16-year-old kid, the youngest player in the National League that season. In parts of two seasons, he will pitch in five games, finishing with a 1-0 record and a 5.87 earned-run average.

1958
Floyd Patterson, a native of Waco in Cleveland County, defends his heavyweight boxing crown with a 13th-round technical knockout of Roy Harris.

Courtesy of the Lew Powell Memorabilia Collection, North Carolina Collection, Wilson Library, UNC-Chapel Hill

1962
Competing in London, former University of North Carolina track star Jim Beatty sets the U.S. record for the mile run at 3:56.5, eclipsing the previous record of 3:57.6.

August 19

1956
More than 10,000 spectators attend the inaugural Highland Games at Grandfather Mountain, launching what will become the largest event of its kind in the country. In addition to performances of Scottish music and dance, the event features athletic competitions such as foot races,

August 19 continued

wrestling, the long jump, the shot put and the caber toss, a traditional Scottish event in which competitors toss a large, wooden pole similar to a telephone pole. A student from nearby Appalachian State Teachers College tosses the 200-pound caber more than 36 feet to win that competition.

August 20

1955

PGA Tour rookie Arnold Palmer, who played collegiately at Wake Forest, wins his first professional title, the Canadian Open—and its $2,400 first prize—with a 23-under-par 265, only two strokes shy of the tournament record.

August 21

1932

Cleveland Indians pitcher Wes Ferrell, a Greensboro native, becomes the first pitcher in the 20th century to win at least 20 games in his first four seasons as he gets an 11-5 victory over the Washington Senators. He will finish the season with 23 wins, following up his first three seasons of 21, 25 and 22 wins.

2008

Former East Carolina University sprinter LaShawn Merritt wins the gold medal in the 400 meters at the 2008 Summer Olympics in Beijing. Merritt competed for one year at ECU before signing an endorsement contract, thus negating the rest of his college eligibility.

August 22

1957

Floyd Patterson successfully defends his heavyweight boxing crown with a sixth-round knockout of Pete Rademacher.

1973

N.C. State basketball star Tommy Burleson, playing for the United States at the World University Games in Moscow, unintentionally triggers a brawl as he scrambles for a loose ball near opponent Cuba's bench. Cuban players rush the court, and the melee continues for five minutes until Soviet police are finally able to restore order. The United States will go on to win the game and the gold medal.

August 23

1934

Christian Adolph "Sonny" Jurgensen III, who will play football at Duke University before moving on to a Hall of Fame career in the pros, is born in Wilmington. Jurgensen will play 18 seasons in the NFL—seven with the Philadelphia Eagles and 11 with the Washington Redskins—racking up more than 32,000 passing yards and winning three individual NFL passing crowns along the way. He will be inducted into the Pro Football Hall of Fame in 1983.

Sonny Jurgensen
Courtesy of North Carolina State Archives

1982

Major-league pitcher—and Williamston native—Gaylord Perry, who for years has been accused of doctoring the baseball, is ejected for that offense for the first time. At age 43, in his 21st major-league season, the Seattle Mariners pitcher is ejected during the seventh inning of a game against the Boston Red Sox, having been warned by the umpire two innings earlier. Perry objects to the ejection, though he never actually denies having doctored the ball.

August 24

1945
Future professional wrestling magnate Vince McMahon is born in Pinehurst. Although McMahon will be best-known as a pro wrestling promoter, he will also found the XFL, a short-lived alternate professional football league intended to complement the NFL during its off-season. The XFL will debut in February 2001 and fold after its initial season, primarily because of low TV ratings.

1989
Charlotte native Tommy Helms replaces Pete Rose as manager of the Cincinnati Reds after Rose is placed on baseball's ineligible list for gambling on games. The team will go 16-21 with Helms as manager, and he'll be replaced after the season by Lou Piniella.

2008
The U.S. men's basketball team, coached by Duke University's Mike Krzyzewski, defeats Spain, 118-107, to win the gold medal at the 2008 Summer Olympics in Beijing. The team features former Duke standout Carlos Boozer and former Wake Forest star Chris Paul. Former N.C. State player Nate McMillan serves as an assistant coach.

August 25

1949
Reidsville Luckies slugger Leo "Muscle" Shoals slams three home runs in a 20-8 rout of the Burlington Bees, bringing his season total to 50. Shoals will go on to hit 55 homers, the most in all of organized baseball for the 1949 season. Sometimes referred to as "the Babe Ruth of the minor leagues," Shoals will end his career with 362 home runs.

1951
The minor-league Granite Falls Rocks of the Western Carolina League make history by fielding what is believed to be the first integrated sports team in North Carolina—and among the first in the South—during a doubleheader at home against Newton-Conover. Three black players—catcher Russell Shuford, pitcher Christopher Rankin and centerfielder Gene Abernathy—all of whom were star athletes at Ridgeview High School in Hickory, play in both games, which struggling Granite Falls loses 9-5 and 6-2. The second game marks the Rocks' 27th consecutive loss, breaking their earlier record of 26 straight.

August 26

1939
Former Duke University baseball player Bill Werber becomes the first major-leaguer to bat in front of a live television audience, as he leads off for the Cincinnati Reds against the Brooklyn Dodgers at Ebbets Field. The game, aired on NBC experimental station W2XBS, is the first televised major-league game and is seen by an estimated 3,000 viewers.

2010
University of North Carolina chancellor Holden Thorp opens a news conference about allegations of academic infractions on the UNC football team with the ominous statement, "To everyone who loves this university, I'm sorry about what I have to tell you." The news conference focuses on "academic misconduct" in which a tutor for the football team allegedly wrote papers for a number of players. The revelation further taints the school's football program, which two months earlier had come under investigation by the NCAA for players possibly receiving improper benefits.

August 27

1978
Cincinnati Reds second baseman Joe Morgan, who played for the minor-league Durham Bulls in 1963, hits his 200th major-league home run, becoming the first player in league history to hit 200 homers and steal 500 bases. Morgan will be inducted into the National Baseball Hall of Fame in 1990.

Did You Know?
Charlie "Choo-Choo" Justice, arguably the greatest halfback in University of North Carolina football history, very well could have been a Duke Blue Devil. After graduating from high school in Asheville, Justice served four years in the Navy during World War II, then began entertaining recruiting efforts from North Carolina, Duke and South Carolina. After eliminating South Carolina from his choices of where he would play college football, Justice sent a proposal to Duke and UNC: as a war veteran, he could attend college with his G.I. tuition money. If either university would allow him to do that—and then give the scholarship he would've received to his wife, Sarah, so she could attend college, too—that's where he would play. UNC accepted Justice's proposal, and the rest is college football lore.

August 28

1954
Twenty-four-year-old golfer Arnold Palmer, who played collegiately at Wake Forest University, wins the U.S. Amateur Championship, a victory that prompts him to turn professional.

1967
San Francisco Giants pitcher—and Williamston native—Gaylord Perry shuts out the Dodgers, 7-0, to begin what will be the longest streak of consecutive scoreless innings in franchise history. Perry will not give up another run over a span of 40 innings.

August 29

1907
Lemuel Floyd "Pep" Young, who will play more than a decade of major-league baseball for the Pirates, Cardinals and Reds, is born in Jamestown.

1952
Durham Bulls pitcher Eddie Neville pitches all 18 innings of a scoreless game, then hits a double and scores the game's only run to get the win.

1988
Former Tar Heel football star Lawrence Taylor, the NFL's most fearsome linebacker, receives a 30-day suspension for violating the league's substance-abuse policy. It's Taylor's second violation; one more will result in a permanent suspension.

August 30

1959
Future Hall of Famer Carl Yastrzemski, a 20-year-old rookie with the minor-league Raleigh Capitals, concludes his phenomenal debut season by winning the Carolina League batting title with his .377 average and his 100 RBIs. "Yaz" also will win the league's Most Valuable Player

award, a sign of the successful major-league career he will enjoy with the Boston Red Sox between 1961 and 1983.

Carl Yastrzemski
Courtesy of Chris Holaday

1986
The powerhouse women's soccer team at the University of North Carolina beats the University of Massachusetts, 4-0. The win is the first of an NCAA record 103-game streak without a loss.

August 31

1992
Sports Illustrated names Chapel Hill the best college town in the country, calling it "the purest example we could find of a town that is defined by a university—and a good university."

2001
Former Durham Bulls player Lawrence "Crash" Davis, who grew up in Gastonia and also played baseball at Duke University, dies at the age of 82, after a long battle against cancer. Davis was made famous by the 1982 movie *Bull Durham*, in which he was played by Kevin Costner.

Did You Know?

Longtime North Carolinian Maxine Allen was one of the most successful female bowlers ever. A student at the Woman's College of the University of North Carolina (now known as the University of North Carolina at Greensboro) in the early 1930s, she began bowling when she was a schoolteacher in Northampton County and was a natural for the sport. She specialized in duckpin bowling, at one time holding dozens of world records in the sport, before moving on to nine-pin bowling, in which she won several national championships during the 1940s and '50s while living in Durham. In 1952, she was ranked as the top female duckpin bowler in the country. She later moved on to ten-pin bowling, and excelled in that, too. Before her death in Greensboro in 1995, Allen was inducted into the National Duckpin Bowling Congress Hall of Fame

Maxine Allen
Courtesy of North Carolina State Archives

SEPTEMBER

September 1

1951

The Granite Falls Rocks, a baseball team in the Class D Western Carolina League, lose their final game of the season, 5-4, to the Morganton Aggies, in 14 innings. The loss gives the Rocks a most dubious distinction: with their paltry 14-96 record—an anemic winning percentage of .127—the Rocks displace the 1899 Cleveland Spiders as the worst team in professional baseball history. Had they won that final game, the Rocks would've finished a few percentage points better than the Spiders and avoided the title of worst team ever. The Rocks end the season with a 33-game losing streak, winning only one of their last 60 games to finish a whopping 57 games behind first-place Morganton in the league standings. Not surprisingly, the Rocks also finish last in attendance for the season.

September 1 continued

1967

The San Francisco Giants' Dick Groat, a former basketball and baseball star at Duke University, draws a bases-loaded walk in the 21st inning to give the Giants a 1-0 win over the Cincinnati Reds in a game that matches the previous major-league record for longest scoreless tie.

1978

Asheville native Sammy Stewart, making his major-league debut with the Baltimore Orioles, strikes out seven consecutive batters against the Chicago White Sox, breaking Karl Spooner's record of six straight strikeouts in a major-league debut. He will remain in the league until 1987, compiling a 59-48 record and winning a World Series ring with the 1983 Orioles.

2007

Appalachian State stuns the college football world with an unprecedented upset—*Sports Illustrated* will dub it "The Mother of all Upsets"—knocking off No. 5 Michigan in a 34-32 thriller at Michigan. Twenty-seven-point underdogs coming into the game, the Mountaineers become the first NCAA Division I-AA team to defeat a ranked team in Division I. Despite Appalachian State outplaying Michigan for most of the game, the Wolverines manage to take a 32-31 lead late in the fourth quarter, and it looks as if they'll be able to escape with a win—even more so when they intercept an Appalachian State pass in Mountaineers territory—but the boys from Boone have a little more magic left in them. First, ASU blocks a Michigan field goal. Then the offense puts together an impressive 69-yard drive—with no timeouts—that leads to a 24-yard field goal and a 34-32 Mountaineers lead with only 27 seconds remaining. On its ensuing drive, Michigan throws a 46-yard pass to the ASU 20-yard-line and lines up for a field goal with only 6 seconds remaining. Again, it looks as if the Wolverines might escape the upset, but ASU's

ASU scores against Michigan
Courtesy of ASU Athletics/Keith Cline

Corey Lynch blocks the field goal and runs the ball to the Michigan 5-yard-line as time expires, silencing most of the 110,000 fans in attendance. Following the upset, an ESPN columnist will write, "We'll still be talking about it a few decades from now. Especially in the locker rooms of every huge underdog, where they'll say, 'If Appalachian State can beat Michigan, why can't we shock the world, too?'"

2007
The longest winning streak in the history of North Carolina high-school football—and the second-longest streak in the nation—finally comes to an end when Independence High School of Charlotte loses to Cincinnati Elder, 41-34, in overtime. Independence had won 109 consecutive games—a streak dating back to 2000—before the loss.

September 2

1931
Detroit Tigers catcher Ray Hayworth, a High Point native, begins his streak of 439 consecutive chances by a catcher without an error, an American League record. The streak will come to an end on Aug. 29, 1932, and the record will later be broken.

1957
Thirty-year-old Winston-Salem racecar driver Bobby Myers dies in a crash during the Southern 500 at Darlington Raceway. On lap 27, when competitor Fonty Flock spins out, Myers tags Flock's car and his vehicle flips end over end down the straightaway, where it will be hit again by

The last photo of Bobby Myers
Courtesy of Chocolate and Caron Myers Photo Collection

September 2 continued

the car of Paul Goldsmith. Myers will die of massive head injuries. Ironically, Myers—who was very superstitious about being photographed before a race—for some reason allowed a photo to be taken before the Southern 500, and it was the last picture he ever posed for.

2000

Burns High School kicker Cline Ingle boots a 61-yard field goal against Shelby, the longest field goal in North Carolina high-school history.

September 3

1936

High Point native Luke Appling's 27-game hitting streak—a Chicago White Sox record at the time—comes to an end against the Boston Red Sox. Ironically, the streak is halted by another North Carolinian, Greensboro native Wes Ferrell.

September 4

1948

Lenoir native Albert Bluford "Rube" Walker, a rookie catcher for the Chicago Cubs, appears on the cover of *The Saturday Evening Post* in Norman Rockwell's now-famous illustration, "The Dugout." Upon learning that Walker had been beaned by a pitch during this afternoon's game, Rockwell will give the young player the original cardboard sketch of the drawing.

Did You Know?

Talk about many happy returns. Charles Johnston of the Eastern North Carolina School for the Deaf tied a national high-school record by returning seven kickoffs for touchdowns in his high-school career, which lasted from 1988 to 1991.

September 5

1960

Lee Calhoun, who excelled as a hurdler at North Carolina Central College in Durham, wins the 110-meter high hurdles at the 1960 Olympics in Rome, becoming the only man ever to win successive Olympic gold medals in the 110-meter high hurdles. He previously won the gold at the 1956 Olympics in Melbourne, Australia. While at North Carolina Central, Calhoun won NCAA titles in the 110-meter high hurdles in 1956 and '57.

Lee Calhoun
Courtesy of NCCU Archives and Records

1961
Bill Bradley, one of the top prep basketball players in the nation, notifies Duke University—only days before the fall semester begins—that he has changed his mind and will enroll at Princeton University. Bradley had announced at his high-school graduation three months earlier that he planned to play at Duke.

1987
A postgame celebration gets out of hand when East Carolina University beats rival North Carolina State, 32-14, at State's Carter-Finley Stadium. ECU fans swarm the field and tear down the goalposts, triggering an ugly confrontation between fans of the two teams that police will struggle to get under control. The incident will lead to the cancellation of the series, though it will eventually be resumed when the N.C. General Assembly passes a law forcing in-state schools to play one another.

2003
Robert L. Johnson, owner of the Charlotte Bobcats, announces that despite much speculation, Michael Jordan will become neither an investor nor a front office employee of the Bobcats. Seven years later, though, Jordan will buy the team and become majority owner.

September 6

1995

Baltimore Orioles star Cal Ripken Jr., who played in the minor leagues for the Charlotte O's in 1979 and 1980, plays in his 2,131st consecutive major-league game, breaking Lou Gehrig's record that was once thought to be unbreakable. Fans will later vote Ripken's achievement as the "Most Memorable Moment" in major-league history. Ripken will play in another 501 consecutive games, extending the streak to 2,632, before voluntarily taking himself out of the lineup for the final home game of the 1998 season.

September 7

1940

Albemarle's American Legion baseball squad wins a Little World Series national championship, defeating a team from San Diego three games to two. After losing the first two games, Albemarle comes roaring back to win the next three, capturing a thrilling 9-8 victory in the deciding game. With the championship, Albemarle becomes one of four North Carolina junior teams that will win the Little World Series, along with Gastonia (1935), Shelby (1945) and Charlotte Post 9 (1965).

1972

Vince Matthews, a former track star at Johnson C. Smith University in Charlotte, wins a gold medal in the 400-meter dash at the Summer Olympics in Munich, West Germany, edging fellow American Wayne Collett by less than two-tenths of a second. Unfortunately, following the medal ceremony, the International Olympic Committee bans both runners from future Olympic competition because of perceived disrespect during the ceremony. As "The Star-Spangled Banner" is played, the two

Vince Matthews
Courtesy of Johnson C. Smith Athletics

men stand casually, chatting and fidgeting, and not facing the American flag. Calling their actions a "disgusting display," the IOC bars them from further competition, which prevents them from competing in the 4 x 400-meter relay. Matthews had won a gold medal in that relay at the 1968 Summer Olympics in Mexico City.

1975

Former University of North Carolina at Greensboro golfer Carol Mann wins the Dallas Civitan Open, the last of her 38 LPGA titles. Mann's wins include two majors, the 1964 Women's Western Open, and the 1965 U.S. Women's Open. She set an LPGA record when she made seven straight birdies at the 1975 Borden Classic, and she will be inducted into the World Golf Hall of Fame in 1977.

2002

University of North Carolina kicker Dan Orner ties an NCAA record by kicking three field goals of more than 50 yards in the Tar Heels' 30-22 win over Syracuse. The three kicks are good from 52, 51 and 55 yards, respectively.

2003

The Carolina Panthers stage their greatest comeback, overcoming a 17-0 halftime deficit to defeat the Jacksonville Jaguars, 24-23. The comeback is led by little-known reserve quarterback Jake Delhomme, who comes off the bench to replace ineffective starter Rodney Peete and throws for three second-half touchdowns. The winning score is a 12-yard TD pass to former Wake Forest star Ricky Proehl with 16 seconds left. Delhomme will remain the Panthers' starting QB and lead the team to the Super Bowl.

Did You Know?

Independence High School quarterback Chris Leak of Charlotte amassed 16,590 career yards (15,593 passing and 997 rushing), the second-best total in the nation. He also holds the national record for career touchdown passes with 185.

September 8

1907

Future Baseball Hall of Famer Walter "Buck" Leonard, who will earn the nickname "The Black Lou Gehrig," is born in Rocky Mount. He will become one of the stars of the Negro National League, best-known for his

September 8 continued

17 seasons with the Homestead Grays. Leonard will be inducted into the Baseball Hall of Fame in 1972.

Buck Leonard
Courtesy of Negro Leagues Baseball Museum

1957
Althea Gibson, who moved to Wilmington as a young woman to hone her tennis game, becomes the first black woman to win the U.S. Open, beating Louise Brough 6-3, 6-2 in the title match. In a dominant display, Gibson breezes through the entire tournament without dropping a set.

1996
Carolina Panthers kicker John Kasay kicks 5-for-5 field goals for the second straight game, becoming only the second kicker in NFL history to go 10-for-10 in a two-game span.

September 9

1954
Walter Davis, who will become a sweet-shooting star at the University of North Carolina—and a six-time NBA All-Star—is born in Pineville.

1972
In a game that will touch off international controversy, the Soviet Union defeats the United States, 51-50, in the gold-medal basketball game at the 1972 Munich Olympics, ending the USA's 63-game Olympic winning streak. Twice the Americans appear to win the game, but the Russians are given second and third chances on dubious calls by the officials, and they eventually score as time expires to get the controversial

win. The U.S. squad files a protest, which is denied by a 3-2 vote. The American players—including North Carolinians Tommy Burleson and Bobby Jones—refuse their silver medals and do not even attend the medal ceremony. Nearly 40 years later, the medals will remain unclaimed.

1999

Hall of Fame pitcher Jim "Catfish" Hunter dies at his home in Hertford, at age 53. A month earlier, Hunter, who had been battling amyotrophic lateral sclerosis (ALS)—better known as Lou Gehrig's disease—fell at his home and hit his head on concrete steps, knocking him unconscious. He had regained consciousness and returned home before his death. Hunter will be buried in a cemetery that lies behind the field where he played high-school baseball, and the state chapter of the ALS Association will be renamed in his memory.

2001

Steve Smith of the Carolina Panthers, making his NFL debut, returns the opening kickoff 93 yards for a touchdown against the Minnesota Vikings. It's the first score in the whole league for that season, and foreshadows what an exciting player Smith will become for the Panthers.

2005

Former Duke University assistant basketball coach Hubie Brown, who went on to greater fame as a two-time NBA Coach of the Year—and later a respected basketball analyst on TV—is inducted into the Naismith Memorial Basketball Hall of Fame. Brown was an assistant coach at Duke from 1969 to 1972.

2009

Former Duke University lacrosse star Zack Greer is the third overall pick—taken by the Minnesota Swarm—in the 2009 National Lacrosse League Draft. At Duke, Greer became the NCAA Division I all-time leading scorer.

September 10

1929

Future Wake Forest University golfer Arnold Palmer, who will become the first Atlantic Coast Conference champion in 1953, is born in Latrobe, Pennsylvania.

September 11

1974

President Gerald Ford, a golf enthusiast whose often wayward tee shots hit spectators on more than one occasion, delivers remarks at the opening ceremony of the new World Golf Hall of Fame in Pinehurst. "I have no background that would justify my professional appearance here," Ford says tongue in cheek, "but I thought maybe by coming, it would be helpful to me to get a little rub-off from some of the people who are inductees and others who are participating." The World Golf Hall of Fame will be located in Pinehurst until 1994, when plans commence for a new facility in St. Augustine, Florida.

1992

Toby Christopherson of Washington High School catches nine passes in a single quarter, a North Carolina high-school record.

2009

The U.S. Military Academy at West Point inducts Duke basketball coach Mike Krzyzewski into its sports hall of fame. Krzyzewski played basketball for the Black Knights, was team captain during his senior season in 1969, and later returned as its head coach before taking over at Duke in 1980. He compiled a 73-59 record in five seasons and led the team to the National Invitational Tournament in 1978.

September 12

1984

The Chicago Bulls sign their top draft pick, former University of North Carolina guard Michael Jordan, to a seven-year, $6.15 million contract. Jordan was only the third overall pick in the 1984 NBA Draft—behind Hakeem Olajuwon (Houston Rockets) and Sam Bowie (Portland Trail Blazers)—but he will turn the struggling Chicago franchise around and ultimately lead the team to six NBA championships.

September 13

1969

High Point native Ken Rush wins the 400 Grand Touring race, the first race ever held at Alabama's legendary Talladega Superspeedway. Rush achieved another significant first in his racing career—he was the NASCAR Rookie of the Year in 1957, the first year the award was given.

1975
Making his collegiate debut as a receiver, East Carolina University's Terry Gallaher sets the NCAA single-game record for receiving yards per catch, hauling in three catches for 218 yards and an astounding 72.7-yard average per catch. All three receptions go for touchdowns, but ECU still loses the game to Appalachian State, 41-25.

1980
East Carolina fumbles and loses the football on five consecutive possessions in the third quarter of a game against Louisiana-Lafayette, setting an NCAA record for fumbles lost in a quarter.

1981
Wilmington native Sugar Ray Leonard stuns Thomas "Hit Man" Hearns with a late rally that leads to a 14th-round technical knockout, giving Leonard the WBC and WBA welterweight crowns.

September 14

1940
Future University of North Carolina basketball star Larry Brown, who will later become one of the most successful basketball coaches in history, is born in Brooklyn, New York.

1976
Asheville native Joe West umpires his first major-league baseball game. West, who played a season of college football on East Carolina University's freshman team and three seasons at Elon College, will become one of major-league baseball's best-known umpires. Career highlights will include working two All-Star Games and four World Series. He will also design and patent the chest protector worn by umpires, which will sometimes be referred to as the "West vest."

September 15

1938
Gaylord Jackson Perry, a future Baseball Hall of Fame pitcher—and confessed spitballer—is born in Williamston.

September 15 continued

1958

Former New York Yankees star George "Snuffy" Stirnweiss—who was an outstanding football and baseball star at the University of North Carolina—dies at 39 when the passenger train that he's riding plunges off a bridge into the Newark Bay. Stirnweiss was an All-America halfback for the Tar Heels in 1939 and was drafted by the NFL's Chicago Cardinals, but he chose to play baseball and signed with the Yankees instead. A two-time All-Star, he captured the American League batting title in 1945 and won three World Series championships with New York.

1962

Steve Denning of Mount Olive High School booms an 87-yard punt against James Kenan High School, a North Carolina high-school record.

1971

Larry Yount, who pitched in eight games for the minor-league Greensboro Patriots in 1968, stakes his major-league claim to fame in a most unusual manner, when he becomes the only player in major-league history to get credit for pitching in a game without actually facing a batter. In what will be his only major-league appearance, Yount is called upon to pitch the ninth inning for the Houston Astros, who are trailing the Atlanta Braves, 4-1. Yount's elbow begins to hurt during warmups, and he has to come out of the game without even throwing the first pitch. Because he has already been announced as the new pitcher, however, he will be credited with having played—even though he never faced a batter.

1991

Former major-league catcher Forrest "Smoky" Burgess, a Caroleen native who once held the major-league record for pinch hits, dies in Asheville at the age of 64. Burgess ended his career in 1967 with 145 pinch hits, which at the time was a major-league record. He was also a nine-time All-Star and won a World Series title with the 1960 Pittsburgh Pirates.

Did You Know?

Albemarle High School kicker Tyler Lewis, who played for the Bulldogs' football team from 2000 to 2003, holds the national high-school record for career points scored by a kicker with 428 (36 field goals, 350 extra points). That's nearly 100 points ahead of the second-place kicker, an Alabama player who finished his career with 334 points. Lewis' 350 extra points are also tops in the nation, and he has the top two individual seasons, with 112 extra points in 2001 and 106 in 2002.

September 16

1979
The New York Yankees hold Catfish Hunter Day at Yankee Stadium, honoring the Hertford native, who has announced he will retire at the end of the season.

September 17

1968
San Francisco Giants pitcher Gaylord Perry, a Williamston native, pitches a no-hitter to beat the St. Louis Cardinals, 1-0, at Candlestick Park.

September 18

1954
Earle Edwards coaches his first football game for North Carolina State, a 30-21 loss to Virginia Tech. Despite a slow start in his first three seasons, Edwards will go on to win five ACC championships during his 17 seasons with the Wolfpack. He will retire in 1971 with 77 wins, the most of any football coach in the school's history. When Edwards dies in 1997 at age 89, he will be cremated and have his ashes scattered on the field at State's Carter-Finley Stadium.

September 19

1970
Fifteen-year-old tennis phenom Chris Evert, still flying beneath the radar on the international tennis scene, serves notice that she's for real by knocking off Australian Margaret Court—the top-ranked woman in the world—at a clay court tournament in Charlotte. Evert's 7-6, 7-6 win comes a day after she defeated Francoise Durr—ranked No. 2 in the world on clay—in a 6-1, 6-0 rout. She will lose her next match 6-4, 6-1 to Nancy Richey, but her two stunning upsets set the stage for the greatness that is to come.

2009
North Carolina State quarterback Russell Wilson sets an NCAA record for consecutive passes thrown without an interception—extending

September 19 continued

his streak to 329 passes—during the Wolfpack's 45-14 win over Gardner-Webb. The previous mark was 325 passes. Wilson's streak will end at 379 passes later in the season, when he throws an interception against Wake Forest.

Russell Wilson
Courtesy of N.C. State Athletics

September 20

1930

North Carolina's first night-time football game is played at North Carolina State's Riddick Stadium, following the installation of lights. State wins the game in a romp over High Point College, 37-0.

1958

Knuckleball relief pitcher—and Huntersville native—Hoyt Wilhelm, making a rare start for the Baltimore Orioles, fires a 1-0 no-hitter against the New York Yankees. Wilhelm whiffs eight batters while giving up only a pair of harmless walks.

1964

Raleigh native John Baker, who played college football for North Carolina Central University and is now a 6-foot-7, 280-pound defensive lineman for the Pittsburgh Steelers, delivers a fierce hit on New York Giants quarterback Y.A. Tittle as he's throwing a pass from his own end zone. The jarring tackle knocks Tittle's helmet off his head, gives him a concussion and cracks his sternum. Right after the hit, a photograph is snapped of Tittle that shows him kneeling in the end zone, dazed and bloodied. The photo will become one of the most iconic sports images of all time, winning numerous awards and being put on display in the Pro Football Hall of Fame. Baker will take advantage of the famous photo, too, when he runs for sheriff of Wake County in 1978 and puts the photo on campaign posters with the slogan, "If you don't obey the law, this is what Big John will do to you." He'll win the election and remain sheriff for 24 years. Baker will die in 2007, at the age of 72.

John Baker
Courtesy of NCCU Archives and Records

1972

Cleveland County's Floyd Patterson loses his rematch with heavyweight boxing champ Muhammad Ali at Madison Square Garden, when Ali scores a 7th-round technical knockout. The loss will convince the 37-year-old Patterson that it's time to retire.

1979

The University of North Carolina women's soccer team plays and wins the first game in its history, crushing Duke 12-0. The program will become the preeminent women's soccer program in the country, win-

Meghan Klingenberg (4) in UNC soccer action
Courtesy of UNC Athletic Communications

September 20 continued

ning 21 national championships—20 NCAA crowns and one AIAW title—including a string of nine straight titles between 1986 and 1994. Head coach Anson Dorrance—the only coach in the program's history—will win National Coach of the Year honors eight times, and the program will produce dozens of All-Americans. In 2003, the magazine *Sports Illustrated on Campus* will dub Tar Heel women's soccer "the greatest college sports program ever."

September 21

1938

Future Tar Heel basketball player and NBA coach Doug Moe is born in Brooklyn, New York.

1949

Artis Gilmore, a future basketball standout at Gardner-Webb Junior College (now University)—and the future NBA career leader in field goal percentage (59.9 percent)—is born in Chipley, Florida. Gilmore will play two seasons (1967-68 and 1968-69) at Gardner-Webb, where he will be a two-time All-America and have his No. 53 jersey retired.

1970

Keith Jackson, Don Meredith and Winston-Salem native Howard Cosell man the booth for the debut of ABC's "Monday Night Football," one of the most popular innovations of all time in sports programming. Cosell will stay with the successful broadcast through the end of the 1983 season.

September 22

1927

Future major-league baseball manager Tommy Lasorda is born in Norristown, Pennsylvania. Lasorda will make his professional baseball debut in 1945 in Concord, where he will pitch for the minor-league Concord Weavers. Though he doesn't exactly show a lot of potential in Concord—he'll have a record of 3-12 in his one season there—he'll go on to become one of the most famous managers in major-league history, leading the Los Angeles Dodgers to two World Series titles, winning two National League Manager of the Year awards, and being inducted into the National Baseball Hall of Fame.

1964
Race car driver Jimmy Pardue, a 33-year-old North Wilkesboro native, dies in a crash during tire testing at Charlotte Motor Speedway. When Pardue blows a tire, he loses control of the car and crashes. Pardue had only two wins in his NASCAR career, but he had 30 finishes in the top five.

1975
For the only time in their major-league careers, Williamston-born brothers Gaylord Perry of the Texas Rangers and Jim Perry of the Oakland A's have identical pitching records. Both have a record of 215-174.

1990
The University of Connecticut defeats the University of North Carolina in women's soccer with a 3-2 overtime victory. The loss ends UNC's incredible 103-game unbeaten streak, an NCAA record.

2009
The Durham Bulls win the Triple-A Baseball National Championship, defeating the Memphis Redbirds, 5-4, in an 11-inning thriller.

> **Did You Know?**
> The boys' soccer team at Sanderson High School in Raleigh played 103 consecutive games without a loss between 1982 and 1987, the second-longest unbeaten streak in the nation.

September 23

1926
Heavyweight boxing champ Jack Dempsey loses a 10-round decision to Gene Tunney, despite an intense month of training in the Hendersonville/Laurel Park area of North Carolina. Dempsey was paid $35,000—plus other benefits totaling about $25,000—to train there, in hopes that his presence would help drum up some publicity for the new Fleetwood Hotel, which was under construction at the time. His entourage included his wife, movie star Estelle Taylor, and an estimated 200 sportswriters who came to cover him.

1983
Major-league pitcher Gaylord Perry announces his retirement from baseball after 22 seasons. Perry will retire to his farm in Martin County.

September 23 continued

He will be elected to the National Baseball Hall of Fame, and the San Francisco Giants—for whom he played from 1962 to 1971—will retire his No. 36 uniform.

2005

Greg Williams of Raleigh's Enloe High School rushes for 484 yards, a North Carolina high-school record, in Enloe's 45-42 loss to Leesville Road High School.

September 24

1950

Former Duke University golf standout Skip Alexander, who grew up in Durham, suffers severe burns over 70 percent of his body when he is the lone survivor of a fiery plane crash in Evansville, Indiana. Alexander, who had won two Southern Conference individual titles while at Duke and three tournaments on the PGA Tour, will find himself no longer able to grip a golf club, even after months of rehabilitation and countless surgeries, so he'll undergo an operation that will essentially mold his badly burned hands into a position that allows him to grip a club. Years later, he will explain to a writer, "My hands were all burned and (now) they're all skin-grafted. The extensors and (other) parts of the fingers were contracted so (tightly) that I didn't have any openings. The doctors opened them up. They took a knuckle out and fused the (remaining) two knuckles together so they would fit a golf club." While Alexander will never recapture the magic he possessed before the crash, only playing a few more Tour events before deciding to become a club professional, he will play at the 1951 Ryder Cup in Pinehurst and help lead the U.S. team to victory. Alexander will die in 1997, at the age of 79.

Skip Alexander
Courtesy of Duke University Athletics

1972
Cherryville native Jack Tatum, of the Oakland Raiders, recovers a Green Bay Packers fumble and returns it 104 yards for a touchdown, the longest fumble return in NFL history. Tatum's record will be tied nearly three decades later.

1980
Former major-league pitcher Ernie Shore, a native of East Bend in Yadkin County, dies at the age of 89. Following a solid career from 1912 to 1920—including a 3-1 record for the Boston Red Sox in the 1915 and 1916 World Series—Shore returned to Forsyth County, where he served as sheriff for many years. In the 1950s, he led the effort to build a minor-league baseball park in Winston-Salem—a park that eventually was named Ernie Shore Field.

September 25

1962
Cleveland County native Floyd Patterson loses his heavyweight title—again—when Sonny Liston knocks him out in the first round at Chicago's Comiskey Park. Patterson had won the title in 1956 and then lost it to Ingemar Johansson in 1959, before winning it back in 1960.

2000
In one of the most memorable dunks in Olympic history, former North Carolina star Vince Carter leaps over 7-foot-2 Frenchman Frederic Weis, barely grazing his head as he slams the ball home during a game in the 2000 Sydney Olympics. French media will refer to the monstrous dunk as "The Dunk of Death." The powerhouse U.S. team, with Carter leading the way, will go on to win the gold medal.

2001
Michael Jordan announces that he's coming out of retirement—again—this time to play with the NBA's Washington Wizards. He will play two seasons for Washington, but the Wizards won't make the playoffs either season.

September 26

1981
University of North Carolina tailback Kelvin Bryant, a Tarboro native, scores four touchdowns against Boston College to complete a

September 26 continued

three-game scoring binge of 15 touchdowns, an NCAA record for TDs scored in three games. Bryant kicked off the season with six touchdowns against East Carolina, then put up five more against Miami (Ohio) and the four against Boston College. Bryant will go on to play three seasons in the USFL—winning the league MVP award as a rookie—and then play five seasons in the NFL with the Washington Redskins.

Kelvin Bryant (44)
Courtesy of UNC Athletic Communications

1999

Tim Biakabutuka of the Carolina Panthers becomes the only running back in NFL history to record two touchdown runs of 60 or more yards in the same game, accomplishing the feat in a 27-3 home win over the Cincinnati Bengals. The first run comes on Carolina's first play from scrimmage, a 62-yard dash to the end zone. The second one, a 67-yard TD, comes in the third quarter.

Tim Biakabutuka
Courtesy of High Point Enterprise/*David Holston*

September 27

1912
Lexington native Harvey Grubb, a journeyman baseball player whose minor-league career will span from 1909 to 1924, gets his one and only at-bat in the major leagues—during a brief stint with the Cleveland Naps—and he's hit by a pitch. He'll never get to the plate again in the majors.

2002
Longtime North Carolina State women's basketball coach Kay Yow, a Gibsonville native, is inducted into the Naismith Memorial Basketball Hall of Fame in Springfield, Massachusetts. Yow won more than 700 games in her coaching career and coached the 1988 U.S. women's team to an Olympic gold medal in Seoul, Korea.

Coach Kay Yow
Courtesy of N.C. State Athletics

September 28

1945
Future college football coaching legend Paul "Bear" Bryant, beginning his career at the University of Maryland, gets the first of his more than 300 career victories—a 60-6 romp over the tiny, overmatched Guilford College Quakers from Greensboro. Years later, former Quakers center Jack Rothrock will recall, "The thing I remember is that the crowd sang 'Maryland, My Maryland' after each touchdown, even the four that they called back. By the end of the first quarter, I knew all the words."

September 28 continued

Before coaching at Maryland, Bryant served on the football coaching staff at the North Carolina U.S. Navy Pre-Flight School, which was housed on the University of North Carolina campus during World War II.

1949

Washington Senators pitcher Ray Scarborough, a native of Mount Gilead, ends Ted Williams' amazing streak of reaching base safely in 84 consecutive games.

1957

Wake Forest gets a bad case of "fumble-itis" in a football game at Florida, fumbling an incredible 13 times and losing six of them.

1964

Future Duke University basketball star Johnny Dawkins is born in Washington, D.C. Dawkins will become Duke's all-time leading scorer—before being surpassed by J.J. Redick—and will win the Naismith College Player of the Year in 1986.

2006

Softball Hall of Famer Don Arndt of Sherrills Ford dies at age 71, following one of the most incredible careers in slow-pitch softball history. Playing for the famous Howard's Furniture-Western Steer team of Denver, North Carolina—a perennial national powerhouse—Arndt slugged nearly 7,000 home runs during his career, which lasted more than three decades. He had his most productive season in 1985—at the age of 50!—when he hit 309 home runs in 185 games. Arndt was inducted into the National Softball Hall of Fame in 1993.

September 29

1949

In what may be the first incident of African-Americans participating in an integrated athletic event in North Carolina, two black members of a Pope Field Army team play in the second half of a football game at High Point College. Many in the crowd greet the two players with boos and threats, forcing the visiting team to retreat to the field house temporarily. They will return, however, to complete the game, which High Point wins, 107-0, for what will be its only victory of the season. The *High Point Enterprise* will report in the next day's afternoon newspaper, "There are no rules banning Negroes from playing with white teams against white teams, but for North Carolina, and that includes High Point, the use of Negroes on white teams has been more or less conceded as taboo. At least, as far as the *Enterprise* was able to learn today, the playing of two Negroes scored a first in North Carolina last night." Years later, the school will install a plaque at the field commemorating the historic game.

1963

Eighteen-year-old John Paciorek turns in what is probably the greatest one-game career in baseball history, playing right field for the Houston Colt .45s in their final game of the 1963 season. Paciorek, who had been called up from the minors earlier in the month, makes the most of his first opportunity to play in the majors, going 3-for-3 with a couple of walks in his five plate appearances, driving in three runs and scoring four more. His 1.000 batting average will be his career average, because after offseason back surgery, he will return to the minor leagues—including stops in Durham, Statesville, Salisbury and Asheville—and he'll never make it back to the big leagues. Of the 20 players to retire with a 1.000 major-league batting average, Paciorek is the only one with more than one at-bat.

1987

New York Yankees first baseman Don Mattingly, who played for the minor-league Greensboro Hornets in 1980, hits his sixth grand slam of the season—a major-league record—in a 6-0 win over the Boston Red Sox.

Did You Know?

Although the University of North Carolina School of the Arts, located in Winston-Salem, doesn't have any officially sanctioned athletic teams, the school does have an official mascot—the Fighting Pickle. The unusual nickname can be traced to the 1970s, when it was created for the school's annual informal game of touch football against a team from Wake Forest University.

September 30

1908

North Carolina State's football team shows no mercy to Wake Forest, defeating the hapless Demon Deacons, 76-0.

1916

New York Giants pitcher Rube Benton, a native of Clinton, beats the Boston Braves in the first game of a doubleheader, 4-0, to extend the Gi-

September 30 continued

ants' winning streak to 26 games, the longest winning streak in baseball history. The streak will end there, however, as the Giants will lose the nightcap.

1927

Babe Ruth swats his record 60th home run of the season, a shot into the right-field bleachers off of Washington Senators left-hander, and Graham native, Tom Zachary. The 60-homer season tops Ruth's previous record of 59, set six years earlier. While Zachary will have a very respectable pitching career—including going 12-0 for the Yankees in 1929—he will always be remembered most for giving up Ruth's historic home run.

Tom Zachary
Courtesy of Steve Hill

1944

The N.C. State football team manages only 10 yards in total offense for the game, but still defeats Virginia, 13-0, setting an NCAA record for fewest yards gained by a winning team.

1970

The final NASCAR-sanctioned dirt-track race is held on the half-mile oval track at the State Fairgrounds in Raleigh. Richard Petty gets the win.

OCTOBER

October 1

1961

On the final day of the regular season, New York Yankees slugger Roger Maris belts his 61st home run, topping Babe Ruth's 1927 record of 60 homers in a season. Who's the unlucky pitcher that gives up the historic homer? It's Boston Red Sox righthander Tracy Stallard, whose minor-league career included a stint with the 1958 Raleigh Capitals.

1978

San Diego Padres pitcher—and Williamston native—Gaylord Perry becomes only the third major-league pitcher to join the 3,000-strikeout club, recording the milestone strikeout against Joe Simpson of the Los Angeles Dodgers. Perry will have a career total of 3,534 strikeouts.

October 1 continued

1997

The former Hartford Whalers franchise plays its first official National Hockey League game as the Carolina Hurricanes, a 4-2 loss at Tampa Bay. Kevin Dineen is the first Hurricane to score a goal.

2001

Three Appalachian State assistant football coaches—Rob Best, Shawn Elliott and Stacy Searels—enter a wrecked van that's engulfed in flames and save two lives, quickly pulling a dazed passenger to safety and freeing the van's trapped driver just before the fire reaches the van's interior. The coaches had been returning to Appalachian following a football game when they came upon the wrecked van, which had been involved in a head-on collision only moments earlier. The NCAA will honor the three men with its Award of Valor, given to coaches, administrators and current or former athletes who perform an act of bravery that puts their own lives in danger.

October 2

1949

Randleman's Lee Petty, the patriarch of the Petty racing family, gets the first of his 54 career wins, taking the checkered flag in a NASCAR race at Heidelberg Raceway, a half-mile dirt track in Pittsburgh, Pennsylvania. With an average speed of 57 mph, Petty is the only driver to complete all 200 laps, finishing five laps ahead of second-place finisher Dick Linder.

2005

In an emotional pregame meeting, Florida Marlins manager—and Elon College graduate—Jack McKeon, 74, tells his players this will be his final game as manager. Florida sends him out with a come-from-behind win over the National League East champion Atlanta Braves, 7-6. Though he never made it to the majors as a player, McKeon managed five different teams in the big leagues, winning National League Manager of the Year honors in 1999 and 2003 and leading the Marlins to a World Series title in 2003.

October 3

1937

Lenoir native Johnny Allen, a pitcher for the Cleveland Indians, comes up one game shy of a perfect 16-0 season, giving up an unearned run in a 1-0 loss to Detroit. His 15-1 record gives him a .938 won-loss percentage, tops in the major leagues at the time.

1949

Life magazine plasters North Carolina football star Charlie "Choo-Choo" Justice on its cover, hailing the zigzagging tailback as "one of the most dangerous players in the game." Indeed, the Asheville native will go down in history as one of the state's greatest college football players, twice finishing second in balloting for the Heisman Trophy—the closest a North Carolinian has ever come to winning it. He'll also be a two-time All-American, will lead the Tar Heels to three major postseason bowl games and will end his career at UNC with 4,883 yards of total offense, an NCAA record at the time. He'll be inducted into the College Football Hall of Fame and will even have a song recorded as a tribute to him, Benny Goodman's "All the Way, Choo-Choo." A statue of Justice will be commissioned and placed outside of Kenan Stadium on the UNC campus honoring his amazing career. Justice will go on to play four seasons with the Washington Redskins, but his pro career will be cut short by injuries. He will die in 2003 in Cherryville, at the age of 79.

1951

Two North Carolinians—Lowell native Whitey Lockman and Lenoir's Rube Walker—play key roles in the fabled "Shot Heard 'Round the World," Bobby Thomson's dramatic three-run homer that gives the New York Giants the pennant over the Brooklyn Dodgers. With the Giants trailing 4-1 in the bottom of the ninth, and runners on first and third, Lockman doubles to drive in a run and set the stage for Thomson's game-winning homer. Meanwhile, behind the plate for the Dodgers is Walker, catching in place of the injured Roy Campanella, when reliever Ralph Branca serves up Thomson's homer. Walker will later say of the Dodgers' postgame reaction, "Me and Branca, we were like a couple of lepers. I called it, he threw it. Nobody wanted to come near us." Even Thomson, the game's hero, has a North Carolina connection, having played third base for the 1942 Rocky Mount Rocks of the minor leagues.

1953

In Game 4 of the World Series between the New York Yankees and the Brooklyn Dodgers, Swepsonville native Don Thompson—having replaced the Dodgers' Jackie Robinson in left field—enjoys a career highlight by throwing out the Yankees' Billy Martin at home plate to end the game, preserving Brooklyn's 7-3 win and tying the series at two games apiece. The Yankees will win the next two games, however, to win the title.

October 3 continued

2006

In girls' high-school volleyball, Dana Griffin of East Lincoln scores 48 consecutive points on her serve in a match against Bessemer City, a North Carolina high-school record. East Lincoln wins 25-0, 25-1, 25-6.

October 4

1970

Stock car driver Curtis Turner, who built the Charlotte Motor Speedway in 1959 with business partner Bruton Smith, dies in a plane crash near Punxsutawney, Pennsylvania. The 46-year-old Turner, who had a residence in Charlotte, dies when the small plane he's piloting crashes not long after takeoff.

1975

After not playing in the first four games of the season, N.C. State freshman running back Ted Brown makes the most of his first collegiate start, rushing for 121 yards and two touchdowns in the Wolfpack's 27-0 win over Indiana. Brown, a High Point native, will remain a starter for all four of his years at State, where he will become the Atlantic Coast Conference's all-time leading rusher with 4,602 career rushing yards.

1992

Arizona Cardinals cornerback Robert Massey, who played his college ball at North Carolina Central University, ties an NFL record by returning two interceptions for touchdowns in a single game, performing the feat against the Washington Redskins.

October 5

1929

Duke University dedicates its new 35,000-seat football stadium, the largest in the South at the time. The debut is an ugly one for the football team—the Blue Devils lose to Pitt, 52-7—but a new era in Duke football lies around the corner with the 1931 arrival of new head coach Wallace Wade, for whom the new stadium eventually will be named.

1972

Future Duke University basketball star Grant Hill is born in Dallas, Texas. Hill will play on Duke's NCAA championship teams in 1991 and 1992, then lead the Blue Devils to another title game in 1994. He will become the eighth Duke player to have his jersey retired, then go on to an outstanding NBA career.

1993

The Charlotte Hornets sign Larry Johnson to a 12-year, $84 million contract extension, at the time the most lucrative contract in NBA history. "I was flipping through the pages looking at it and finally said, 'You'd better hurry and sign this, big guy, before somebody changes their mind,'" Johnson tells reporters.

2001

Duke University basketball coach Mike Krzyzewski is inducted into the Naismith Memorial Basketball Hall of Fame. Coach K's incredible success at Duke will include four NCAA championships—including back-to-back titles in 1991 and 1992—11 appearances in the Final Four, and 12 National Coach of the Year awards.

Mike Krzyzewski
Courtesy of Duke University Athletics

2007

Olympic gold medalist Marion Jones, who played basketball and ran track at the University of North Carolina, pleads guilty in U.S. District Court to lying under oath about her use of performance-enhancing drugs. In admitting she lied, Jones acknowledges that she used steroids before the 2000 Sydney Olympics, where she won three gold medals and two bronzes competing in sprints, relays and the long jump. Following her court appearance, she'll announce her retirement from track and field. In January 2008, she will be sentenced to a six-month prison term, which she'll serve from March through September. The International Olympic Committee will strip Jones of her five Olympic medals and ban

October 5 continued

her from attending the 2008 Summer Olympics in any capacity. The president of the International Association of Athletics Federations, Lamine Diack, will state, "Marion Jones will be remembered as one of the biggest frauds in sporting history."

October 6

1993

North Carolina's Michael Jordan announces his retirement from the NBA, saying he has nothing left to prove. The surprise announcement comes on the heels of the Chicago Bulls' third straight NBA title and Jordan's seventh consecutive league scoring title. Following a brief career in professional baseball, however, Jordan will return to the Bulls.

2001

North Carolina A&T running back Maurice Hicks rushes for an astounding 437 yards against Morgan State University, falling only four yards shy of the all-time collegiate rushing record.

October 7

1967

The North Carolina State football team's famed "White Shoes Defense" holds second-ranked Houston to only six points as the Wolfpack pulls off a stunning 7-6 upset. The game is played in the Houston Astrodome before a crowd of 52,483—the largest crowd ever to see an indoor football game at the time. About 7,000 jubilant State fans will greet the players at the airport when they return to Raleigh the next day. The "White Shoes Defense"—a name given to the squad after they painted their black cleats with white shoe polish, a la Joe Namath and his white shoes, prior to their first game—will give up only 8.5 points per game on the season.

1969

Major-league veteran Curt Flood is one of four players traded by the St. Louis Cardinals to the Philadelphia Phillies. Flood, whose professional career began in the minors with the Hi-Toms of High Point/Thomasville, will refuse to report to Philadelphia, instead opting to challenge baseball's reserve clause. In a letter to baseball commissioner Bowie Kuhn, Flood demands to be declared a free agent, writing: "After twelve years in the major leagues, I do not feel I am a piece of property to be bought and sold irrespective of my wishes. I believe that any system which produces that result violates my basic rights as a citizen." When Kuhn denies Flood's request, he will file a $1 million lawsuit against Kuhn and Major-League Baseball. The Supreme Court ultimately will rule in favor of MLB, but Flood's case will set in motion events that eventually will nullify the reserve clause, ensuring that he will be remembered more for what he did off the field than what he did on it.

October 8

1966

North Carolina State University dedicates its new Carter Stadium, later to be known as Carter-Finley Stadium, during halftime of the Wolfpack's first home game of the season. Despite the festive atmosphere, State loses to South Carolina, 31-21.

1999

Legendary basketball coach John McLendon, whose first college coaching job was at N.C. College for Negroes (now N.C. Central University) in Durham—and who was the first African-American coach elected to the Naismith Memorial Basketball Hall of Fame—dies at the age of 84.

Did You Know?

Ricky Lanier of Hayes High School in Williamston accounted for 13 touchdowns—five rushing and eight passing—in an 80-0 win over Snow Hill in a 1967 football game. His 13 touchdowns tied the national record set in 1927 and, according to the National Federation of State High School Associations, remains tied for first in the nation.

October 9

1944

Denton native Max Lanier gets the win as the St. Louis Cardinals clinch the 1944 World Series with a 3-1 victory over the St. Louis Browns. The Cards win the series four games to two.

1971

Wake Forest quarterback Larry Russell comes off the sidelines to tackle N.C. State's Bill Miller, who appears headed for a touchdown on

October 9 continued

the final play of the game. The fluke play occurs when the Demon Deacons, trailing 15-14 with 22 seconds remaining, line up for a potentially game-winning 52-yard field goal. Wake's kicker slips on the soggy field, however, and the flubbed kick ends up in the hands of Miller, who sprints toward the end zone until Russell comes off the sidelines to stop him. An official recognizes what has happened and awards the Wolfpack a touchdown, giving State a 21-14 victory.

Larry Russell
Courtesy of Wake Forest Media Relations

1983

Randleman's Richard Petty wins the Miller High Life 500 at Charlotte Motor Speedway, his 198th career win, but the victory comes amid a cheating scandal that will change the future of the sport. Following the race, an inspection reveals that left-side tires had been put on the right side of Petty's racecar—a violation of NASCAR rules—and that his engine is significantly larger than the rules allow. Surprisingly, Petty—who denies any knowledge of the cheating efforts—will be allowed to keep the victory, but he'll be fined a record $35,000 and stripped of 104 points. Three days later, NASCAR will announce that any team caught using an illegal engine will be suspended for a minimum of 12 weeks or three races, whichever comes first—a decree that will dramatically curb the practice of using big motors.

1997

Dean Smith, the most successful coach in the University of North Carolina's basketball program—and, at the time, the all-time wins leader in NCAA Division I history—stuns the college basketball world by announcing his retirement. After 36 seasons as head coach of the Tar Heels, Smith leaves with 11 trips to the Final Four, including NCAA championships in 1982 and 1993. Longtime UNC assistant Bill Guthridge will be named as Smith's successor.

Did You Know?

The North Carolina state high-school record for fumbles recovered in a game is eight. That's how many Maiden High School fell on during a 1986 game against Bunker Hill.

October 10

1964

Third-ranked Alabama thumps North Carolina State 21-0, but the Crimson Tide's star quarterback, Joe Namath, injures his knee. The injury marks the first of many occasions in his illustrious college and pro career that Namath will suffer from knee problems. He will come to believe the injury is a result of not adhering to his usual superstition of wrapping his cleats with white tape, something he did for all of his college games—except this one.

1974

Future NASCAR star Dale Earnhardt Jr. is born in Concord. He will become a third-generation driver, following in the tire tracks of his grandfather, Ralph Earnhardt, and his legendary father, Dale Earnhardt Sr.

1997

The Carolina Hurricanes get their first win since the franchise—formerly the Hartford Whalers—moved to North Carolina, picking up a 2-1 victory over the New Jersey Devils.

1997

Vishone Kennion of East Duplin High School returns three punts for touchdowns against Richlands, a state high-school record.

October 11

1975

Lenoir-Rhyne and Davidson combine to set an NCAA single-game rushing record in Lenoir-Rhyne's 69-14 win over the Wildcats. The

October 11 continued

Bears rush for 837 yards, while Davidson gains another 202 yards on the ground, allowing the teams to set an NCAA record with 1,039 combined rushing yards on 111 attempts. Lenoir-Rhyne finishes with 914 yards in total offense.

1975

The University of North Carolina football team appears headed for an upset over Notre Dame in Chapel Hill, until little-known sophomore quarterback Joe Montana comes off the bench to perform some fourth-quarter magic. Entering the game with about six minutes remaining—and the Fighting Irish trailing 14-6—Montana quickly completes a 38-yard pass to set up a 2-yard touchdown run, then throws for the 2-point conversion to tie the game. When Notre Dame gets the ball back with about a minute remaining, Montana completes a short pass that turns into an 80-yard touchdown; the extra point gives the Irish a 21-14 lead, and then the defense preserves the stunning come-from-behind victory. Montana's numbers on the day? Three-of-four passing for 129 yards, one touchdown and one conversion ... and a miserably memorable "Joe Cool" moment for the Kenan Stadium faithful. Montana will go on to an outstanding college career and a Hall of Fame career as a pro, winning four Super Bowls and three Super Bowl MVPs.

1991

Fayetteville native Chip Beck shoots only the second 59 in PGA tournament history, recording 13 birdies and five pars in the third round of the Las Vegas Invitational.

1994

Former UNC head basketball coach Frank McGuire, who led the Tar Heels to the 1957 NCAA title, dies in Columbia, South Carolina.

October 12

1894

North Carolina and N.C. State (at the time known as A&M College) meet for the first time on the football field, with UNC claiming a convincing 44-0 win. The Tar Heels will either win or tie the next 12 games, before A&M finally gets its first win in the series in 1920, a 13-3 victory.

1905

Future Baseball Hall of Fame catcher Rick Ferrell is born in Durham. He will play in the major leagues from 1929 to 1947, and will be inducted into the Hall of Fame in 1984.

1916
In Game 5 of the World Series, Boston Red Sox pitcher—and East Bend native—Ernie Shore baffles the Brooklyn Robins with a masterful three-hitter and a 4-1 win. The victory gives Boston its fourth title in the 13-year history of the World Series. Shore also won the first game of the series for the Red Sox.

2008
Buddies Brian Lilley and Daniel Maloney set a world record for the longest billiards marathon, playing for 53 hours and 25 minutes at a VFW post in Spring Lake. The two men play more than 600 games during the marathon, which will be certified by Guinness World Records.

October 13

1982
The International Olympic Committee votes to restore the two gold medals won by Jim Thorpe at the 1912 Olympics in Stockholm, Sweden. The medals, won in the decathlon and pentathlon, had been stripped from Thorpe in January 1913 after it was discovered he had been paid to play minor-league baseball in North Carolina before the Olympics, a violation of amateur rules. During the summers of 1909 and 1910, Thorpe had played for the Rocky Mount Railroaders and the Fayetteville Highlanders, thus negating his amateur status. After countless attempts to get the medals returned to Thorpe, the IOC finally agrees, based on a rule stating that officials had 30 days to contest an athlete's amateur status, but Thorpe's baseball past wasn't discovered until some six months after the Olympics. Unfortunately, the IOC's ruling comes nearly 30 years after Thorpe's death, so replicas of the medals will be presented to his family instead.

2000
Greensboro native Bob McAdoo, who played one season of college ball at the University of North Carolina, is enshrined in the Naismith Memorial Basketball Hall of Fame. McAdoo had a stellar NBA career, winning Rookie of the Year in 1973 and league Most Valuable Player in 1975, as well as winning two NBA championships. He was also a five-time All-Star and a three-time league scoring champion.

2006
Mooresville High School defeats Lake Norman, 68-61, in a football game that goes seven overtimes, a North Carolina high-school record. The teams are deadlocked at 26 at the end of regulation.

October 14

1951
Two North Carolina television stations—WBTV in Charlotte and WFMY in Greensboro—broadcast a Washington Redskins game for the first time. The Redskins lose to the Browns, 45-0, but this broadcast and the ones that follow will fuel a long love affair between North Carolinians and Washington. Even when the Carolina Panthers arrive in 1995, many fans will still find it difficult to give up their loyalties to the Redskins.

1998
San Diego Padres pitcher—and Fayetteville native—Sterling Hitchcock is named Most Valuable Player of the National League Championship Series as the Padres beat the Atlanta Braves, four games to two. Hitchcock won both of his starts in the series and posted a terrific 0.90 earned-run average.

2006
Wake Forest University kicker Sam Swank ties an NCAA record by kicking three field goals of 50 yards or more during a game against North Carolina State.

October 15

1946
Roxboro native Enos "Country" Slaughter of the St. Louis Cardinals makes his famous "mad dash" around the bases—one of the most memorable plays in World Series history—to score the winning run in Game 7 of the World Series against the Boston Red Sox. After Slaughter singles to lead off the bottom of the eighth inning of a 2-2 game, the next two batters make outs. Then, when Harry Walker lines the ball into left-center field, Slaughter takes off around the bases and doesn't even slow down at third, despite the base coach's signal to hold up. Slaughter's bold running apparently catches the Boston defense sleeping. The delayed relay throw is off the mark, allowing Slaughter to score what proves to be the winning run, and the Cardinals win the Series. A statue will be placed outside Busch Stadium in St. Louis to commemorate the "mad dash."

1970
The tradition of "Midnight Madness" begins in College Park, Maryland, courtesy of former North Carolinian Charles "Lefty" Driesell. Be-

226   ≡   Instant Replay

cause the NCAA does not allow basketball teams to practice before Oct. 15, Driesell—who played at Duke University and coached at Davidson College—becomes the first coach to have his team's first regular-season practice begin at 12:01 a.m.

1971

Julius Erving, who will become one of the greatest, most popular basketball players of all time, makes his professional debut at the Greensboro Coliseum. Playing for the ABA's Virginia Squires against the Carolina Cougars, "Dr. J" scores 21 points and grabs 22 rebounds in leading the Squires to a 118-114 win.

1982

The boys' soccer team at Sanderson High School in Raleigh gets a win that will be the first of 103 consecutive games in which the team will go unbeaten, a North Carolina high-school record. The streak will continue through Nov. 17, 1987.

1995

The expansion Carolina Panthers win their first regular-season game in franchise history, defeating the New York Jets, 26-15.

2006

Defensive end Julius Peppers records two sacks against the Baltimore Ravens, bringing his career total to 48.5 sacks and making him the all-time sack leader for the Carolina Panthers. Peppers, a Wilson native, joined the Panthers in 2002, after being chosen second overall in the NFL Draft, and he earned the league's Defensive Rookie of the Year Award. Prior to his NFL career, Peppers played football and basketball at

Julius Peppers
Courtesy of UNC Athletic Communications

October 15 continued

the University of North Carolina. He has the unique distinction of being the first athlete ever to play in the NCAA men's basketball Final Four (with the Tar Heels in 2000) and the Super Bowl (with the Panthers in 2004).

October 16

1976

Duke University kicker Vince Fusco drills a school-record six field goals—including a 57-yarder, also a school record—to give Duke a hard-earned 18-18 tie with Clemson. Fusco's other kicks are from 27, 22, 22, 25 and 37 yards out.

October 17

1966

Future Duke University basketball standout Danny Ferry is born in Bowie, Maryland. At Duke, Ferry will lead the Blue Devils to the Final Four in 1986, 1988 and 1989, and will win several National Player of the Year honors in 1989. He'll also set Duke's single-game scoring record, racking up 58 points against Miami on Dec. 10, 1988. Ferry's jersey will be retired at Duke, and he'll play more than a decade in the NBA before going into an executive career in NBA team management.

Danny Ferry
Courtesy of Duke University Athletics

2003
Former University of North Carolina football star Charlie "Choo-Choo" Justice, who was twice a runner-up for the coveted Heisman Trophy, dies at his home in Cherryville at the age of 79.

October 18

1888
In the state's first intercollegiate game of football—or "foot ball," as the local press called it—Wake Forest College defeats the University of North Carolina, 6-4, at the State Fairgrounds in Raleigh.

1895
The faculty votes to ban football games on the grounds of Wake Forest College. After playing the state's first intercollegiate game in 1888, the school banned football briefly in June 1890 before reviving it the next year. This time, though, the ban will last more than a decade, with Wake Forest trustees—in response to student demand—finally restoring intercollegiate football in May 1908.

1973
Duke University names assistant basketball coach Neill McGeachy its head coach for the 1973-74 season, in the wake of the sudden departure of Bucky Waters, who resigned in September to take an administrative job at Duke Medical Center. Only a day before the announcement, legendary Kentucky coach Adolph Rupp—at age 72—had been considering coming out of retirement to take the job. McGeachy, a Charlotte native who grew up in Statesville, will last only one season as Duke's head coach.

Did You Know?
Duke University football has two of the 10 longest losing streaks in NCAA history—23 games from 1999 to 2002 (tied for seventh-longest losing streak) and 22 games from 2005 to 2007 (ninth-longest streak).

October 19

1965
Future Tar Heel and NBA basketball star Bradley Lee Daugherty is born in Black Mountain. He will be a first-team All-American at North

October 19 continued

Carolina and will be the number-one overall pick in the 1986 NBA Draft, selected by the Cleveland Cavaliers.

1994

For the first time in the program's 16-year history, the juggernaut University of North Carolina women's soccer team loses a home game, as Duke knocks off the Tar Heels 3-2.

1998

St. Louis Rams linebacker Leonard Little—an Asheville native who was a high-school All-American at Asheville High School—kills 47-year-old Susan Gutweiler in a drunk-driving crash in downtown St. Louis. Little, who had been drinking to celebrate his 24th birthday, will plead guilty to involuntary manslaughter and be sentenced to 90 days in jail instead of the four-year sentence requested by prosecutors. The sentence will outrage critics, who say it's far too lenient.

October 20

1938

The Raleigh Junior Chamber of Commerce finds a unique way to give out free tickets to N.C. State's homecoming football game against Furman. The organization releases a bevy of balloons with instructions attached for the finders, telling them how they can claim their free tickets.

2003

Soccer star Matt Smith of Eastern Alamance High School scores 11 goals in a single game, a North Carolina high-school state record.

October 21

1968

North Carolina State swimmer Stephen Rerych wins a gold medal in the men's 4 x 200-meter freestyle relay, his second gold of the 1968 Summer Olympics in Mexico City. Four days earlier, he won a gold medal in the 4 x 100-meter freestyle relay. In both events, one of his teammates is Mark Spitz, who will famously win seven gold medals at the 1972 Summer Olympics.

2006
Raleigh native Candyce Marsh hits a top speed of 208.55 mph during qualifying for a drag-racing competition in Rockingham, though she comes up just short in her attempt to qualify. Marsh is the first African-American woman to compete in professional drag racing.

October 22

1994
Monroe native Richard Huntley, a running back at Winston-Salem State University, rushes for 361 yards—at the time a national record for historically black colleges and universities—and scores four touchdowns in a 56-14 win over Virginia Union. Huntley will go on to play six seasons in the NFL.

2004
Deangelo Ruffin of South Johnston High School hauls in 25 passes in a single game against Harnett Central, a North Carolina high-school state record and the fourth-best performance in the nation.

2010
Raleigh native Josh Hamilton of the Texas Rangers wins the Most Valuable Player award for the American League Championship Series. Hamilton hits four home runs in the series as the Rangers defeat the New York Yankees four games to two.

October 23

1922
Lenoir College (now Lenoir-Rhyne University) suffers one of the worst defeats in college football history, losing 206-0 to King College of Bristol, Tennessee.

1953
At a university banquet in the ballroom of the Carolina Inn, Andy Griffith (UNC, Class of '49) provides the evening entertainment with an original monologue titled "What It Was, Was Football." The monologue—a humorous description of a college football game through the eyes of a country preacher who is experiencing the sport for the first time—will be made into a recording, which will help launch Griffith's career in entertainment.

October 23 continued

1987

Major-league pitcher Dickie Noles, a Charlotte native, has the unusual distinction of being traded for himself. In September, the Chicago Cubs had traded Noles to the Detroit Tigers for "a player to be named later." However, when the two clubs are unable to agree on who that player will be, the Tigers send Noles back to the Cubs, meaning he was traded for himself.

October 24

1992

Columbus County native Otis Nixon, an outfielder for the Atlanta Braves, makes the final out of the 1992 World Series on a bunt attempt, giving the Toronto Blue Jays a 4-2 series win over the Braves. It's believed to be the only time a World Series has ended on a bunt.

October 25

1924

The original Charlotte Speedway, a 1¼-mile oval track in Pineville built out of wooden two-by-fours, hosts its inaugural race. More than 50,000 spectators come to see the race, a 250-miler that features many of the same drivers from the Indianapolis 500—including Tommy Milton, the first two-time winner of the Indy 500. Milton wins the Charlotte race, averaging 118.7 mph. According to historical accounts, the track was built of green pine so the boards would cure and shrink, which would allow enough ventilation to keep tires from burning during the races. Unfortunately, the speedway will be closed in 1927 when the track begins to deteriorate and crowds begin to dwindle.

Opening day, Oct. 25, 1924 at the Charlotte Speedway
Courtesy of North Carolina State Archives

1937

Duke University football coach Wallace Wade appears on the cover of *Time* magazine. Inside, an article profiles how he's turned the football program around at Duke.

Wallace Wade
Courtesy of Duke University Athletics

1978

Williamston native Gaylord Perry, a pitcher for the San Diego Padres, wins the National League Cy Young Award, making him the first major-league pitcher to win the Cy Young in both leagues. He previously won the award in 1972 with the Cleveland Indians. For the Padres, Perry earned the award with a record of 21-6 and a 2.72 earned-run average.

2003

The Florida Marlins win the World Series, making 72-year-old Jack McKeon the oldest manager ever to win a World Series title. The Marlins beat the Yankees, 2-0, to win the series four games to two. McKeon is an Elon College graduate who still lives in Elon.

October 26

1895

A University of North Carolina punter throws—and completes—what is believed to be the first forward pass in the history of college football. And it's witnessed by no less an authority than John Heisman, the longtime college football coach for whom the Heisman Trophy will be named. The pass occurs during a game played in Atlanta between the Tar Heels

October 26 continued

and the Georgia Bulldogs. With the game deadlocked at 0 and UNC deep in its own territory, the Tar Heels line up to punt, but when Georgia closes in to block the kick, the panic-stricken punter takes a few steps to his right and heaves the ball in the direction of teammate George Stephens, who catches it and runs 70 yards for a touchdown. Georgia protests the play, but the referee claims not to have seen the pass, and Carolina ends up with a 6-0 win. More than 30 years later, Heisman—who says he was watching from less than 10 yards away when the punter threw the ball—will write in *Collier's Weekly*, "I had seen the first forward pass in football. It was illegal, of course. Already Warner (Georgia coach Glenn "Pop" Warner) was storming at the referee. But the referee had not seen the North Carolina lad, goaded to desperation, toss the ball. A touchdown had been made and a touchdown it remained."

1920

After a 25-year absence, intercollegiate football returns to Trinity College—the forerunner of Duke University—as Trinity defeats Guilford College, 20-6. In 1895, at the urging of college president John C. Kilgo, Trinity's board of trustees had banned football at the school because it had become "too dangerous physically to be a college sport and, too, it distracts from academics." Students staged a number of protests through the years—including a 1917 bonfire so large that local firefighters thought the college was on fire—until finally, in the spring of 1918, trustees voted to reinstate the school's football program.

1921

Future North Carolina A&T star running back Robert "Stonewall" Jackson is born in Mineral, Virginia. Following an outstanding career at A&T that will earn him Little All-America honors in 1949, Jackson will become the first player ever drafted into the NFL from a historically black college in 1950, when he's selected by the New York Giants. He'll play two seasons with the Giants before moving on to a coaching and teaching career at North Carolina Central University. He will die in 2010 at age 88.

1984

Former Tar Heel hoops star Michael Jordan makes his NBA debut, scoring 16 points to help the Chicago Bulls defeat the Washington Bullets, 109-93.

1993

At their league meeting in Chicago, NFL owners unanimously award an expansion franchise—the league's 29th franchise—to Charlotte. The selection makes Jerry Richardson, a native of Spring Hope, the first former NFL player since George Halas to become a team owner. Richardson, a flanker and halfback, played for the Baltimore Colts in 1959 and 1960.

Jerry Richardson
Courtesy of High Point Enterprise/*David Holston*

1995
Cardinal Gibbons High School in Raleigh defeats the Eastern North Carolina School for the Deaf, 100-42, to tie a state high-school record for most combined points in a football game. In 1930, the same number of points were also scored when Windsor defeated Creswell, 142-0.

October 27

1969
Future Carolina Panthers kicker John Kasay is born in Athens, Georgia. Kasay will be the last remaining member of Carolina's inaugural team to continue playing for the Panthers, and he will also become the Panthers' all-time leading scorer.

2008
Professional golfer John Daly is detained by Winston-Salem police after he passes out drunk at a local Hooters restaurant. He will be taken to the Forsyth County Jail for 24 hours to sober up.

> **Did You Know?**
> Early athletic squads at Davidson College were alternately referred to as Presbyterians, Preachers and the Red & Black. It wasn't until 1918 that they became known as the Wildcats, the nickname Davidson employs today. The college even had a live wildcat mascot beginning in the 1920s, a tradition that lasted into the 1960s.

October 28

1995

Wake Forest quarterback Rusty LaRue completes an NCAA-record 55 passes in a 42-26 loss at Duke. LaRue, a Winston-Salem native, completes 55 of 78 passes for 478 yards and four touchdowns.

Rusty LaRue
Courtesy of Wake Forest Media Relations

October 29

1982

After leaving the University of North Carolina a year early to play in the NBA, James Worthy makes his debut with the Los Angeles Lakers. The Gastonia native, taken by the Lakers as the number-one overall pick in the 1982 NBA Draft, will have a stellar rookie season, averaging

James Worthy
Courtesy of UNC Athletic Communications

13.4 points per game and 5.2 rebounds per game en route to making the NBA All-Rookie first team.

1996

A distinguished panel's list of the "50 Greatest Players in NBA History"—named to honor the league's 50th anniversary—includes several North Carolina players: Michael Jordan, James Worthy and Billy Cunningham (University of North Carolina), Sam Jones (N.C. Central University), Earl Monroe (Winston-Salem State University), Pete Maravich (Broughton High School in Raleigh), and Robert Parish (Charlotte Hornets).

October 30

1935

Future major-league baseball pitcher—and 1970 American League Cy Young Award winner—Jim Perry is born in Williamston.

1974

Oakland A's pitcher Jim "Catfish" Hunter, a Hertford native, caps an impressive 25-win season by capturing the prestigious American League Cy Young Award.

1992

Earvin "Magic" Johnson plays what he believes will be his final game as a Los Angeles Laker, a preseason exhibition game played in Chapel Hill against the Cleveland Cavaliers. Johnson had tried to make an NBA comeback—despite having tested positive for HIV a year earlier—but when he scratches his arm in the Chapel Hill game, he senses fear and hysteria surrounding him and decides to retire for good. Four years later, though, he'll come back one more time, play 32 games for the Lakers, and then really retire for good.

1996

The WNBA announces that Charlotte is one of eight cities that will host a team in the league's inaugural season. The women's team, the Charlotte Sting, will finish the season with a 15-13 record.

Did You Know?

On two occasions, the Duke men's and women's basketball teams were the top-ranked teams in the country. The unusual distinctions happened Jan. 7-14, 2003, and Feb. 21, 2006.

October 31

1972
Cleveland Indians pitcher Gaylord Perry, a Williamston native, wins the American League Cy Young Award. Perry finished the season with a 24-16 record and a 1.92 earned-run average.

2009
Appalachian State University's Armanti Edwards becomes the first quarterback in NCAA Division I history to throw for 9,000 yards and rush for 4,000 yards in a career, accomplishing the feat during a 52-27 win at Furman. Later in the season, he'll push his passing total over the 10,000-yard milestone. Edwards will also be the first two-time winner of the Walter Payton Award, given to the Football Championship Subdivision's most outstanding offensive player, receiving the award in 2008 and 2009. After graduating, he will go on to play for the NFL's Carolina Panthers.

Armanti Edwards avoids a tackler
Courtesy of ASU Athletics/David Scearce

2010
Caldwell County native Madison Bumgarner, a pitcher for the San Francisco Giants, pitches eight shutout innings—surrendering only three hits—against the Texas Rangers in Game 4 of the 2010 World Series, a 4-0 win that gives the Giants a 3-games-to-1 series lead. Bumgarner, a 21-year-old rookie, becomes the fourth-youngest pitcher ever to win a World Series game. The Giants will go on to win the championship in Game 5.

NOVEMBER

November 1

1946

Former High Point College basketball player George Nostrand plays in the first game in NBA history. The game, played in Toronto, features Nostrand's Toronto Huskies vs. the New York Knickerbockers. The league is known as the Basketball Association of America, which is the forerunner to the National Basketball Association. The Knicks win, 68-66. With the Maple Leafs' image to contend with and only one Canadian player on its roster, Toronto had tried hard to promote the game, using a photo of the team's tallest player—the 6-foot-8 Nostrand—in three-column newspaper ads that asked, "Can You Top This?" According to the ads, any fan taller than Nostrand would be granted free admission to the season opener. Regular tickets were priced from 75 cents to

November 1 continued

$2.50, and a crowd of nearly 7,100 turned out for the event—not bad for a game played in the middle of hockey country. Nostrand plays and scores in the game, but he will be better known for those innovative newspaper ads than for his playing career, which will last only four seasons, during which he'll average 8.2 points per game. Nostrand played on High Point's freshman team in 1941-42—freshmen could not play on the varsity during that era—and was elevated to the varsity for his sophomore and junior years, before playing his final season for the University of Wyoming.

1994

The Chicago Bulls unveil a sculpture of Bulls superstar—and former University of North Carolina star—Michael Jordan outside the United Center. The sculpture features the inscription, "The Best There Ever Was. The Best There Ever Will Be."

November 2

2010

Clyde King, who played college baseball at the University of North Carolina and whose career in baseball spanned more than six decades, dies at the age of 86 in his native Goldsboro. King pitched seven seasons in the major leagues—the first six of them with the Brooklyn Dodgers—between 1944 and 1953, compiling a mediocre 32-25 record. He would never leave the game, however, first becoming a manager for several teams, then joining the New York Yankees' front office in 1976. He would remain with the Yankees in some capacity—scout, pitching coach, general manager, special advisor, interim manager—for nearly 30 years.

November 3

1985

Future Tar Heel basketball star Tyler Hansbrough is born in Columbia, Missouri. During a stellar four-year career at North Carolina, Hansbrough will become the school's and the Atlantic Coast Conference's all-time leading scorer with 2,872 points, as well as the NCAA's all-time free throw leader. He will earn multiple National Player of the Year honors in 2008 and will lead the Heels to an NCAA championship in 2009. Following his departure for the NBA, Hansbrough's No. 50 jersey at Carolina will be retired.

November 4

1951

Team USA crushes Team Great Britain, 9½ to 2½, in the 1951 Ryder Cup, played at Pinehurst Resort in Pinehurst—the only time the international competition has been played in North Carolina. The U.S. team, led by captain Sam Snead, includes two North Carolinians, Charlotte native Clayton Heafner and former Duke University standout Skip Alexander, who grew up in Durham. Both contribute to the win. Heafner scores 1½ points for Team USA, winning his foursomes match with partner Jack Burke Jr. and halving his singles match against Fred Daly. It's Alexander, though, who pulls off the stunner of the Ryder Cup, defeating British standout John Panton in the match-play singles competition. Only 14 months before the Ryder Cup, Alexander had suffered severe burns over much of his body in a plane crash, and he had undergone surgery to mold his badly burned hands into a position that allowed him to grip a golf club. Both hands bleed during his match against Panton, but Alexander perseveres and wins the match by the largest margin in Ryder Cup history, 8 and 7 (eight strokes up with seven holes to play).

A button from the 1951 Ryder Cup
Courtesy of the Lew Powell Memorabilia Collection, North Carolina Collection, Wilson Library, UNC-Chapel Hill

1987

Fisherman Robert Cranton catches a world-record Spanish mackerel, a 13-pounder, at Ocracoke Inlet.

1988

Playing in a sold-out Charlotte Coliseum, the Charlotte Hornets play their first-ever NBA game, a 133-93 loss to the Cleveland Cavaliers. The expansion Hornets will struggle to a 22-62 record in their inaugural season.

November 4 continued

2009

The New York Yankees win their 27th World Series title, and the so-called "Core Four"—Yankee veterans Derek Jeter, Mariano Rivera, Andy Pettitte and Jorge Posada—win their fifth World Series ring. All four of the "Core Four" played for the minor-league Greensboro Hornets before ascending to the Yankees. Jeter played for the Hornets in 1992 and '93, the latter year being voted "Most Outstanding Major League Prospect" by South Atlantic League managers. Rivera pitched for the Hornets in 1991 and '93, and Pettitte and Posada played for the 1992 Hornets.

November 5

1996

NASCAR legend Richard Petty, known for winning races, loses this one—the race for the North Carolina Secretary of State. The Randleman native, running as a Republican, comes up more than 200,000 votes shy of Democratic candidate Elaine Marshall.

Courtesy of the Lew Powell Memorabilia Collection, North Carolina Collection, Wilson Library, UNC-Chapel Hill

1999

Carolina Hurricanes captain Ron Francis becomes only the sixth player in NHL history to reach 1,500 points.

2004

A statue of North Carolina football great Charlie "Choo-Choo" Justice is unveiled at a dedication ceremony in front of UNC's Kenan Football Center. Justice, an Asheville native, was an All-American at Carolina in 1948 and 1949, and finished second in the Heisman Trophy balloting both years.

November 6

1970

Long before breaking backboards will become more commonplace, ABA player Charlie "Helicopter" Hentz breaks two backboards during a single game—believed to be the only time that's ever happened—at Raleigh's Dorton Arena. Hentz, of the ABA's Pittsburgh Condors, breaks the first backboard late in the first half of the game against the Carolina Cougars, and play is delayed about an hour while the backboard is replaced. Then, late in the game, Hentz does it again. This time the remainder of the game is cancelled, with Carolina being declared a 122-107 winner. According to some accounts, the Cougars will send Hentz a bill for the two shattered backboards, but he will refuse to pay.

2002

Durham native Morgan Wootten, the winningest high-school basketball coach of all time, announces his retirement from DeMatha Catholic High School in Hyattsville, Maryland. In 46 seasons at DeMatha, Wootten compiled a record of 1,274 wins against only 192 losses—an 87-percent winning percentage—and his teams won the mythical high-school national championship in 1962, 1965, 1968, 1978 and 1984. In 1965, DeMatha pulled off a stunning upset, ending the 71-game winning streak of Power Memorial Academy, which was led by Lew Alcindor (later known as Kareem Abdul-Jabbar). In announcing his retirement, the 71-year-old Wootten says, "There is a time under the heavens for everything. This is the time for me to step down at DeMatha."

November 7

1984

Fisherman David Deuel catches a world-record red drum, or channel bass, off of Avon, North Carolina. The trophy fish weighs in at 94 pounds, 2 ounces. Ironically, the previous world-record red drum, weighing 90 pounds, was caught by Elvin Cooper at Rodanthe—on the *exact same date*, 11 years earlier.

November 7 continued

1986

The Philadelphia 76ers retire the No. 24 uniform of Charlotte native and former Tar Heel Bobby Jones, one of the best defensive players in NBA history. A four-time NBA All-Star, Jones made the league's All-Defensive first team eight times and won the NBA's Sixth Man of the Year Award in 1983. Philadelphia general manager Pat Williams once said of Jones, "Bobby Jones gives you two hours of his blood, showers and goes home. If I was going to ask a youngster to model after someone, I would pick Bobby Jones."

2007

Tiny, unheralded Gardner-Webb University goes to Rupp Arena to challenge No. 20 Kentucky—NCAA Division I's winningest program—and blows the Wildcats off their home court, 84-68. The Bulldogs show no fear against the favored Wildcats, opening the game with a 14-0 run and never looking back. Grayson Flittner leads the way with 22 points for Gardner-Webb. Rick Scruggs, head coach of the Bulldogs, acknowledges after the game what an upset his team has just pulled, saying, "A lot of people will think this is a misprint."

November 8

1914

Future Hall of Fame college basketball coach Frank McGuire, who will lead the North Carolina Tar Heels to the 1957 NCAA title, is born in New York City.

1924

Rameses the Ram, the University of North Carolina's woolly mascot, leads the Tar Heel football team onto the field for the first time and proves to be a good-luck charm against favored Virginia Military Institute. Late in the fourth quarter, with the game a scoreless tie, UNC's Bunn Hackney enters the game to attempt a field goal—but as he trots onto the field, he pauses to rub the ram's head for good luck. Sure enough, Hackney makes the 30-yard drop kick and the Tar Heels pull off a 3-0 upset win.

1970

With only two seconds remaining, Tom Dempsey kicks an NFL-record 63-yard field goal to give the New Orleans Saints a dramatic 19-17 win over the Detroit Lions. Making the all-important hold for Dempsey's amazing kick is former North Carolina State defensive back Joe Scarpati.

244 ≡ Instant Replay

1988

Kansas University becomes the only NCAA basketball program prohibited from defending its title, one of several severe sanctions levied against Kansas because of recruiting infractions committed while Larry Brown was coach. However, Brown—the former University of North Carolina star and Carolina Cougars coach—had moved on to coach the San Antonio Spurs of the NBA.

1992

Forbes magazine names former Tar Heel Michael Jordan the highest-paid athlete in the world, with an estimated annual income of $35.9 million. According to the magazine, only $3.9 million of his income comes from his Chicago Bulls salary—the rest is earned through product endorsements.

November 9

1950

Duke University grants a leave of absence to head basketball coach Gerry Gerard, who is dying of cancer. Gerard, head coach since 1943, will die two months later, at age 47. In the meantime, with the news of Gerard's leave of absence, Duke announces the hiring of Harold Bradley as his replacement. Bradley will last nine seasons, but Duke fans will always be left to wonder what might have been, because Gerard's replacement could've been the great Red Auerbach of Boston Celtics fame. Duke had hired Auerbach as an assistant coach for the 1949-50 season, with intentions of promoting him to head coach when Gerard died. Auerbach became uncomfortable with that arrangement, however—he didn't like the idea of becoming a head coach at Gerard's expense—so he left after only three months, and of course went on to win nine NBA titles as coach of the Celtics.

1982

Sugar Ray Leonard, a 26-year-old Wilmington native, announces his retirement from professional boxing because of a partially detached retina suffered during his last fight. Leonard's ophthalmologist gave him permission to fight again, but strongly discouraged it. A little more than a year later, Leonard will change his mind and announce he's coming out of retirement.

1984

Duplin County native James "Bonecrusher" Smith loses an International Boxing Federation title fight to reigning champion Larry Holmes,

November 9 continued

who comes into the fight with a 45-0 record, including 18 consecutive title fights.

1985

Fayetteville native James Earl "Air" Harvey, a freshman quarterback for North Carolina Central University, sets an NCAA Division II record for touchdown passes thrown in a single game by a freshman, throwing six TD passes against Johnson C. Smith.

2008

The Guinness World Record for the longest tennis singles marathon is set by George Bolter and Athos Rostan III, who play for 31 hours, 35 minutes and 30 seconds at a YMCA fundraising event in Hickory.

November 10

1918

The North Carolina State football team gets obliterated at Georgia Tech, losing 128-0 in a game that's called early in the fourth quarter. State, which had lost numerous players to the nation's war effort and to the Spanish flu pandemic, is one of three teams to give up more than 100 points to Georgia Tech during the 1918 season.

November 11

1989

Duke University wide receiver Clarkston Hines sets an NCAA record for career touchdown receptions, scoring twice in a 35-26 Blue Devil win over North Carolina State. Hines will finish his college career with 38 touchdown catches, tops in the NCAA at the time.

1996

Space Jam, an animated motion picture starring Bugs Bunny and former University of North Carolina basketball star Michael Jordan, premieres in Hollywood. While Jordan gets top billing—along with Bugs, of course—other players with North Carolina connections who make brief appearances in the movie are Charlotte Hornets players Muggsy Bogues, Larry Johnson and Alonzo Mourning. The movie will gross $230 million worldwide.

November 12

1927

The newly constructed Kenan Memorial Stadium makes its debut on the University of North Carolina campus, with the Tar Heels easily defeating Davidson College, 27-0. UNC's Edison "Satchel" Foard scores the first touchdown. The new stadium will be dedicated on Nov. 24, after which the Heels will beat Virginia, 14-13.

November 13

1965

The N.C. State football team gives Riddick Stadium a fond farewell in the stadium's final game, defeating Florida State, 3-0. Harold Deters kicks the winning field goal for the Wolfpack.

1998

Talk about a potent ground attack...South Columbus High School rushes for a state-record 745 yards against Eastern Guilford. The performance also ranks as fifth-best in the nation for rushing yards in a game by one team.

Did You Know?

Surry Central High School soccer player Michael Richardson set a national record by scoring 92 goals during the 2002 season. His career total of 205 goals between 2000 and 2002 is third-best in the nation.

November 14

1936

Just when it appears that North Carolina's football team will give powerful Duke a challenge, Duke's game-changer—Clarence "Ace" Parker—changes the game. After Carolina ties the game at 7 with a third-quarter touchdown, Parker takes the ensuing kickoff five yards deep in the end zone and runs it all the way back for a touchdown. The 105-yard return—a Duke record—crushes the Tar Heels' momentum and silences the Kenan Stadium crowd, and the Blue Devils go on to a 27-7 win.

November 14 continued

1966

Wilmington native Roman Gabriel—a former star quarterback at North Carolina State and the NFL's Los Angeles Rams—makes his television acting debut as a headhunter on an episode of "Gilligan's Island" titled "Topsy-Turvy." Trying to launch an acting career, Gabriel will also appear in the "Ironside" TV series and in the movies *Skidoo* and *The Undefeated*.

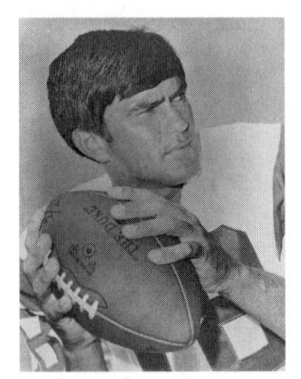

Roman Gabriel
Courtesy of North Carolina State Archives

1970

On second thought, sharing a basketball arena with a cattle show may not be such a good idea after all. When the ABA's Carolina Cougars host the Indiana Pacers at Dorton Arena in Raleigh—the day after a large cattle show was held in the same arena—the two teams and their fans are greeted by multitudes of flies, still hanging around after the cattle left. The flies are so bad that many fans depart at halftime, but the players and officials on the court have no such option. The Pacers survive the infestation and win the game, 128-119.

1970

Seventy-five people, including the Marshall University football team and coaching staff, die when Southern Airlines Flight 932—carrying the team back to Huntington, West Virginia, after its game in Greenville against East Carolina University—crashes and burns near Huntington's Tri-State Airport. It's the worst such tragedy ever involving an athletic team. Among the dead players are two from North Carolina—Bob Patterson, a junior from Louisburg, and Art Shannon, a junior from Greensboro. Also killed are two coaches with North Carolina ties—head coach Rick Tolley, who was a defensive line coach at Wake Forest in 1968 before taking the head job at Marshall, and offensive line coach Al Carelli Jr., who played football at Lenoir-Rhyne College in the early

1960s and was a graduate assistant coach at the University of North Carolina in 1968 and '69. A number of Thundering Herd supporters aboard the plane also die, including UNC graduate Parker Ward. Back at ECU, where the Pirates had defeated Marshall, 17-14, a few hours earlier, the team gathers in a campus dorm to mourn the Marshall players, coaches and supporters who had died. Years later, ECU will dedicate a plaque outside the visitors' locker room at Dowdy-Ficklen Stadium that memorializes the crash victims.

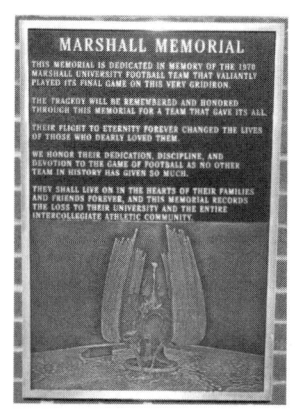

The Marshall Memorial Plaque at ECU
Courtesy of ECU Athletic Media Relations

2001
Head basketball coach Mike Krzyzewski signs a lifetime contract with Duke University. Athletic director Joe Alleva says, "We think he is the best coach in America and are delighted he is committing to remain at Duke until he decides to retire."

November 15

1974
Winston-Salem native Harold "Happy" Hairston, a forward for the Los Angeles Lakers, sets an NBA record for defensive rebounds in a quarter, recording 13 against the Philadelphia 76ers. Hairston also played for the 1971-72 Lakers squad that many consider to be the greatest basketball team of all team; the team won 33 games in a row at one point en route to an NBA title. During that same season, Hairston and teammate Wilt Chamberlain each grabbed more than 1,000 rebounds, the only time that's ever happened in NBA history.

November 15 continued

2004

Charlotte native Charlie Sifford becomes the first African-American inducted into the World Golf Hall of Fame. Sifford—whose interest in golf began as a caddie and who was shooting par by the time he was 13—won the National Negro Open five years in a row (1952-56), even as he tried to break through professional golf's color boundaries. He finally shattered the PGA Tour's Caucasian-only clause in 1961 to become the Tour's first black player. Sifford won twice on the PGA Tour—the 1967 Greater Hartford Open and the 1969 Los Angeles Open—and won the PGA Seniors' Championship in 1975. Sifford later told his story, the highs and the lows, in his autobiography, titled *Just Let Me Play*. At the Hall of Fame induction ceremony, South African golfer Gary Player introduces Sifford: "Tonight we honor a man not only for his accomplishments on the course, but the course he took in life. Persistence is an ingredient that is essential to success, and Charlie had that persistence." Fighting back tears, the 82-year-old Sifford tells the audience, "This makes me feel like I'm a worthwhile professional golfer."

2007

In his first game for North Carolina State, freshman J.J. Hickson shoots 12-for-12 against William & Mary, setting an NCAA record for field goal percentage in a player's collegiate debut.

J. J. Hickson
Courtesy of N.C. State Athletics

Did You Know?

T.A. McLendon, who played for Albemarle High School from 1999 to 2001, was one of the top high-school running backs of all time. He was the first high-school player anywhere to score more than 1,000 points in his career (he finished with 1,076, which once led the nation but is now second), and his 71 touchdowns in the 2001 season is still a national record. Furthermore, the Bulldogs' 903 points during that 2001 season still ranks first in the nation.

November 16

1999

Cherica Adams, the 8-months-pregnant girlfriend of Carolina Panthers wide receiver Rae Carruth, is shot four times in a drive-by shooting in Charlotte. Adams will slip into a coma at the hospital and die a month later, but doctors will save the child—Chancellor Lee Adams—in an emergency Caesarean section. Carruth, a first-round pick for the Panthers in the 1997 NFL Draft, will be found guilty of conspiracy to commit murder, shooting into an occupied vehicle, and using an instrument to destroy an unborn child. He'll be sentenced to 18 to 24 years in prison, with a projected release date of October 2018.

November 17

1960

Pittsburgh Pirates shortstop Dick Groat, who played baseball and basketball at Duke University, wins the National League's Most Valuable Player award after capturing the league batting crown with a .325 average. Groat was an All-American in both sports at Duke and was the Helms National Player of the Year for basketball in 1952. By the time his major-league career is over, he'll be an eight-time All-Star and a two-time World Series champion.

Dick Groat
Courtesy of Duke University Athletics

2006

Former Tar Heel basketball coach Dean Smith is inducted as a member of the founding class of the National Collegiate Basketball Hall of Fame, in recognition of his many contributions to the game.

November 18

1985

New York Giants linebacker Lawrence Taylor, a former All-America at the University of North Carolina, violently sacks Washington Redskins quarterback Joe Theismann, inadvertently breaking Theismann's right leg in the process—an injury that will lead to the veteran quarterback's retirement. Occurring during a "Monday Night Football" broadcast, the gruesome injury will be voted the NFL's "Most Shocking Moment in History" in an ESPN poll.

November 19

1999

The North Carolina State men's basketball team plays its first game at the new RBC Center in Raleigh and christens the facility with a win, defeating Georgia 67-63.

November 20

1951

Future home run king Hank Aaron's professional baseball career begins when he signs a contract with the Indianapolis Clowns of the Negro American League. Aaron, only 17 when he signs, will board a bus in his hometown of Mobile, Alabama, and ride it to Winston-Salem, where the Clowns hold spring training. Aaron's time in Winston-Salem will not be remembered fondly. Decades later, in his autobiography *I Had A Ham-*

Hank Aaron in Indianapolis Clowns uniform
Courtesy of Negro Leagues Baseball Museum

mer, he will write: "They called it spring training, but there wasn't much training involved and the weather in Winston-Salem didn't feel like any spring I'd ever known. The wind ripped across the field without mercy, cutting right through the threadbare shirt I practiced in. The veterans had jackets, but they weren't about to hand one over to an eighteen-year-old rookie. The Clowns didn't think too much of rookies. They had a lot of veterans on the team, and they had won the Negro League championship the last couple of years without any 150-pound teenagers. I was just a nuisance to most of them, a raggedy kid who was in the way. They made fun of my worn-out shoes, and they asked me if I got my glove from the Salvation Army. They didn't bother to find out if I could hit." They would find out soon enough, though, as another player's injury will give Aaron a chance to play; he will produce almost immediately, helping lead the Clowns to the 1952 Negro League championship. It's also during Aaron's brief stint with the Clowns that he will be discovered by the Boston Braves, and it won't be long until he's on his way to a Hall of Fame career in the major leagues.

November 21

1944

Playground legend Earl "The Pearl" Monroe is born in Philadelphia. Monroe will play basketball at Winston-Salem State University, where he will lead the Rams to the NCAA College Division championship and be named the NCAA College Division's Player of the Year, thanks in part to his gaudy 41.5-points-per-game scoring average.

2000

East Mecklenberg High School defeats Harding 124-121 in triple overtime. The two-team total of 245 points is a record for North Carolina high schools.

2001

The Denver Nuggets call up Chris Andersen from the Fayetteville Patriots – a team in the NBA's Development League—making him the first D-League player to be called up to the NBA.

Did You Know?

The Triangle once fielded a professional football team, but the results were less than stellar. The Raleigh-Durham Skyhawks, coached by former N.C. State and NFL star quarterback Roman Gabriel, played a season in the World League of American Football. Unfortunately, the Skyhawks went 0-10 and folded at the end of the season.

November 22

1965
Heavyweight boxing champion Muhammad Ali scores a 12th-round technical knockout over two-time former champ—and Cleveland County native—Floyd Patterson in a title fight at the Las Vegas Convention Center. Prior to the fight, Ali angrily called Patterson an "Uncle Tom" because of Patterson's refusal to call the champ Muhammad Ali, instead choosing to continue referring to him by his given name, Cassius Clay. During the fight, Ali toys with Patterson and mocks him throughout, before finally knocking him out in the 12th round.

1981
The University of North Carolina women's soccer team wins the first of its 20 national championships, defeating Central Florida, 1-0, in Chapel Hill, for the AIAW title. The Tar Heels will win additional NCAA titles in 1983 and 1984, 1986-1994, 1996-1997, 1999-2000, 2003, 2006, 2008 and 2009, making their case as perhaps the most dominant dynasty in all of college athletics.

2003
North Carolina State retires the jersey of quarterback Philip Rivers before the Wolfpack's final game of the season. Rivers will finish his college career ranked second in NCAA history with 13,484 passing yards and 13,582 yards of total offense, both Atlantic Coast Conference records. He will be named the 2003 ACC Player of the Year after setting an NCAA Division I record for career starts by a quarterback with 51.

2003
New Tar Heel head basketball coach Roy Williams wins his first official game, leading North Carolina to a 90-64 home win over Old Dominion University.

2003
Mia Hamm, the former University of North Carolina women's soccer star—as well as an Olympian and World Cup champion—marries Boston Red Sox shortstop Nomar Garciaparra.

2006
Seven-foot-seven Kenny George makes his debut for the University of North Carolina at Asheville, becoming the tallest player in the history of NCAA Division I basketball. Unfortunately, George's career will be cut short prior to the 2008 season when a nasty staph infection forces the partial amputation of his right foot.

November 23

1957

North Carolina State football star Dick Christy enjoys a game for the ages, scoring all 29 points—including a game-winning 47-yard field goal as time expires—in the Wolfpack's 29-26 win over South Carolina. Christy runs for four touchdowns and kicks two extra points before booting the dramatic field goal—the first field goal of his career. The win gives the Wolfpack its first Atlantic Coast Conference title.

2002

Star point guard Chris Paul of West Forsyth High School scores 61 points against Parkland as a tribute to his late grandfather, Nathaniel Jones, who had been murdered a few days earlier. Prior to the game, Paul had decided he would try to score exactly 61 points—one point for each year of his beloved grandfather's life. With less than two minutes remaining, and Paul's point total at 59, he drives to the basket and makes a tough shot as he's fouled, giving him the 61 points he'd set as his goal. He intentionally shoots an air ball on the free throw, then comes out of the game to a standing ovation.

Chris Paul
Courtesy of Wake Forest Media Relations

2010

Texas Rangers outfielder—and Raleigh native—Josh Hamilton wins the 2010 American League Most Valuable Player award. The 29-year-old slugger led the major leagues with a .359 batting average and a .633 slugging percentage, and was among the American League leaders in on-base percentage, total bases, hits, multi-hit games, extra-base hits and home runs. He helped the Rangers win the American League West

November 23 continued

for the first time in more than a decade, and he was voted the MVP of the American League Championship Series.

November 24

1949

Future UCLA basketball star Henry Bibby is born in Franklinton. Bibby will help lead the Bruins to three straight NCAA championships between 1970 and 1972.

1959

The girls' basketball team at Bailey High School defeats Red Oak, 4-3, in the lowest-scoring girls' game in the six-player era of North Carolina high-school basketball.

1985

North Carolina's Brad Daugherty shoots 13 of 13 against UCLA, an ACC record, as the Tar Heels open their 1985-86 season with a 107-70 victory over the Bruins in Carmichael Auditorium. Daugherty, a 6-11 senior center, will finish his playing days at UNC with a career field-goal percentage of 62.0.

Did You Know?

More than two dozen basketball players with North Carolina connections have played for the world-famous Harlem Globetrotters. In addition to the two best-known players—Wilmington native Meadowlark Lemon and Greensboro native Curly Neal—other former Globetrotters connected to North Carolina have included such players as Clyde "The Glide" Austin of North Carolina State, Charles "Tex" Harrison of North Carolina Central University, Orlando Melendez of the University of North Carolina, Kendal "Tiny" Pinder of North Carolina State, Raleigh native James "Twiggy" Sanders, Donald Williams of the University of North Carolina, and Barton College star Anthony Atkinson.

November 25

1980

Wilmington native Sugar Ray Leonard recaptures his WBC welterweight title—the title he lost to Panama's Roberto Duran five months earlier—by defeating Duran in a rematch. With Leonard leading on points, Duran surrenders in the eighth round, turning to the referee and saying, *"No más, no más,"* meaning "no more." Duran will claim he quit because of stomach cramps, caused by overeating after the weigh-in, but Leonard and many fight observers believe otherwise. "I *made* him quit," Leonard will say. "To make a man quit—to make Roberto Duran quit—was better than knocking him out."

1988

Former Duke University basketball coach, football coach and athletic director Eddie Cameron—for whom Duke's Cameron Indoor Stadium is named—dies at his home in Durham, at age 86. Cameron coached the basketball team from 1929 to 1942, compiling a record of 226-99. He coached the football team from 1942 to 1945, leading the Blue Devils to a 25-11-1 record, including a win over Alabama in the 1945 Sugar Bowl. He served as athletic director from 1951 to 1972. According to Duke lore, in 1935 Cameron and then-football coach Wallace Wade sketched out the plans for Duke's new indoor stadium on the cover of a book of matches. The facility opened in 1940 and was renamed for Cameron in 1972, the year he retired.

1989

After nearly a decade of "home" basketball games in Greensboro rather than Winston-Salem, the Wake Forest University basketball team debuts in its new home—Lawrence Joel Veterans Memorial Coliseum—and routs Davidson, 84-65. The new facility stands on the site of the old Winston-Salem Memorial Auditorium.

1990

The NBA's two newest franchises, the Charlotte Hornets and the Minnesota Timberwolves, square off in their first-ever meeting, with the Hornets taking an 85-73 win.

1993

Future NCAA Player of the Year Tim Duncan, an unheralded freshman at Wake Forest, starts the first game of his college career against Division II Alaska-Anchorage and scores, um, *zero* points. In fact, he plays only 10 minutes and doesn't even take a shot—though he does grab seven rebounds—and the Demon Deacons lose, 70-68. The very next night, however, Duncan will record his first double-double—the first of 13 double-doubles that season and the first of 87 in his college career—finishing with 12 points and 12 rebounds in Wake's 78-49 win over Hawaii.

1993

Tarboro native Burgess Whitehead, the last surviving member of the St. Louis Cardinals' famed "Gashouse Gang" that won the 1934 World

November 25 continued

Series, dies at age 83 in Windsor. Whitehead was also a two-time National League All-Star.

November 26

1932

East Carolina University wraps up an uninspired first season of football, finishing 0-5 without scoring a single point. The season includes losses to Presbyterian (39-0), the Wake Forest freshman squad (20-0), Guilford College (79-0), the North Carolina State freshman team (28-0) and, on this day, Appalachian State (21-0).

1959

The Duke and North Carolina football squads face off in Durham with identical 4-5 records, capping off a disappointing season for both, but the Tar Heels end the season on a high note. UNC coach Jim Hickey implores his team to win for their former coach, Jim Tatum, whose coaching career at UNC had been cut short when he died the past July, and the Heels respond with a 50-0 blowout.

November 27

1919

Wake Forest football captain Harry Rabenhorst unleashes a thundering 110-yard punt—believed to be the longest punt in college football history—during a Thanksgiving Day game at North Carolina State (a

This College Football Hall of Fame exhibit honors Harry Rabenhorst's punt
Courtesy of the College Football Hall of Fame

21-7 State win). In the first quarter, with Wake Forest backed up to its own 1-yard-line, Rabenhorst punts from 10 yards deep in the end zone. According to at least one newspaper account, the ball sails 85 yards in the air, landing at State's 25-yard line and then bounding toward the end zone, as State's punt returner and two Wake Forest defenders give chase. The State player catches up to the ball at the goal line and touches the ball, but he can't hold on to it, and one of the Wake players falls on the ball in the end zone for Wake's only score of the game. The next day, Wake's student newspaper—*Old Gold and Black*—will proclaim on its front page, "Rabenhorst Breaks World's Punting Record," and include a photo of him. The claim will remain unofficial—college stats will not become official until the late 1930s—but the game ball and Rabenhorst's cleats, along with a Wake Forest pennant and a copy of the *Old Gold and Black* article will be put on display at the College Football Hall of Fame in South Bend, Indiana. Meanwhile, the official record-holder for Wake Forest's longest punt will be Sam Swank, who will boot a mere 86-yarder against Duke on Sept. 9, 2006.

1972

Heavily recruited basketball star David Thompson, making his varsity debut at North Carolina State, does not disappoint, scoring 33 points and grabbing 13 rebounds in a 130-53 win over Appalachian State. A consistently prolific scorer, the Shelby native will top the 30-point mark in each of his first four games and go on to accumulate a career scoring average of 26.9 points per game. All three years of his varsity career, Thompson will be the Atlantic Coast Conference Player of the Year and a consensus first-team All-American, and he'll lead the Wolfpack to the 1974 NCAA championship. He will also have an outstanding professional career in the ABA and the NBA, which will include winning the ABA's Rookie of the Year honors in 1976. Thompson will also be the only player to win Most Valuable Player in the ABA All-Star Game (1976) and the NBA All-Star Game (1979). He will be inducted into the Naismith Memorial Basketball Hall of Fame in 1996.

1997

Former Negro National League star Buck Leonard dies at age 90 in his native Rocky Mount. Best-known for his years with the Homestead Grays, Leonard helped lead the Grays to nine consecutive Negro National League championships between 1937 and 1945. In 1948, he led the league with a sizzling .395 batting average, and he consistently finished first or second in the league in home runs. Leonard was inducted into the National Baseball Hall of Fame in 1972.

2000

Former Seattle SuperSonics star Nate McMillan, who played his college ball at North Carolina State, is named head coach of the Sonics.

November 28

1929
Davidson College football captain Thad Brock fakes a punt against Duke and runs 102 yards—without scoring a touchdown. Taking the snap seven yards deep in his own end zone, Brock scrambles around and through the entire Duke defense and carries the ball to the Duke 5-yard-line, where he's finally brought down. Davidson wins the game, 13-12, and Brock's amazing run will be featured in *Ripley's Believe It Or Not* as the longest and "nerviest" non-touchdown play ever.

1983
The University of North Carolina's Michael Jordan and Sam Perkins appear on the cover of *Sports Illustrated*, which has made the Tar Heels its preseason No. 1 in college basketball. The photo marks Jordan's first time on the cover, and he will eventually appear on 57 covers—far more than any other athlete in the magazine's history.

2008
Durham native Rodney Rogers, a former basketball star at Wake Forest University and in the NBA, is paralyzed in a dirt bike accident in Vance County when he hits a ditch, flies over the handlebars and breaks his neck. Doctors say Rogers—the 1993 Atlantic Coast Conference Player of the Year and the 2000 NBA Sixth Man of the Year—has only about a 5-percent chance of ever walking again. In 2010, he will establish the nonprofit Rodney Rogers Foundation to assist others who are paralyzed.

Did You Know?
Several of "Pistol" Pete Maravich's Broughton High School teammates once bet him he couldn't make a half-court hook shot during a game. The future college and NBA star took the bet, and, in true Maravich fashion, made a half-court hook at the first-half buzzer of a game against Wilson.

November 29

1928
President Calvin Coolidge watches the University of North Carolina football team knock off Virginia, 24-20, in Charlottesville, marking the first time a president has attended a football game in the South.

1980

Ronnie Carr of Western Carolina University makes college basketball's first three-point field goal in a regulation game, burying a 23-foot jumper in the early minutes of a home game against Middle Tennessee State. The Southern Conference—with the NCAA Rules Committee's approval—is conducting a season-long experiment with a 22-foot three-point line, to see if three-pointers could become a viable addition to the college game. When Carr makes the shot, referees halt the game and retire the ball, which will be sent—with Carr's autograph on it—to the Basketball Hall of Fame. During his two seasons with the three-point line, Carr will shoot 46 percent from behind the arc.

Ronnie Carr's historic 3-pointer
Courtesy of WCU Public Relations

1980

Charismatic Jim Valvano makes his debut as head basketball coach at North Carolina State, leading the Wolfpack to an 83-59 win over the University of North Carolina at Wilmington.

November 30

1956

Cleveland County native Floyd Patterson, only 21 years old and a heavy underdog, becomes the youngest heavyweight boxing champion in history when he scores a 5th-round technical knockout of Archie

November 30 continued

Moore in a title fight in Chicago. Moore hits the mat twice in the fifth round before the referee stops the fight and awards the title to Patterson.

1971

Brian's Song, the story of former Wake Forest University football star Brian Piccolo, debuts on television as the ABC Movie of the Week. Piccolo, who led the nation in rushing at Wake Forest and went on to play four seasons with the Chicago Bears, was stricken with terminal cancer and died in 1970, at the age of 26. The movie portrays the close friendship between Piccolo (played by James Caan) and Bears superstar Gale Sayers (Billy Dee Williams). The movie will earn seven Emmy Award nominations—three of which will win—and will go on to be released in theaters.

1979

Wilmington native Sugar Ray Leonard, 23, wins the world welterweight boxing championship with a 15th-round technical knockout of previously unbeaten Wilfred Benitez. The victory is Leonard's 26th consecutive win since turning pro.

Did You Know?

Randolph County native Augustus E. Staley founded the football team that would eventually become the Chicago Bears. Born in 1867, Staley left North Carolina and founded a food starch company that was based in Decatur, Illinois. In 1920, he founded a football league, and his team—made up of men who worked in his factory—was called the Decatur Staleys. The company hired George Halas, who eventually took full control of the team. In 1921, the team relocated to Chicago, where it was renamed the Chicago Staleys and later the Chicago Bears. In Staley's memory, the Bears' official mascot is named Staley Da Bear.

DECEMBER

December 1

1985
Duke wins the inaugural NIT Season Tip-Off championship—at the time known as the Big Apple NIT—with a 92-86 win over Kansas.

2008
North Carolina State quarterback Russell Wilson becomes the first freshman in Atlantic Coast Conference history to be named the All-ACC first-team quarterback. Wilson led the ACC in passing efficiency, touchdown passes and total offense en route to also winning ACC Rookie of the Year honors.

December 2

1949

Some fans have to sit on cement tiers for the debut of Reynolds Coliseum—the new home of the North Carolina State men's basketball team—because not all of the seats have been installed yet. They'll go home happy, though, after watching the Wolfpack destroy Washington and Lee, 67-47.

1961

North Carolina kicks off a new basketball season with an impressive 80-46 win over Virginia in UNC's Woollen Gymnasium, marking the first career victory for the team's new coach, 30-year-old Dean Smith. By the time he retires in 1997, Smith will have 879 career wins against only 254 losses, giving him a winning percentage of nearly 80 percent.

1989

Wrestler Landry McDuffie of Lumberton High School, wrestling in the 119-pound division, ties a national high-school record for fastest pin, pinning his opponent in an amazing three seconds.

December 3

1945

Army fullback Felix "Doc" Blanchard, whose college career began at the University of North Carolina, becomes the first junior to win the coveted Heisman Trophy. Blanchard originally enrolled at UNC in 1942, where he played on the freshman team (freshmen were not allowed to play varsity football). But then he changed his mind and decided to enroll at West Point, where he teamed with Glenn Davis to form one of the most potent backfields in college football history. His immense success—including the Heisman—will leave disappointed Tar Heel fans wondering what might have been had he stayed at Carolina.

2002

South Johnston High School's girls' basketball team beats West Johnston 50-0, marking the first time in the history of North Carolina girls' high-school basketball that a team has been shut out.

2008

The University of North Carolina basketball team travels to Detroit's Ford Field for a sneak preview of the Final Four venue at the end of the season, and the top-ranked Tar Heels obviously like what they find, destroying Michigan State, 98-63. Tyler Hansbrough leads the way with 25 points and 11 rebounds. Ironically, UNC will return to Ford Field for the Final Four, and will play Michigan State again in the title game—and destroy the Spartans again.

December 4

1954

The N.C. Central University Eagles football team defeats Tennessee State, 19-6, to earn the title of National Black College Champions. The squad, coached by Herman Riddick, went 7-1-1, then avenged its only loss of the season with the win over Tennessee State.

1956

The powerful University of North Carolina men's basketball team crushes Furman University, 94-66, the first win in what will be a perfect 32-0 season. The icing on the cake will be the Tar Heels' triple-overtime win over Wilt Chamberlain and the Kansas Jayhawks in the 1957 NCAA championship game.

1961

Cleveland County native Floyd Patterson successfully defends his heavyweight boxing crown with a fourth-round knockout of Tom McNeeley.

1965

Basketball standout Henry Logan of Western Carolina University breaks the 40-point barrier for the first time in his collegiate career, scoring 41 points against Catawba College. By the time he's done at WCU, the Asheville native will have scored 40 or more points in 20 games, 50 or more points in six games, and his top scoring game—the all-time WCU record—will be his 60-point outburst against Atlantic Christian College on Jan. 7, 1967. He will also set the school single-game records for assists (22) and steals (9), but scoring will al-

Henry Logan
Courtesy of WCU Public Relations

December 4 continued

ways be what he's most remembered for. In the 1967-68 season, he'll lead the nation in scoring with a 36.2 points-per-game average. Logan will also be remembered as the first black intercollegiate athlete to play for a predominantly white institution in the Southeast.

1994

University of North Carolina women's basketball phenom Charlotte Smith becomes only the second woman ever to dunk during a regulation game, accomplishing the feat in the Tar Heels' 113-58 rout of N.C. A&T State University. Playing in front of a home crowd in Carmichael Auditorium, the 6-foot-tall star—who just happens to be the niece of N.C. State legend David Thompson—intercepts a pass, dribbles the length of the floor and gets the dunk with only 17 seconds remaining in the game.

Charlotte Smith's dunk
Courtesy of UNC Athletic Communications

1997

North Carolina head football coach Mack Brown leaves the Tar Heels for the University of Texas. Brown, who came to UNC in 1988 and led the team to national respectability, will lead Texas to the 2005 national championship.

2001

Eric Williams of Wake Forest-Rolesville High School shoots a blistering 18 for 18 vs. Northern Durham, a state record for North Carolina high-school basketball.

December 5

1974
North Carolina State's All-American senior hoops star, David Thompson, scores a career-high 57 points against Buffalo State.

1980
Two legendary college basketball coaches, North Carolina's Dean Smith and Duke's Mike Krzyzewski, meet head-to-head for the first time at the Greensboro Coliseum. Carolina wins 78-76 behind James Worthy's 26 points. Smith will win 24 head-to-head matchups to Krzyzewski's 14, but Coach K will eventually pass Smith on the all-time wins list.

December 6

1967
Playing in Chapel Hill, Doug Grayson of Kent State University hits 16 consecutive field goals—and 18 of 19 overall—against North Carolina, for an NCAA record for consecutive field goals. The Tar Heels, however, still get the win, 107-83.

2000
Former UNC star Antawn Jamison, now playing for the Golden State Warriors, matches Los Angeles Lakers superstar Kobe Bryant's 51 points, leading the Warriors to a 125-122 overtime win. The offensive showdown marks the first time in nearly four decades – and only the third time in NBA history – that opposing players each score at least 50 points in a game. It is also Jamison's second straight game of scoring 51 points, having performed the feat three nights earlier against Seattle.

December 7

1964
Everett Case, the winningest men's basketball coach in North Carolina State history, steps down after being diagnosed with inoperable cancer. Later that season, when the Wolfpack wins the ACC Tournament, the players will roll him in his wheelchair from press row to the net-cutting festivities, then hoist him on their shoulders so he can cut the last strand of the net. Case will die on April 30, 1966, and be buried at Raleigh Memorial Park. Per his instructions, his body was to be laid in

December 7 continued

the grave facing N.C. Highway 70, so he could wave to future State teams traveling to Durham and Chapel Hill.

2003

The University of North Carolina women's soccer team beats Connecticut 6-0 for its 18th national championship. The win caps an undefeated season (27-0-0) and an amazing postseason in which the Tar Heels score 32 goals while allowing none.

2007

Appalachian State University quarterback Armanti Edwards rushes for 313 yards—an NCAA record for quarterbacks—to lead the Mountaineers to a 55-35 playoff win over the Richmond Spiders.

December 8

1981

Former Guilford College basketball standout Lloyd Bernard Free legally changes his name to World B. Free, explaining that "that's what people were calling me anyway." The nickname came from his high-school days in Brooklyn, where a friend dubbed him "World" because of his impressive 360-degree dunks. As a freshman at Guilford, Free led the Quakers to an NAIA national championship in 1973—earning the tournament's Most Valuable Player honors in the process—before going on to a stellar 13-year career in the NBA.

World B. Free
Courtesy of Guilford College Athletics

1992
Atlanta Hawks superstar Dominique Wilkins, who played his high-school basketball in Beaufort County, goes 23-for-23 from the free throw line, setting an NBA record for most free throws in a game without a miss.

2002
Carolina Panthers wideout and punt returner Steve Smith has a banner day, returning two punts for touchdowns against the Cincinnati Bengals. The returns go for 61 and 87 yards, respectively.

2006
Red Springs High School point guard Amanda Sinclair pulls off what is believed to be the first quadruple-double in North Carolina girls' high-school basketball history. Sinclair records 14 points, 14 assists, 12 rebounds and 11 steals—plus four blocked shots, for good measure—in a 79-32 win over South Robeson.

> #### Did You Know?
> The Wake Forest Demon Deacons were originally known as the Tigers—and later the Old Gold & Black or the Baptists—until 1923, when a school newspaper editor began referring to the team as the Demon Deacons because of their "devilish" play on the football field.

December 9

1980
Winston-Salem native Howard Cosell breaks the news of John Lennon's murder during a "Monday Night Football" game between the New England Patriots and the Miami Dolphins. "Remember, this is just a football game, no matter who wins or loses," Cosell says. "An unspeakable tragedy confirmed to us by ABC News in New York City. John Lennon, outside of his apartment building on the west side of New York City—the most famous, perhaps, of all of the Beatles—shot twice in the back, rushed to Roosevelt Hospital, dead on arrival. Hard to go back to the game after that news flash."

2006
North Carolina basketball coach Roy Williams picks up his 500th victory—a 94-69 win over High Point University—becoming the first coach ever to reach that milestone in fewer than 20 seasons.

December 10

1990
In a battle between the two all-time winningest programs in college basketball, North Carolina and Kentucky square off against each other with 1,483 victories apiece. The Tar Heels, playing at the Dean Smith Center in Chapel Hill, take an 84-81 win to break the tie.

1995
The Los Angeles Lakers retire the No. 42 jersey of longtime Laker—and Gastonia native—James Worthy, making him only the sixth player in Lakers history to have his jersey retired. Worthy, who played his college ball at the University of North Carolina, spent his entire 12-season NBA career from 1982 to 1994 with Los Angeles, playing in 926 regular-season games and 143 playoff games. A number-one overall draft choice of the Lakers, he also won NBA titles with the team in 1985, 1987 and 1988. He will be inducted into the Basketball Hall of Fame in 2003.

2010
Former University of North Carolina basketball standout George Karl becomes only the seventh coach in NBA history to record 1,000 wins, reaching the milestone when his Denver Nuggets beat the Toronto Raptors, 123-116. During the previous season, Karl took a leave of absence from the Nuggets while being treated for neck and throat cancer, but he eventually returned and was able to join the 1,000-win club.

December 11

1965
The longest basketball game in Atlantic Coast Conference history begins as North Carolina State visits Wake Forest. The game will not be completed until more than 10 weeks later. With 10:05 remaining in the first half, the game is delayed and then suspended because of a transformer fire in the lobby at the Winston-Salem Memorial Auditorium. Play will resume on Feb. 23, 1966, and State will come away with a 101-75 victory.

1968
Duke University basketball coach Vic Bubas notifies assistant coaches Chuck Daly and Hubie Brown that he plans to retire at the end of the season, though the news will not become public for another two

months. Bubas will finish with a record of 213-67—a 76-percent winning percentage. Neither Daly nor Brown will replace the legendary coach; instead, he'll be replaced by former Duke assistant—and former North Carolina State player—Bucky Waters.

1982

The previously undefeated Duke University men's soccer team loses a heart-stopper, falling 2-1 to Indiana in the NCAA championship game, in a record *eight overtimes*.

December 12

1937

Former major-league pitcher Rube Benton, a 47-year-old Clinton native, dies in a head-on automobile collision in Dothan, Alabama. In 15 seasons, Benton's record was 150-144.

1986

Duplin County native James "Bonecrusher" Smith claims the World Boxing Association's heavyweight championship with a stunning first-round technical knockout over reigning WBA champ Tim Witherspoon. The win makes Smith—who holds a bachelor's degree in business administration from Shaw University—the first heavyweight champion to hold a college degree.

1997

Dean Smith becomes only the second college coach to receive *Sports Illustrated*'s coveted Sportsman of the Year honors.

December 13

1966

Earl "The Pearl" Monroe, Winston-Salem State's flashy, high-scoring basketball star, scores a state-record 68 points as the Rams defeat Fayetteville, 112-97, at Winston-Salem State's Whitaker Gymnasium. Monroe's scoring feat includes a 44-point outburst in the second half, 16 of them in a particularly torrid 3-minute stretch. He finishes the game 29 of 42 from the field and 10 of 13 from the free throw line.

December 13 continued

1977

All 14 players on the University of Evansville basketball team—as well as the team's coaches, trainers and sportscaster—die when their chartered plane crashes and burns about 90 seconds after takeoff in Evansville, Indiana. Among the players killed are two freshmen from Goldsboro—Warren Alston and Barney Lewis.

1994

Bryan Kerchal, reigning champion of the Bassmaster Classic fishing tournament, dies in a plane crash near Raleigh. Only a few months earlier, in Greensboro, the 23-year-old Connecticut angler had become the first amateur to win the prestigious Bassmaster Classic competition, landing a 36-pound, 7-ounce bass.

December 14

1985

The Utah Jazz retires the No. 7 uniform of hoops phenom Pete Maravich, who played at Broughton High School in Raleigh. In his 10 NBA seasons, Maravich averaged 24.2 points per game.

2007

Appalachian State ends its amazing football season with a historic victory, crushing Delaware 49-21 to win its third consecutive NCAA Division I-AA national championship—the first team in that division to win a "three-peat." Delaware is led by future NFL quarterback Joe Flacco, but Mountaineers quarterback Armanti Edwards outshines Flacco on this night, throwing for three touchdowns to lead Appalachian State to the rout.

Appalachian State celebrates its "three-peat"
Courtesy of ASU Athletics/Courtney Burchett

2010
Former North Carolina star Michael Jordan is *finally* inducted into the N.C. Sports Hall of Fame at halftime of a Charlotte Bobcats home game. Jordan was elected into the Hall of Fame in 1993, but he was never able to attend the induction ceremony, so Hall of Fame officials decided to bring the induction ceremony to him in Charlotte, where he is majority owner of the Bobcats.

Did You Know?

Colton Palmer, a wrestler for Durham Riverside High School from 2004 to 2007, finished his career with 284 victories, tops in the nation. He suffered only six defeats.

December 15

1948
Charlie Scott, who will be the first black scholarship athlete at the University of North Carolina, is born in New York City. After averaging more than 22 points per game at UNC, Scott will go on to an outstanding pro career as well, playing in two ABA All-Star games and three NBA All-Star games.

1973
It's a battle of the winning streaks—UCLA's monstrous 79-game streak against North Carolina State's 29-game streak—at the St. Louis Arena. UCLA, despite star center Bill Walton sitting out more than half of the game with foul trouble, still clobbers the Wolfpack, 84-66. State will get its revenge at the Final Four, when the Wolfpack will knock off the Bruins and go on to win the NCAA championship.

1987
Former Baltimore Colts receiver Jerry Richardson, a native of Spring Hope in Nash County, announces his bid for an NFL franchise. Six years later, his dream will become a reality when the NFL awards him the franchise now known as the Carolina Panthers.

1991
Trash-talking Florida State guard Sam Cassell, after leading the Seminoles to an 86-74 road victory over North Carolina, mocks the Tar Heel faithful for what he deems to be lukewarm support. "This is not a Duke kind of crowd," he says. "It's more like a cheese-and-wine crowd, kind of laid-back."

December 15 continued

1994

The first batch of original Carolina Panthers are signed—Matt Campbell, Randy Cuthbert (who played at Duke), Kevin Farkas, Mike Finn, Willie Green, Carlson Leomiti, Darryl Moore, Tony Smith, Lawyer Tillman and Eric Weir.

2003

For the first time in its history, *Sports Illustrated* selects two basketball players for its coveted Sportsmen of the Year honors—San Antonio Spurs teammates David Robinson and former Wake Forest star Tim Duncan.

December 16

2000

Newland native Paul Johnson, head football coach at Georgia Southern University, leads the Eagles to their second consecutive NCAA Division I-AA national championship with a 27-25 win over Montana. A graduate of Western Carolina University, Johnson previously led Georgia Southern to the 1999 championship win over Youngstown State, 59-24.

December 17

2008

New Orleans Hornets guard Chris Paul, a Winston-Salem native, gets a steal in his 106th consecutive game, an NBA record. He'll go on to get steals in his next two games—setting the record at 108—before the streak finally ends.

2009

Cincinnati Bengals wide receiver Chris Henry, 26, dies one day after falling from the back of his fiancée's truck on a Charlotte street and suffering massive head injuries. The two had been arguing at the home of his fiancée's parents. No charges will be brought against his fiancée.

Did You Know?

When the North Carolina State football team played its first game on March 12, 1892, the Farmers—as they were called at the time—wore pink and blue uniforms. The team would not begin wearing the traditional red and white that it wears now until 1895.

December 18

2002
The NBA Expansion Committee unanimously recommends awarding an expansion franchise to Charlotte, the former home of the Charlotte Hornets. The new franchise, to be owned and operated by Robert L. Johnson, will become the Charlotte Bobcats. The Bobcats will begin play in the 2004-05 season and will get their first win on Nov. 6, 2004, a 111-100 win over the Orlando Magic.

2008
Reigning National Player of the Year Tyler Hansbrough scores 20 points to become the University of North Carolina's all-time leading scorer, surpassing Phil Ford, who had held the record for 30 years. Ford, who finished his career at UNC in 1978 with 2,290 points, is on hand to congratulate Hansbrough with a playful bow and a hug.

December 19

2005
The Dallas Mavericks assess a $1,000 fine against guard Darrell Armstrong—a Gastonia native who played college basketball at Fayetteville State University—for having a little too much fun at the Dallas fans' expense. The previous night, Armstrong had grabbed a microphone before a Mavs home game and shouted, "How 'bout those Redskins!" A few hours earlier, the Washington Redskins had crushed the rival Dallas Cowboys, 35-7, prompting Armstrong, who grew up in North Carolina as a Redskins fan, to talk some junk. Mavericks officials announce the money will be given to a charity—a charity to be determined by the Cowboys organization.

December 20

1985
Famed sportscaster Howard Cosell, a Winston-Salem native, retires from ABC Sports after 20 years with the network. Cosell's departure from ABC is bitter, stemming largely from his 1985 autobiography, *I Never Played the Game*, which was highly critical of many of his ABC colleagues.

December 20 continued

1985

North Carolina sets an NCAA Division I record for blocked shots in a game, chalking up 18 blocks against overmatched Stanford. The Heels win, 87-55.

1994

Former U.S. Secretary of State Dean Rusk, age 85, dies at his home in Athens, Georgia. Rusk was a 1931 graduate of Davidson College, where he participated in tennis and track and was a four-year letterman on the varsity basketball team.

Dean Rusk
*Courtesy of Davidson
College Archives*

December 21

1963

North Carolina State loses to Mississippi State, 16-12, in the 1963 Liberty Bowl. Played in Philadelphia, the game is so cold and so poorly attended that it will lead to the 1964 Liberty Bowl being the first college bowl game ever played indoors. With temperatures of 22 degrees at kickoff and 15 degrees by the end of the game, the Liberty Bowl suffers from horrible attendance—only slightly more than 8,300 fans watch the game in the 102,000-seat Philadelphia Stadium. Organizers take an estimated $40,000 loss on the so-called "Deep Freeze Bowl," and next year the venue will be moved to the Atlantic City Convention Hall in Atlantic City, New Jersey.

276   ≡   Instant Replay

December 22

1969

Former Broughton High School basketball star Pete Maravich, now playing for Louisiana State, sets the NCAA Division I record for most free throws made, sinking 30 of 31 against Oregon State. Maravich finishes the game with 46 points, and LSU gets the win, 76-68.

1996

Carolina Panthers kicker John Kasay makes three field goals against the Pittsburgh Steelers in an 18-14 Carolina win in Charlotte. The field goals give Kasay 37 for the season, a new single-season NFL record (which eventually will be broken). In the same game, Pittsburgh's Kordell Stewart runs 80 yards for a touchdown—the longest scoring run by a quarterback in NFL history.

December 23

1972

Oakland Raiders defensive back—and Cherryville native—Jack Tatum's defensive play nearly clinches an AFC divisional playoff game against the Pittsburgh Steelers, but instead results in one of the most miraculous plays in NFL history, dubbed "The Immaculate Reception." Trailing 7-6, the Steelers have 4th-and-10 from their own 40-yard-line with 22 seconds left in the game. A scrambling Terry Bradshaw passes downfield to Frenchy Fuqua for what would be a first down, but Tatum—one of the fiercest hitters in the game—jars the ball loose with a perfectly timed hit. That would essentially win the game for the Raiders, except that the ball is snatched out of mid-air by Steelers running back Franco Harris, who fends off a would-be tackler and sprints to the end zone for a touchdown and an improbable 13-7 Pittsburgh victory.

1976

Philadelphia Eagles defensive lineman Blenda Gay, a 26-year-old Greenville native who played college football at Fayetteville State University, is murdered by his wife, Roxanne, at their home in Clementon, New Jersey. As the 6-foot-5, 255-pound athlete sleeps, his wife slits his throat with an 8-inch kitchen knife. He manages to crawl to a phone and call police—implicating his wife in the crime—but he'll be dead within half an hour. Roxanne will allege her husband had physically abused her on a regular basis, and her cause will be taken up by the feminist movement. She will be deemed innocent by reason of insanity, and will be released in 1980 after completing psychiatric treatment. In 1992,

December 23 continued

Gay will be posthumously inducted into the Fayetteville State University Athletic Hall of Fame.

1988

In Michael Jordan's first return to North Carolina as a professional, the expansion Charlotte Hornets greet him and his Chicago Bulls teammates rudely, pulling off a 103-101 upset win at the buzzer at "The Hive"—a.k.a. the Charlotte Coliseum. In what will be the Hornets' only nationally televised game of the season, they stun the Bulls with a Kurt Rambis putback at the buzzer for the win, setting off pandemonium throughout the coliseum. "It was an extraordinary experience," Carl Scheer, the Hornets' general manager at the time, will tell a reporter years later. "That was our playoff to our fans. We had arrived. It was a very, very credible experience that authenticated pro basketball in Charlotte."

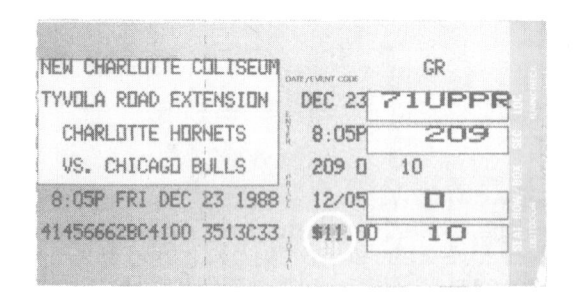

A ticket stub from the Hornets-Bulls game on Dec. 23, 1988
From the Author's Collection

December 24

1974

Future major-league pitcher Kevin Millwood is born in Gastonia. A graduate of Bessemer City High School, Millwood will debut with the Atlanta Braves in 1997, joining a dominant rotation that includes Greg Maddux, John Smoltz and Tom Glavine. He'll make the All-Star team in 1999 and pitch a no-hitter for the Philadelphia Phillies in 2003.

2004

Former major-league catcher and manager Johnny Oates, a native of Sylva in Jackson County, dies at age 58 after battling brain cancer for three years. Oates played 11 seasons in the majors, but was better-known for his managerial success. As manager of the Texas Rangers, he was named American League Manager of the Year in 1996, and three times he led the Rangers to the American League Western Division title. In August 2003, he received a standing ovation at The Ballpark in Arlington as he was inducted into the Texas Rangers Baseball Hall of Fame.

December 25

1931
Future college basketball coach Charles "Lefty" Driesell is born in Norfolk, Virginia. Driesell will play center for Duke University in 1953 and 1954 before moving on to a college coaching career that will include a successful stint at Davidson College during the 1960s.

Did You Know?
In boys' swimming and diving, Greensboro's Grimsley High School won 16 straight state titles from 1965 to 1980, the seventh-longest streak in the nation.

December 26

1964
Boston Celtics head coach Red Auerbach starts five African-Americans, the first time that's ever happened in NBA history. Among the starters is Wilmington native and former North Carolina Central star Sam Jones.

1973
Ted "Hound-Dog" McClain, a feisty guard for the Carolina Cougars, sets an ABA single-game record with 12 steals against the New York Nets during a game in Raleigh.

1986
Hall of Fame stock car driver—and Wilkes County native—Junior Johnson, age 54, receives a pardon from President Ronald Reagan for a 1956 moonshining conviction. Johnson had been convicted of manufacturing non-tax-paid whiskey—and had served 11 months in a federal

December 26 continued

penitentiary—after revenue officers arrested him at his father's still. It was after he got out of prison that Johnson made a name for himself as one of the stars of NASCAR. He was inducted into the National Motorsports Press Association Hall of Fame in 1972.

Junior Johnson
Courtesy of High Point Enterprise/*Sonny Hedgecock*

2004
Retired NFL defensive superstar Reggie White dies at age 43, after suffering a cardiac arrhythmia at his home in Cornelius. Remembered most for his Pro Bowl years with the Philadelphia Eagles and Green Bay Packers, the "Minister of Defense" also played the 2000 season with the Carolina Panthers, his final year in the NFL. White will be buried at Glenwood Memorial Park in Mooresville.

December 27

1892
The nation's first black intercollegiate football game is played on the campus of Livingstone College in Salisbury, where Biddle University (now Johnson C. Smith University) defeats Livingstone by a score of either 4-0 or 5-0 (sources differ over the correct score). The teams play two 45-minute halves on the snow-covered field, with Biddle scoring the only touchdown of the game. In 1956, a marker will be placed on the Livingstone campus at the site of the game, commemorating the historic showdown between the two schools.

1989
The North Carolina Tar Heels give up an NCAA record 21 three-point field goals to Kentucky, but still manage a 121-110 win.

December 28

1990
Talk about a physical game...Greene Central and North Lenoir high schools shoot a combined 124 free throws in a single game, the most in the history of girls' high-school basketball in North Carolina.

1991
McDowell High School shoots 79.2 percent (38 of 48) in its 85-61 win over Freedom. In the second half, McDowell shoots a sizzling 87.5 percent (21 of 24). Both shooting percentages are state records for North Carolina high-school basketball.

2008
John Kasay kicks a last-second, 42-yard field goal to give the Carolina Panthers a 33-31 win over the New Orleans Saints—and, more importantly, the NFC South division title. The Panthers finish the regular season with 12 wins, equaling the franchise record, but they'll get blown out in their first playoff game by the Arizona Cardinals, 33-13, in a game marred by quarterback Jake Delhomme's six turnovers (five interceptions and a fumble).

December 29

1959
Tar Heel basketball player York Larese knocks down 21 of 21 free throws against Duke. His effort comes up shy of the NCAA single-game record for free throws (24-for-24), but the Heels still enjoy a 75-53 win over their arch rivals.

2010
Duke basketball coach Mike Krzyzewski passes North Carolina's Dean Smith on the all-time wins list, picking up his 880th victory with a 108-62 rout of the University of North Carolina at Greensboro. The milestone win puts Krzyzewski in second place on the list, trailing only his former mentor, Bobby Knight.

December 30

1950

Duke astonishingly overcomes a 32-point deficit to beat Tulane, 74-72, at the Dixie Classic basketball tournament in Raleigh, marking the largest deficit overcome in NCAA history. Tulane leads by 32 with two minutes to play in the first half, leads by 29 at halftime, and still leads by 20 (72-52) with only eight minutes remaining, but Duke finishes with a torrid run, scoring the final 22 points of the game to get the win.

December 31

1974

The New York Yankees sign Jim "Catfish" Hunter, a 28-year-old righthander from Hertford, to a five-year contract worth a reported $3.75 million—which is at least three times the salary of any other major-league player. The deal comes after a high-stakes bidding war that drew numerous teams to a law office in Ahoskie, near Hunter's hometown, hoping to sign the free agent. Hunter, who won the American League Cy Young Award in 1974, will make two All-Star teams and win two World Series titles as a Yankee before retiring in 1979.

Jimmy Tomlin is a native of Statesville, North Carolina. He holds a journalism degree from the University of North Carolina and has worked as a newspaper and magazine journalist for more than 25 years, winning numerous state and national writing awards. He is currently a feature writer and columnist for the *High Point Enterprise*. His articles have been published in *Our State*, *Sky*, *Rails To Trails* and several other magazines. *Instant Replay* is his first book, but he contributed to *North Carolina's Shining Hour: Images and Voices From World War II* and *North Carolina Churches: Portraits of Grace*, both published by Our State Books. He lives in Greensboro with his wife, Becky, and their two daughters, Ashley and Caroline.